HITLER'S
Atlantic Wall

Anthony Saunders

SUTTON PUBLISHING

First published in 2001 by
Sutton Publishing Limited . Phoenix Mill
Thrupp · Stroud · Gloucestershire · GL5 2BU

British Library Cataloguing in Publication Data
A catalogue record for this book is available from the British Library

ISBN 0 7509 2544 2

Typeset in 10.5/13.5 pt Times.
Typesetting and origination by
Sutton Publishing Limited.
Printed and bound in England by
J.H. Haynes & Co. Ltd, Sparkford.

Contents

Acknowledgements

Jonathan Falconer at Sutton gave me the opportunity to write this book and took some of the photographs that appear in it. My thanks are due to fellow members of Site O (an Internet site dedicated to the study of fortifications): Neil Short, Marcus Massing of Germany and Joe Kaufmann of the USA, who generously allowed me to use their photographs. I would especially like to thank another Site O member, Ruud Pols of the Netherlands, who, despite family commitments, drew scale plans of some of the bunkers for me. Beverley Williams, Assistant Curator at the Royal Engineers Museum, Chatham, supplied me with information from *The Royal Engineers Journal* and Maggie Magnuson, Assistant Librarian at the Royal Engineers Library, Chatham, provided me with copies of drawings in an unpublished report written in 1945. Patricia Crampton, Fellow of the Institute of Translation and Interpreting, kindly translated some of the more abstruse German for me, for which I thank her.

Introduction

The Atlantic Wall was Hitler's vision of an impregnable coastal rampart to protect the western part of the Greater German Reich. This rampart was meant to be the barrier against which the enemies of the Third Reich would batter themselves to destruction should they attempt an invasion in the West. It was intended to stretch in an unbroken line from the Spanish frontier all the way to Norway's North Cape inside the Arctic Circle, some 2,800 miles of coastline. From mid-1940 to mid-1944, this vision was made real, its reality made more potent by the engine of propaganda. Thousands of gun emplacements, fire-control bunkers, command posts, ammunition bunkers, observation posts, anti-aircraft batteries and radar stations were built in thick ferroconcrete up and down the coasts of occupied Europe. Some were truly massive structures. By the beginning of 1942, Hitler and the German High Command (*Oberkommando der Wehrmacht* – OKW) recognized that it was only a matter of time before the Allies launched an invasion and that it was most likely to occur in France. It is not surprising then that the most important part of the Atlantic Wall was built along the Channel and Atlantic coasts of France. It is these defences that are the subject of this book.

Other structures were built along the Channel and Atlantic coasts during the war besides the defences of the Atlantic Wall, notably the U-boat pens at Brest, Lorient and la Pallice on the Biscay coast, as well as the launching ramps for V-1s and sites for launching V-2s located around Cherbourg and in the Pas-de-Calais. These are often claimed as part of the Atlantic Wall. However, their purpose was very different from that of the purely defensive structures along the coast and were never considered by Hitler to be part of the Atlantic Wall. Hence, neither the U-boat bases nor the V-weapon sites are included here. Massive structures were also built on the Channel Islands. A disproportionate amount of building work was carried out on the Islands before militarily more important sites in France received attention because Hitler was convinced that the British would attempt to wrest them back. These are also outside the scope of this book for the simple reason that the Channel Islands are not part of France.

Today, much of the Atlantic Wall still stands. Although ferroconcrete is gradually eroded by the elements, it does not fade away in a few decades. Most structures have walls and ceilings at least 2 m thick. Considering that external dimensions usually exceed 10 m in length and 5 m in height that makes each structure a substantial mass of concrete. The Atlantic Wall may prove as resistant to complete destruction as the concrete blockhouses of the First World War which still blot the landscape of northern France. Some of the Atlantic Wall structures were severely damaged during the fighting following D-Day but their remains have been remarkably resistant to complete eradication. Some casemates and bunkers were dynamited by US and British engineers after the war in order to remove them. Others are being slowly buried by drifting sand or are being swallowed by the sea. Post-war industrial development projects and improvements to harbour facilities have led to the destruction of many structures in ports like Dunkirk, le Havre and la Rochelle. Most traces of these bunkers have gone. More recently, three of the massive Pas-de-Calais gun casemates disappeared, buried by work for the Channel Tunnel. But a few structures have been turned into museums, thus ensuring their continued existence, while many of those at sites along the Normandy coast, for example, have been preserved because they are tourist attractions. Many, however, are completely neglected and overgrown while some are inaccessible to the public because they are inside military zones or are on private property.

Some sites can be difficult to find without the aid of a map. The IGN 1:25,000 series are detailed enough to show individual bunkers. They are essential for the serious enthusiast. But a warning: anyone thinking of exploring a site, especially an overgrown one, should be cautious. The most innocent-looking site can be far from safe. There are hidden dangers, not the least being concealed holes – hidden emergency exit shafts, for example – down which the unwary explorer can fall. Walls are sometimes partially collapsed and structurally unsafe. There are also exposed steel reinforcement bars in unexpected placess. The interiors of some bunkers can be dangerous due to the accumulation of rubble and modern rubbish. Although ferroconcrete is not quickly eroded, it is nevertheless damaged by water and temperature changes which can cause it to weaken and disintegrate. Serious structural damage can occur without any obvious sign to indicate that the building is unsafe. Always treat all sites with caution as few are maintained with public safety in mind.

Considering the ever-growing interest in the Atlantic Wall, it is perhaps surprising that so little has been written about it in English. This book is a critical look at the history of the Atlantic Wall, how it was built, what was built and the role it played in the Second World War, as well as a guide to what remains of it today in France.

CHAPTER I

The 'Great Wall' of Greater Germany

The Atlantic Wall has been described as the most ambitious building project in the Western World for two thousand years. This claim was based on the findings of a British Intelligence report written in 1945 but, rather than singling out the Atlantic Wall for this accolade, it encompassed all the building work carried out by the Organization Todt, the principal builder. This included its work behind the Eastern Front and in Italy, which included not only the construction of bunkers but also roads and bridges. It also built several massive headquarters bunker complexes for Hitler, some of which he never used, as well as the command bunkers and shelters 'needed' by others in the Nazi heirarchy. And, of course, there were the U-boat pens and other naval facilities at a number of locations in France, as well as V-weapon sites. However, the Atlantic Wall formed a major part of the Organization Todt's construction work and probably amounted to about 65 per cent of the work it carried out in the West. It was, indeed, a monumental project, both literally and figuratively.

Nevertheless, describing it as the most ambitious building project for two millennia is misleading as it implies the existence of a masterplan. Indeed, it seems to be a common misconception that the Atlantic Wall was built according to such a plan. There is no doubt that the Wall's construction involved a prodigious effort. It required the preparation of fortification designs, the surveying of prospective sites, the excavation of those sites, the dispersal of millions of cubic metres of earth, the production of huge quantities of concrete and steel reinforcement, the development of building techniques, the transportation of materials, the building of complex shuttering for the liquid concrete at hundreds of locations, and the marshalling of manpower to carry out these tasks, all of which needed to be organized and managed. Equally, steel components such as reinforcement bars, doors, embrasure closures and turrets as well as ancillary equipment for electrical and water supplies, for example, had to be manufactured, transported to the right places and fitted. The artillery pieces, radar equipment, communications equipment and observation equipment all had to be ordered, transported and installed.

But what was built and where and the order in which the sites were selected for the construction work was not the result of a carefully prepared blueprint that was painstakingly followed and intelligently adapted according to local conditions. On the contrary, the fortifications tended to be built piecemeal and haphazardly, often without regard for the most tactically advantageous locations and with a heavy emphasis on ports with the coast inbetween largely devoid of protection, unless there were beaches on which a landing could take place. It is, in fact, very difficult to rationalize it all as a single project. This is hardly surprising when it is realized that it was not a single project at all but a combination of several unrelated building programmes, large and small, that were only later brought together under one name.

The work carried out between 1940 and 1944 was carried out by at least three different agencies, namely the Heer (army), the Kriegsmarine (navy) and the Organization Todt. There was a distinct lack of inter-service cooperation between the Heer and Kriegsmarine until late 1942 when Hitler instructed them to bury their differences. The Organization Todt was a law unto itself and did not need to cooperate with anybody. According to General Speidel, it often did not. It was in a unique position, being a civilian organization that took its orders from the Ministry of Armaments and was consequently outside the military chain of command.

The Kriegsmarine was mostly concerned with the construction of offensive positions (because it had guns big enough to fire on the southern coast of England whereas the Heer did not) while the Heer was concerned with those of a defensive nature. Because of this, much of the work on the Channel coast between the Fall of France and the Battle of Britain was often carried out independently and with little coordination. Indeed, there was little reason to coordinate the work in the summer of 1940. This state of affairs continued up to about mid-1942. A plan drawn up by Hitler in September 1942 emphasized ports and the Channel Islands as the main sites for the bunkers and casemates of what he now called the Atlantic Wall, which prior to about spring 1942 had no such grandiloquent name. He expected the work to be completed by 1 May 1943, a totally unrealistic target. Building work of the Atlantic Wall type that had been underway on the Channel Islands and elsewhere long before the idea of the Atlantic Wall was born was now brought together but in name only. Operationally, there was a considerable gulf. Defences for the U-boat bases being built in France were now also classified as part of the Atlantic Wall while the bases themselves remained part of the offensive apparatus.

Even before the Atlantic Wall (also referred to as the New West Wall) was born and given its name in autumn 1942, the OKW fully realized that it was impossible to build fortifications everywhere and choices had to made; it was too big an undertaking. However, there was no consensus about which areas were the important ones regarding a future invasion – although Hitler's plan put the ports at the highest priority because he believed that the Allies would need to capture one in the event of an invasion. This was compounded by the Allied raids on Saint-Nazaire in March 1942 and at Dieppe the following August. Such raids had an impact on German thinking about what should built and where. Certain areas were inevitably given low priority because they were not recognized as potential invasion sites. This is one of the reasons why the fortifications between the mouth of the Seine and the Cotentin were incomplete at the time of the invasion. The Normandy region was only recognized relatively late on in the building programme as a likely place for the invasion.

Two Wehrmacht soldiers relax in deckchairs on a beach at Cap Blanc Nez. Behind them is a fire-control post. (599/1043/31. Bundesarchiv)

It is arguable whether any of the construction work carried out on the coastline of occupied Europe before about December 1942 was part of the Atlantic Wall concept, although all of it was subsequently incorporated into the rampart and made to appear as though it was part of a grand design. These elements of the Wall were incorporated as much for propaganda purposes as for practical ones. The inflation of the Atlantic Wall into a potent image of impregnability has been dismissed as mere propaganda, partly because of the Wall's failure to prevent the invasion. When the boot was on the other foot, however, and the Allies were attempting to deceive the Germans about the time and place of the invasion, this was not called propaganda but deception (and consequently legitimized). Although conducted on different scales and executed in different ways, the purpose of the deceit in both cases was essentially the same – hoodwinking the enemy. The Nazi deception was not some fortunate by-product of overblowing the strength of the Wall for the purpose of Nazi aggrandizement; on the contrary, the Nazi hierarchy fully intended to deceive the enemy about the Wall's strength because it was well aware of its weaknesses. The propaganda about the Atlantic Wall was effective as it helped to dictate where the Allies mounted the invasion. Unfortunately, it backfired as it helped the Allies to choose Normandy, one of the less well-protected sections of the Channel coast.

The inauguration of Lindemann battery in 1942 while construction work was still in progress. Note the dapple-pattern paintwork and the camouflage netting. (364/2314/161. Bundesarchiv)

The most enduring image of the Atlantic Wall is that of the huge gun casemates built in 1942 and 1943 in the Pas-de-Calais. These casemates and their guns were replacements for earlier batteries of cross-Channel guns that had been sited here on Hitler's instructions in preparation for an invasion in the other direction. The big guns were intended to command the Dover Straits and for the bombardment of southern England. The first of these guns were mounted in open emplacements with no protection against air attack and as railway guns in equally exposed positions – there was no need to worry about air attacks in 1940. The very idea that Hitler should put up some sort of defence in 1940 against an English invasion of Europe was unthinkable. By 1942, circumstances had changed and the big guns needed to be protected from not only air attack but bombardment by the Kent batteries; so they were housed in massive casemates. At the same time, they were incorporated into the Atlantic Wall by Nazi propaganda, which represented the whole Atlantic Wall as being as formidable as the Pas-de-Calais guns. In reality, it was for all practical purposes non-existent in some places (for example, parts of Britanny and the Biscay coast); by June 1944, the Atlantic Wall was far from complete. The propaganda was more effective than anyone could ever have hoped. Not only did it have an impact on the Allies at the time but today's impression of the Atlantic Wall is largely based on this hyped-up image.

Although Hitler had the seeds of the idea in December 1941, it was not until September 1942 that he gave the Atlantic Wall a tangible shape. And it was not until the end of the year that a formal instruction was issued for its construction. Work probably started around spring 1942 but it is unclear because of the way Hitler formulated military ideas and issued orders based on them. The Atlantic Wall was the pulling together of existing coastal works, built between summer 1940 and summer 1942 (the usual defence works that the army constructed when it became static), with new works to be carried out at designated sites. An anti-invasion rampart took shape in Hitler's mind between late 1941 and September 1942; its birthday is usually given as 23 March 1942, the date on which Hitler issued Führer Directive 40. In reality, ascribing a single date to the birth of the Atlantic Wall is misleading as the concept clearly evolved over many months and owed its existence to a number of different ideas from different sources. This was all something of a muddle and hardly reflected a masterplan.

The nature of the Atlantic Wall changed as the war progressed because Hitler's strategic perceptions changed. It could be argued that the Atlantic Wall evolved in both concept and form according to these changing circumstances but with a common objective. However, that was not the case. If the Atlantic Wall is viewed as originating in 1940, then the rampart can be seen to have gone through several unrelated building phases until mid-1944 when construction ceased. These phases corresponded with Hitler's reactions to particular events and were not developments of a well-thought out anti-invasion strategy. No matter how the development of the Atlantic Wall is viewed, it is difficult to cast it as a coherent single project: the disparate components do not fit into the same jigsaw. The only way that they come together is through the filter of Nazi propaganda. It is inexorably intertwined with myth which has tended to grow with the passage of time, reinforced by the fact that all the structures look alike because they are built of the same material.

The construction of the Atlantic Wall was made unnecessarily complicated by the lack of a mechanism for cooperation between the Heer, Kriegsmarine and the Luftwaffe, the services that were to use the facilities. As early as the mid-1930s, each had established its own links with industry for the supply of equipment and these independent lines of procurement usually operated in competition with one another. This state of affairs continued well into 1942 when Speer as Armaments Reichsminister endeavoured to simplify matters by pulling procurement together. But he faced considerable opposition from within the services and the party heirarchy. Despite Speer's efforts, procurement of weapons and equipment for the Atlantic Wall remained competitive for the most part. This competitiveness also extended to the procurement of cement. One service would requisition a whole consignment for its own purposes without regard for the needs of the other services. Speer endeavoured to rectify this absurd situation in September 1942 and made his ministry solely responsible for the allocation of cement, creating monthly quotas.

Rommel with his entourage posing for the camera in front of a bunker on one of his inspections of the Atlantic Wall in 1944. (295/1596/12. Bundesarchiv)

Neither was there a means for the three services to cooperate directly with the Organization Todt. This came under the auspices of the Armaments Ministry and as such was Speer's responsibility, not OKW's. General Speidel, Rommel's chief of staff in Normandy, complained after the war that the Organization Todt often built what it liked, where it liked and without regard for military necessity, sometimes building just for the sake of it. Speidel put this down to mismanagement. Local army commanders and even the commander of Army Group B, Generalfeldmarschall Rommel, who had responsibility for about 1,300 miles of coastline and for supervising and improving the defences of the Atlantic Wall from late 1943, could not order the Todt to carry out construction work. Rommel could only convey his wishes to OKW or to Hitler directly. Protesting about this unwieldy and inefficient system made not one jot of difference.

This was a consequence of the way in which the Nazi state functioned. It started at the top with Hitler's method of working, a combination of amateurishness, wild inspiration and authoritarianism, while surrounding himself with sycophants who would diligently turn his desires into reality. His subordinates then acted on the will of the Führer, the catch-all justification that swept aside argument and dispensed with a sense of responsibility. Not only did this abnegation of responsibility allow them to attempt to absolve themselves from blame during the war if something went amiss, and at the end of the war when they were held accountable for the conduct of the Nazi state, but it encouraged them to execute Hitler's wishes without scruple.

At military conferences, Hitler would often use masses of memorized statistics and figures to bludgeon into submission anyone who disagreed with him. These numbers were intended to demonstrate the Führer's superior knowledge on a subject but Albert Speer thought they only demonstrated his amateurishness. Hitler could be persuaded to alternative views by real experts on a subject. These experts were almost always civilians from industry. Strangely, Hitler had a particular dislike of specialists in government. By the outbreak of war in September 1939, Hitler had become accustomed to getting his own way and to getting any project completed on a timescale of his choosing. This was especially true of building projects which were often very dear to his heart. In January 1938, Hitler demanded that Speer design and build a new chancellery of majestic proportions, one that would overawe the world. He told Speer that he wanted it ready for use by 10 January 1939. Speer promised that it would be done although he later regretted the decision as the target date seemed unattainable when he stopped to consider the size of the undertaking. It took 4,500 workers and two shifts a day on the site for a year to complete the project on time. In fact, it was completed two days ahead of schedule. But this was nothing less than what Hitler expected. He was not in the least interested in how the target was achieved. Or, indeed, the cost.

Hitler mistrusted bureaucrats, convinced that the bureaucracy of government merely hindered action and stifled initiative. This led to a military-style chain of command throughout the Nazi hierarchy and government. Curiously, the bureaucracy lower down the chain actually increased and sometimes became almost a parody of itself because of its convolutions. These were partly a consequence of everyone wanting to cover his own back and avoid taking responsibility in case anything went wrong. This was a system ripe for corruption and mismanagement, made worse by the fact that if anything did go wrong scapegoats were sought by the Nazi heirarchy; genuine mistakes in the war industries, for example, could lead to charges of sabotage and treason. Even discussing production problems could lead to accusations of defeatism, a serious offence likely to result in a visit from the Gestapo. This did not encourage critical discussion which in turn did not provide an environment in which maximum efficiency could even be pursued, let alone attained.

Speer only became Armaments Minister by chance. The previous incumbent, Fritz Todt, died in an air crash in February 1942 when his aircraft was taking off for Berlin after a conference with Hitler in Rastenburg, East Prussia. Speer had been on his way back to Berlin from Dnepropetrovsk behind the Eastern Front but because the aircraft in which he was a passenger was not his personal plane he had to go where the aircraft was going, namely Rastenburg. Hitler was pleased to see him and had him stay up to the early hours of the following day talking about architectural projects and what he had seen on the Eastern Front. Consequently, Speer overslept the next day and missed the fatal Berlin flight. Hitler saw Speer's lucky escape and his presence at Rastenburg – which he had never visited before – as the hand of fate. Thus, as far as Hitler was concerned, he was only following through what fate had ordained in appointing Speer to take over Todt's responsibilities. Other members of the Nazi hierarchy did not share his view.

The construction of the Atlantic Wall proper occurred during Speer's time as Reichsminister. When he took the appointment, Speer was amazed to discover that although he knew nothing about armaments or the business of running the Ministry – he had tried to turn it down on these grounds – he could do more or less as he pleased because there was no mechanism for critical discussion within its corridors. Speer changed matters by introducing a form of democratic administration, increasing departmental responsibility. This had little effect on the way the Organization Todt operated and it was not popular with the Nazi heirarchy. The Organization Todt was run autonomously by Xaver Dorsch, a department head who had formerly been Fritz Todt's assistant.

Speer's staff and department chiefs and the heads of the businesses that fell within his jurisdiction had to be protected from the attentions of Bormann and the Gestapo. This Speer successfully achieved, until the failed attempt on Hitler's life in July 1944, by getting Hitler to issue a decree that exempted them from political interference, which, in effect, allowed critical discussion. However, Dorsch disapproved and often undermined Speer's reforms. He was an old party man whose membership of the Nazi party went back to the 1920s. Dorsch did what he could to prevent the measures being implemented, covertly at first, so that Speer only discovered by accident that Dorsch owed greater loyalty to the party than to Speer. With Bormann's backing, Dorsch attempted to undermine Speer's standing with Hitler in early 1944 when the Reichsminister was ill in hospital. Although Dorsch never succeeded in ousting Speer, this kind of relationship did not improve efficiency. The building of personal prestige at the expense of everything else was typical of the way in which the old Nazis behaved. Before Speer began to fall from grace with Hitler, he had to invoke Hitler's decree from time to time, even to the extent of freeing a miscreant sent to a concentration camp as a punishment for some imagined crime against the state as insignificant as voicing an unpalatable opinion. Often it was Dorsch's handiwork that led to industrialists or ministry officials needing Speer's intervention.

Speer's appointment to a post for which he lacked the appropriate expertise, in a time of war when experts were needed more than ever to increase efficiency and productivity, was typical of Hitler. Hitler mistrusted experts in government posts but he expected others to recognize his own superior expertise on any subject, an expertise that he demonstrated by his memory for figures and statistics. Moreover, Speer's precise role as Reichsminister was never clearly defined. Hitler was vague about who was responsible for what unless pushed. There were conflicts between the Reichsministers because of apparent overlaps of jurisdiction, as well as conflicts between the armed services because of competition for weapons and ammunition production. Right from the moment of his appointment, Speer found himself in conflict with the ostentatious, unpredictable and ultimately unreliable Göring. The Reichsmarschall had responsibility for the war economy (another individual in a post for which he was unqualified) and friction arose from an overlap of jurisdiction in running the war industries, a conflict that predated Speer's appointment and which was not helped by the fact that Göring had hoped to expand his own power base by taking over much of what Hitler's appointee, Speer, was now unequivocally given. It was further complicated by the fact that Walter Funk was the Reichsminister of Economics so that there was a threefold overlap. Those in Hitler's immediate circle manoeuvred and intrigued to increase their own power and prestige and diminish that of rivals. The interests of the party came second while the interests of the state came a very poor third.

Hitler seemed to encourage this behaviour while remaining aloof from it, only intervening when it suited him. He tended to listen to those who buttered him up the most, dismissing those who argued with him too much, filling posts according to who was least likely to cause him problems; in the end, negative selection was at the heart of the Nazi government. The Army Chief of Staff, General Halder, was removed by Hitler for being too difficult and replaced by someone more amenable, General Zeitzler. Generalfeldmarschall Keitel, OKW Chief of Staff, was a wet rag when it came to disagreeing with Hitler. But the Führer could be manipulated by the more cunning of his intimates, such as Göbbels and Bormann. Bormann, in particular, was a ruthless intriguer and not only manoeuvred himself into Hitler's confidence over many years but succeeded in making himself the agency through whom all others had to pass to reach Hitler. Bormann and Speer clashed from time to time because of the latter's methods of running his ministry and over the means by which Speer wanted to increase productivity. Hitler tended to vacillate, a tendency that became more evident as Germany's situation worsened following the defeat at Stalingrad in early 1943. It paid to prevent your rivals from getting to him first. Stratagems were commonplace and often necessary to get even commonsense decisions from Hitler, which became less and less frequent.

Dorsch, through the Organization Todt, took control of the construction of the Atlantic Wall. Speidel reckoned that the designer in the Todt was militarily unqualified for the job. Input from the Heer and the Kriegsmarine was often ignored although they were all supposed to be working together with a common goal. Attempts by individuals to increase their prestige within the hierarchy were often at the root of this. Hitler himself drew up some bunker designs, probably for personnel bunkers, which were used with only minor alterations. He was fascinated by architecture and fancied himself to be the equal of the best architects. It is doubtful that anyone would have had the courage to question the suitability of Hitler's bunker designs because of their 'architectural' nature and his 'expertise' on such matters due to his First World War experiences, although Speer thought they were sound. Hitler believed that his designs were without fault. But it was absurd that a country's leader in a time of war should spend his time making sketches of bunkers.

It was in this climate that the Atlantic Wall was conceived and built.

A personnel bunker at Brest, taken over by US medics during the investment of the port in August 1944. The concrete blocks from which the bunker was constructed and the curved tops of the vertical reinforcement bars are clearly visible, as are the remains of camouflage netting. Note the crack in the wall on the right and the damage bottom right. (NARA)

CHAPTER 2

The Greatest Builder of Fortifications of all Time

Three events led to the creation of the Atlantic Wall. The first was the Luftwaffe's failure to defeat the RAF in the Battle of Britain in the summer of 1940. The second was the Wehrmacht's failure to defeat the Soviet Union by the onset of winter in 1941. And the third was Hitler's declaration of war on the United States on 11 December 1941. The first led to the cancellation in October 1940 of Operation Sealion, the proposed invasion of Britain, which allowed Britain to stay in the war. The second meant that the war against the Soviet Union was clearly going to extend well into 1942, while the third meant that Britain now had an ally in the West. Hitler dismissed America as no more than a collection of immigrants and disparaged the fighting qualities of the American soldier because of America's late arrival in the First World War, factors which encouraged him to declare war on the USA. These events added up to a very real possibility of Germany having to fight on two fronts at some future date. This led Hitler to demand a bastion in the West so that he could concentrate on defeating Bolshevism in the East.

In December 1941, Nazi Germany was still in the ascendancy. Most of Western Europe had been conquered by the apparently invincible might of its armed forces. They were, even now, at the gates of Moscow, thousands of miles to the east, the harsh Russian winter merely postponing until 1942 inevitable victory over the Soviet Union. In the west, only Britain had yet to succumb and in late 1941 Britain's prospects seemed decidedly bleak. She continued to fight, notably in North Africa, but the war in the desert was going Germany's way in late 1941. The intervention of the Afrika Korps in early 1941 had tipped the balance in favour of the Axis and it seemed only a matter of time before the British were finally driven from Africa. Hitler's belief that Britain was too weak to pose a serious threat to his plans was a factor in his decision to invade the Soviet Union on 22 June 1941. But Generalfeldmarschall von Rundstedt, who had commanded Army Group A during the invasion of France and was subsequently appointed to command Army Group South for the invasion of Russia, believed that Britain was still a force to be reckoned with and fully expected her to intervene in the west after Germany had turned east.

The Japanese attacked Pearl Harbor on 7 December and, four days later, in a fit of overoptimism bred of ignorance, Hitler declared war on the United States. Three days after that, he issued orders for a defensive posture to be established along the coast of occupied Europe. This did not mean that permanent defences were to be built along the coast, however, merely that the troops along the Channel were to assume a defensive stance. The French coast between Belgium and the Cotentin had been occupied for the past nine months by the Fifteenth Army and it was already making use of existing fortifications built by the French. In fact, OKW had been building defensive positions along the Channel coast since the spring but these were in accordance with normal military practice and had little to do with a bastion against invasion.

In March 1942, von Rundstedt was recalled to active duty (he had been dismissed by Hitler from command of Army Group South in Russia in November 1941 for withdrawing from Rostov-on-Don without orders) and given command of Army Group West which included the Low Countries and France. Later the same month, Hitler issued Führer Directive 40 which set out the sort of permanent defences that should be constructed along the coast but without specifying where they should be located. This was a matter of some contention. The arguments centred on where a prospective invasion might occur while taking into account the regions of coastline that appeared to be especially vulnerable to assault from the sea, irrespective of its scale. These questions were never fully resolved, even after the construction work had been under way for more than a year. The lack of a definitive answer helped to ensure that some regions were poorly protected.

The Directive also increased the rivalry between the Kriegsmarine and the Heer. The former had the greater responsibility of the two services for coastal defence because coastal defence was a traditional role for the Kriegsmarine. Consequently, it was given priority for weapons and equipment for these new defences although hitherto it had been more concerned with offensive capabilities along the occupied coasts. The Directive meant that the Kriegsmarine would get new weapons and equipment while the Heer would have to make do with a range of old, new and captured stores; the guns which equipped the positions under army control came from as many as ten different countries. The Heer was, in fact, saddled with a huge variety of artillery pieces which presented enormous logistical problems for ammunition and parts. Many of the Heer's guns were obsolescent field guns that had to be modified to allow them to be mounted on a pedestal in an emplacement. Among the commonest were the 105 mm, which was acceptable for enfilading a beach but unsuited to firing on ships, and the First World War 155 mm which was too inaccurate and had too slow a rate of fire for shooting at ships. The Kriegsmarine, on the other hand, received a modern 150 mm gun which was accurate and quick although few batteries were equipped with it. The Vasouy and Longues-sur-Mer batteries in Normandy were; on D-Day they proved to be very capable of inflicting damage.

It fell to von Rundstedt to implement the new building programme. The Generalfeldmarschall was made Commander in Chief West which meant that not only the Heer but the Kriegsmarine in the region came under his command. All three services were instructed to cooperate in the building programme. Typically, von Rundstedt was answerable directly to OKW rather than to OKH. Oberkommando der

Wehrmacht had been created by Hitler in 1938 and was, in effect, his own war staff. Keitel was his chief of staff with General Jodl his operations officer. Oberkommando des Heeres was the army's staff; the Luftwaffe and the Kriegsmarine had their own staffs. It meant that there were in effect two competing army high commands with Hitler at the head of both.

Work on defensive positions along the coast had been under way on a limited scale ever since the Fall of France in summer 1940. These, however, had not been intended for anything other than local defence. For the most part, they consisted of no more than field works – trenches and weapons pits with barbed wire and mines – although some structures were built in concrete. The works arose independently of each other at various locations. Their coordination subsequently became the responsibility of Generalleutnant Schmetzer, Inspector General Land Defence West, who was subordinate to the General of Engineers at OKH. The number of concrete structures began to increase. Schmetzer gave responsibility for the continental coastal defences to the General of Engineers on von Rundstedt's staff at Army Group West, while retaining responsibility for the Channel Island defences. These coastal defences were built by army construction battalions and garrison troops. It was not until September 1941 that a proper plan for coastal defence began to be formulated to take in work being carried out by the Organization Todt at Kriegsmarine sites. The defences varied considerably in strength and many sites were only weakly protected. Von Rundstedt instructed local commanders to improve the defences. By December 1941, Schmetzer had at last established suitable coordinating and planning organizations to direct the work.

OKW now took a hand and ordered the existing defences along the coasts to be consolidated and made stronger, using all available labour for the construction work. This meant that concrete bunkers capable of withstanding the heaviest of bombardments were to be built. The Organization Todt now took control of the supply of labour and materials, the design of the structures and their construction. Nevertheless, the Inspector General of Defences West was supposed to be in overall control of what was built and where. Thus, in theory, no installation, irrespective of whether it was to be operated by the Kriegsmarine, Heer or Luftwaffe, could be built anywhere if it was not part of the coordinated coastal defence plan. The Inspector General of Land Defence West had a staff of twenty made up army officers and technicians. To ensure that the construction of defences followed the plan, local army commanders with responsibility for the defence sectors into which the coast had been divided were assigned senior fortress engineers to their staffs. These officers reported to the Inspector General of Land Defence West. Local army commanders had no authority over them and they could not order construction work to be carried out in an area that they felt was underdefended. They had to submit requests for construction work to the Paris headquarters of Army Group West rather than through the fortress engineers on their staffs. This was inefficient and unwieldy.

The Inspector General of Land Defence West made decisions on what was to be built according to these competitive requests. But he did not have the final say

A Seetakt radar (using the same antenna as the Freya radar) near Brest protected by a stone enclosure and sandbags. (MW 4980/16. Bundesarchiv)

as the matter had to go to OKW for approval. Ultimately, this meant Hitler had the final say on the finer details of what was built and where. In practice, this was not always the case, however. Moreover, what was approved was not necessarily what was built because it was the Organization Todt, the builder of the bunkers, that decided. Approval by OKW meant that the Coastal Defence Staff at Army Group West issued orders to the fortress engineers in the sectors concerned to carry out surveys of the prospective building sites to ascertain the strengths and weaknesses of the terrain with regard to assault from the sea and from the landward flanks and rear. Having done this, they submitted recommendations for the types of weapon needed for defence of the area, as well as a fire plan – which must have been rather tricky before weapons had been allocated, since what was requested and what was assigned did not necessarily match. In theory, the fortress engineers in any locality were allowed to determine the most appropriate defensive positions. Weapons procurement was the responsibility of the General of Engineers at OKH.

Although the order from OKW in December 1941 can be seen as an instruction to build an Atlantic rampart with concrete shelters and bunkers, a continuous

Cap Fréhel west of Saint-Malo was the site of a major Luftwaffe radar station codenamed Goldfish. This shows a bunker that mounted one of the five radars. (Marcus Massing)

rampart was not the intention at this stage. However, it had become the objective by March 1942 when Hitler issued Directive 40. Almost as soon as the Atlantic Wall programme got under way in response to this, the British attacked the docks at Saint-Nazaire and caught the German defenders by surprise. The timing was an unfortunate coincidence but it convinced Hitler that the danger of attacks on ports was not only serious but that they could be highly effective if the ports lacked good defences, especially if there was no warning of the assault. This should have demonstrated the need for an effective radar system but the lesson was not learned. Although radar installations were set up along the coast of France, the radars were too few in number and often unsuited to directing fire on sea targets even assuming they could detect ships – most radars were designed to detect aircraft. They were also vulnerable to attack from the air. There was a lack of co-ordination between the radar stations and the gun positions. This was an organizational problem that arose from a lack of cooperation between the three services but it was also due to Hitler's inability to understand the technicalities of radar early warning systems.

A light Flak emplacement, part of the Cap Fréhel radar station. (Marcus Massing)

This failing of German radar, which was partly technical in that the equipment was not always of the right type to detect targets at sea or to direct fire on them with any degree of accuracy, was demonstrated in August when the British and Canadians attacked Dieppe. Again, this should have warned Hitler that it was all very well building positions in concrete but if an attack could not be detected early there was a good chance that the defences would be overwhelmed. However, the Dieppe raid was not an unqualified success for the Allies and this served to demonstrate to Hitler the value of permanent defences. The raid merely confirmed Hitler's belief that the Atlantic Wall would be successful in defeating an Allied invasion. The Allies, on the other hand, took a different view. The raid also demonstrated to Hitler that the Allies would launch an invasion at a location that possessed flat sandy beaches near a port.

In May 1942, Hitler held a conference about the Atlantic Wall in his Vinnitsa headquarters, at which Speer was present. He emphasized to his new Reichsminister that the work on the Channel Islands being carried out by the Organization Todt should not be scaled down to allow for the increase in building work assigned to the Todt on account of the Atlantic Wall. Speer promised to provide 400,000 m³ of concrete each month. It was not until late September 1942 that the Atlantic Wall was discussed in more detail at another conference convened by Hitler specifically to deal with defence in the West. Present were Speer, Göring,

An Obergefreiter observing from a tobruk on a beach in front of an anti-tank wall in 1943. There is a bunker with a machine-gun embrasure in the background to enfilade the beach. (78/35/2. Bundesarchiv)

von Rundstedt, General Jacob of the OKW Ordnance Board and Generalleutnant Schmetzer. Such conferences were, however, conferences in name only since Hitler did most of the talking and rarely paid much notice to the opinions of others; he often did not allow anyone else to speak. However, Speer was still very much a favourite and Hitler was prepared to listen to him at this stage of the war. He was prone to dismiss difficulties as minor hiccups because of Speer's proven ability to get things done on time (later, he would dismiss them because of Speer's proven skill in getting the armaments industry to increase production despite heavy air raids that caused serious damage). This became something of a burden for Speer. Hitler now expected 15,000 bunkers and emplacements to be constructed from Norway to Spain and these were to be manned by 300,000 soldiers. He gave top priority to the ports and lowest priority to areas of open beach that were nowhere near a port. He demanded that the work be completed by 1 May 1943, which allowed just seven months. To make matters more difficult, he insisted that the construction of the U-boat bases should not be compromised by this new undertaking.

A fire-control post on the Channel coast in the summer of 1942, camouflaged with grass attached to netting. Note the glass panels in the observation slit and how the hastily-applied paint has run. (291/1213/12. Bundesarchiv)

This time he could not rely on Speer to pull a rabbit out of a hat and present him with the completed task on or before the appointed deadline. From a technical standpoint alone, it was not feasible to fulfil Hitler's wishes because the construction industry as a whole could not cope with the undertaking in that time frame. But even assuming that the bunkers could be built on such a scale, there was simply insufficient manpower to garrison the positions. Considering the timescale in which Hitler expected the work to be completed, it is a little surprising that he left it until mid-December to issue the orders to carry out the work. As Commander in Chief West, von Rundstedt issued the appropriate operational orders four days later. Thus it was not until the end of 1942 that the Atlantic Wall was formalized as a coastal defence against the threat of invasion. Having set the plans in motion, Hitler now wanted to be constantly updated on progress, demanding detailed reports on consumption of concrete, the type of concrete and its thickness, methods of construction and all the minutiae that would enable him to spout yet more statistics. These reports were sometimes ten or more pages long.

Inevitably, although a remarkable amount of work was completed by May 1943, the defences were very far from finished when the deadline was reached. To ascertain just how incomplete they were, a survey was conducted over several months and a report prepared for Hitler which von Rundstedt delivered to him at the end of October, a year after the Atlantic Wall had become an imperative. The report was not good. Not only did it show the weaknesses of the Atlantic Wall in terms of numbers of bunkers and strongpoints and their locations but also in terms of the quality of the troops who manned them. Von Rundstedt concluded that a mobile reserve that could launch powerful counterattacks was essential if an invasion was to be defeated. Nevertheless, he conceded that the Atlantic Wall could play a useful role in slowing down the assault which would then allow the reserves time to deploy where were needed. This was not what Hitler wanted to hear. The immediate consequence of this report was an order to the three services to take whatever steps were necessary to improve the defences as quickly as possible. Nothing was done about mobile reserves.

In the meantime, Rommel was transferred from Italy to take up command of Army Group for Special Employment in the West but rather than coming under von Rundstedt's command he was to report directly to OKW and Hitler as, indeed, did von Rundstedt. At the same time, Rommel was also appointed Inspector General of Defences. This inevitably led to a conflict of jurisdiction between von

An array of anti-tank obstacles, 1943. (293/1480/25. Bundesarchiv)

Beach defences, constructed from curved rails, opposite the casino at Trouville. They are 2.4 m tall, 6.41 m long and spaced at 1.42 m intervals. Note the barbed wire among the obstacles. (293/1487/10a. Bundesarchiv)

Erecting beach obstacles at low tide. (297/1716/28. Bundesarchiv)

Rundstedt and Rommel. Rommel and his staff conducted a survey much like the one already carried out by von Rundstedt. He reported the results of the first part of this survey, which dealt with Denmark, to Hitler in mid-December. Von Rundstedt was not pleased by this apparent dilution of his authority and he complained. The consequence of this was that Rommel was made commander of Army Group B which comprised the Fifteenth Army in the Pas-de-Calais, the Seventh Army in Brittany as well as the LXXXVIII Army Corps in the Netherlands. This comprised the major portion of Army Group West. Later, Generaloberst Blaskowitz was given command of Army Group G which included the Biscay coast and the South of France. However, although on paper it appeared that Rommel's command was now subordinate to von Rundstedt's, Rommel still reported directly to OKW and Hitler.

Unlike von Rundstedt, Rommel was in favour of permanent coastal defences to repel an invader and because of this, from December 1943, he became the most important figure in the construction of the Atlantic Wall. However, he told Hitler soon after his appointment that the Atlantic Wall as it stood at that time, with the major protection going to the ports, would not be enough to stop an invasion especially with Allied air superiority. He pressed for primitive beach obstacles to be used in large numbers to wreck landing craft. Von Rundstedt did not share this view. The difference of opinion between the two men was to lead to indecisiveness and confusion on the ground which was not helped by the fact that both men reported independently to Hitler. Nevertheless, Rommel was punctilious in observing the correct etiquette with von Rundstedt. But etiquette could not resolve their differences. On the one hand, von Rundstedt wanted to use mobile reserves to counterattack whereas Rommel was well aware of the power of Allied air superiority from his experience of the North African campaign that had ended with a German defeat in Tunisia in May 1943. He suspected that mobility would be lost to the dominance of Allied fighter-bombers and it was advisable to have the forces to repel the invaders already in place. Von Rundstedt respected Rommel's loyalty and courage but he had a lower opinion of his strategic skills. Hitler and von Rundstedt shared the same belief that the Pas-de-Calais would be the site of the forthcoming invasion and it was merely a matter of determining when it would be launched. Rommel came to the belief that the invasion would most likely come in Normandy and that the enemy had to be destroyed before he got off the beaches.

Following his inspection of the Atlantic Wall, Rommel concluded that only 30 per cent of the required bunkers, gun emplacements and other installations had been completed. He also discovered that there were still problems owing to a lack of cooperation and coordination between the Heer and the Kriegsmarine which resulted in confusion over who was responsible for what. Because Rommel believed that the Atlantic Wall had to be strong enough to halt the invasion rather than merely hinder it, he set about improving the defences but then encountered his own problems with the Organization Todt. More concrete structures were needed but urgency and tactical considerations could not persuade the Todt to build where Rommel would have liked it to build. Because of these difficulties, he instigated the construction of field defences by army engineers close to the beaches to link the positions already built despite the fact that Hitler had forbidden the construction of field defences sometime before the end of 1943. Rommel also had obstacles planted on the beaches that might be used to land troops. These were produced and placed by army engineers.

Hitler, who was by this stage of the war more indecisive and more prone to vacillation under the constant dripping of counter arguments than hitherto, had come round to Rommel's view that Normandy was a likely site for an invasion. Because of Hitler's changing views about its location, he made different demands during late 1943 and early 1944. His focus went from the Pas-de-Calais to Normandy to Cherbourg to Brest and other ports according to his pet idea of the moment. In early 1944, Hitler issued orders that ports that might be Allied targets in an invasion were to be designated fortresses and were to fight to the last man to deny the facilities to the Allies. Hitler believed that denying the Allies a port would seriously undermine their invasion plans. But this sort of order entrenched the notion of immobility of the German defence. Von Rundstedt was not alone in opposing Rommel's views about the location of the invasion and the use of static defence at the expense of mobile reserves. General Guderian, Inspector of Panzers, disagreed with Rommel's approach and several times tried to dissuade Hitler from such a reliance on the obviously weak static defences of the Atlantic Wall. He was concerned about the disposition of panzer forces which would be used in a counterattack in the West. Hitler would not listen. On one occasion in January 1944 Hitler flew into a hysterical rage and proclaimed 'I am the greatest builder of fortifications of all time. . . I built the West Wall. I built the Atlantic Wall'. Hitler then spouted statistics about tonnes of concrete. Guderian was not impressed. The Atlantic Wall of Hitler's imagination did not match the Atlantic Wall of reality. But there was no telling him what he did not want to hear.

In the two years from mid-1942 to mid-1944, the Organization Todt used 13,234,500 m³ of concrete in building the Atlantic Wall along the coasts of the Netherlands, Belgium and France. The cost of this was 3.7 billion Deutschmarks. In addition to the concrete, 1,200,000 tonnes of steel were used. This represented 5 per cent of Germany's annual production. At a time when the German armaments industry needed every tonne of steel for the production of tanks, guns and ammunition the diversion of this amount of steel from armaments production made a significant impact on the production figures. Speer later commented that 'All this expenditure and effort was sheer waste' because of the successful invasion of Normandy and the Allies' use of artificial harbours to bring supplies ashore which obviated the immediate need to capture a port, but he had the benefit of hindsight. At the time, it seemed like a good idea – although Speer was not happy about the effect the loss of steel had on armaments production, especially as he was continually being pressed by Hitler to improve output.

During 1940, the Organization Todt consumed only 122,000 m³ of concrete in building bunkers and gun emplacements in the West. In 1941, it used a mere 72,700 m³ of concrete. But this rose to 2,425,300 m³ in 1942, most of this being consumed from June onwards, reaching a peak of 453,400 m³ in December. Consumption in 1943 rose to 5,705,100 m³ with a peak of 769,100 m³ in April and only fell off slightly in May when Speer reassigned 7,000 workers from the Atlantic Wall to help repair the Eder and Möhne dams which had been badly damaged by the RAF attacks. Towards the end of the year, consumption of concrete fell to mid-1942 levels. Between January 1944 and the end of May, consumption started to rise again and another 2,061,400 m³ were consumed. The invasion in June inevitably brought construction to a halt.

Despite this enormous expenditure of materials, by early 1944 only a few places along the coast were equipped with defences that could be described as adequate and fewer still had defences of the strength close to that originally conceived for the whole of the Atlantic Wall. Not surprisingly, these mostly corresponded to those places that Hitler had at various times considered to be likely Allied targets for an invasion, including the Pas-de-Calais, the coast around the estuary of the Seine, the area round Cherbourg, and Brest and Lorient. Cherbourg became important because of the siting of V-1 launching ramps, while the last two were U-boat bases as well as ports. But perhaps more serious than this was the continued absence of a means to coordinate the defences operated by the Kriegsmarine with those operated by the Heer. This went all the way to the top of Army Group West. Von Rundstedt lacked the means to conduct an organized and coordinated defence because he did not control what the Kriegsmarine did despite being nominally in overall command. Like Rommel having to relay requests to OKW for the Organization Todt to build at specified sites, so von Rundstedt had to relay requests to OKW for assistance from the Kriegsmarine.

This problem went back to the summer of 1940. Coastal defence had always been the Kriegsmarine's domain but this rule had been established long before the prospect of having to protect such an enormous length of coastline had become necessary and long before an Atlantic Wall was conceived. The Kriegsmarine had neither the equipment nor the manpower to garrison the whole coastline on its own. It was, however, the first service to build concrete structures on the coast of occupied Europe, partly because the guns of the necessary calibre and range belonged to the Kriegsmarine. These were the guns that were to fire on southern England as a prelude to Operation Sealion. The Heer more or less drifted into a coastal defence role because of Hitler's orders for a defensive posture in late 1941. However, some eighteen months earlier, army coastal artillery units (*Heeres Küsten Batterien*) had been created because of the Kriegsmarine's lack of manpower for coastal defence. These came under Kriegsmarine control following Führer Directive 16 in July 1940 which had brought them into existence. Thus the Kriegsmarine and the Heer artillery coastal units coexisted to fulfil the same function but a coordinated plan of operation was never worked out. Until March 1941, the Heeres Küsten Batterien were subordinated to the Kriegsmarine but army field artillery sited for coastal defence came under Heer control. By the time the Atlantic Wall was being built, this problem had not been addressed. To make matters worse, neither service shared the other's approach to artillery tactics and fire-control. Indeed, they used different guns and equipment and operated under different procedures which complicated the subordination of Heeres Küsten Batterien to Kriegsmarine control; the army's were not suited to shooting at moving targets at sea. These guns were not housed in casemates until late 1943 by which time Allied fighter-bombers had made adequate air-raid protection imperative. Prior to this, most of the army guns had been in open emplacements.

The first permanent Kriegsmarine batteries had been erected in the summer of 1940 but the first permanent Heer batteries were not constructed until March 1941 when the Heer's mobile artillery was moved to different theatres. The remaining artillery included railway guns. These had sufficient range to shoot at targets on the coast of southern England and were based in the Pas-de-Calais, the part of France that was closest to England.

The rear of a type 669 casemate for a 105 mm gun at Fort de la Varde. (Marcus Massing)

CHAPTER 3

Defence of the French Coast

B efore the Organization Todt assumed responsibility for the construction of the Atlantic Wall in early 1942, construction of permanent positions along the coast had been undertaken independently by Kriegsmarine and Heer fortress engineers. Even after Directive No. 40, the Heer fortress engineers, attached to the staffs of local commanders, were theoretically responsible for deciding what was built. In practice, this seldom happened. Before Führer Directive 40 there had been no reason for the two services to work cooperatively since a coordinated defensive 'wall' was not a common goal. The Kriegsmarine placed its guns in the Pas-de-Calais, on some of the French islands in the Bay of Biscay and around the bigger ports, while the Heer's guns were placed in the coastal regions in between. Although this suggested that there was a clear distinction between which areas of the coast each service's guns were intended to protect, in practice the overlap of responsibilities made an effective defensive fire plan difficult to achieve.

This was complicated by the fact that the shoreline was used as an arbitrary dividing line of responsibility; the Heer was in charge inland of this line while the Kriegsmarine was in charge seaward of the line. It was known as the Main Battle Line. Such a distinction was possible because the navy fired at ships at sea while the army fired at troops and tanks on land. The army's guns were usually placed much further inland than the navy's, which were mostly right on the coastline to enable the guns to engage targets as far out to sea as the guns' range would allow. Targets were acquired visually from a fire-control post which might be some distance from the battery. The Heer, on the other hand, was more concerned with shooting at predetermined zones according to its usual practice for defensive fire, using indirect shooting with the aid of forward artillery observers, although some army guns were placed closer to the shoreline in order to enfilade beaches. Unfortunately, the Heer and Kriegsmarine could not agree upon when, in the event of an invasion, command should be transferred. The Heer's position in respect of command control was further complicated by the fact that Heer guns located to engage sea targets came under navy control. The fact that the two services perversely adopted different methods of classifying artillery according to calibre did not help matters. The Heer used two categories, light (up to 120 mm) and heavy (above 120 mm), whereas the Kriegsmarine used three, light (up to 105 mm), medium (105–200 mm) and heavy (above 200 mm).

The OKW seemed incapable of sorting out this tangle. Although Hitler had instructed the Kriegsmarine and the Heer to cooperate with each other over the requisition of concrete, it was not until late 1943 that a degree of cooperation and coordination was achieved concerning the use of artillery in the event of a landing. This followed a series of conferences held during the summer of that year and attended by representatives of the parties concerned. That it needed more than one to agree on a plan of operations is an indication of the difficulties involved and the intransigence of the participants. Even so, the problems were not completely resolved. All they managed to agree upon was the designation of the term Sea Battery Fire to fire in front of the Main Battle Line while fire behind it was designated Landing Battery Fire, the former under the direction of the local sea commandant, the latter under the direction of the divisional artillery commander. They even went so far as to define the use of flares at night to show the line of demarcation. What none of this settled, of course, was the question of when command responsibility should be handed from the navy to the army.

The coasts of the occupied territories were arbitrarily divided into Strategic Coastal Defence Sectors of two sorts, the most important of which was intended to protect 6–10 km of coastline most vulnerable to assault from the sea. This included the major ports as well as river estuaries such as the Seine and the Gironde. Each of these Sectors was garrisoned by an artillery regiment, a battalion of coastal artillery comprising two and sometimes three batteries and any Kriegsmarine batteries that were located within the Sector. It also had an anti-tank brigade and a number of Luftwaffe anti-aircraft units. A slightly different version of the Strategic Coastal Defence Sector was intended for the protection of the less vulnerable lengths of coastline and was garrisoned by a single infantry division. The length of coastline that the division was supposed to protect was anything from 15 km to 20 km. In practice, this increased to 80 km for some divisions of the Fifteenth Army and to as much as 350 km for some divisions of the Seventh Army in Brittany. For artillery, each division had only its own artillery regiment along with an anti-tank battalion, neither of which could engage targets before they landed on the beach.

By the end of May 1942, three main types of coastal defensive position within these Sectors had been devised. These took into account the fact that it was not feasible to protect the entire length of coastline with the available manpower, while acknowledging that some places were strategically more important than others. The level of protection afforded to any place was determined not by local army commanders or even by the Commander in Chief West but by OKW and ultimately by Hitler. The idea was to combine the permanent defences that were now being built with mobile reserves that could counterattack when they were needed. This use of reserves was firmly rooted in German military doctrine which stressed the importance of quickly recapturing ground that was lost and this idea was naturally extended to the concept of repelling an invasion from the sea. However, the relative importance of static defences based on reinforced-concrete buildings at the expense of mobile reserves increased so that by early 1944 the permanent defences had acquired an importance in the defensive plan that they had not possessed in 1942. Moreover, the mobile reserve had largely become strategic in nature and now came under the direct control of OKW, and consequently Hitler, not Army Group West.

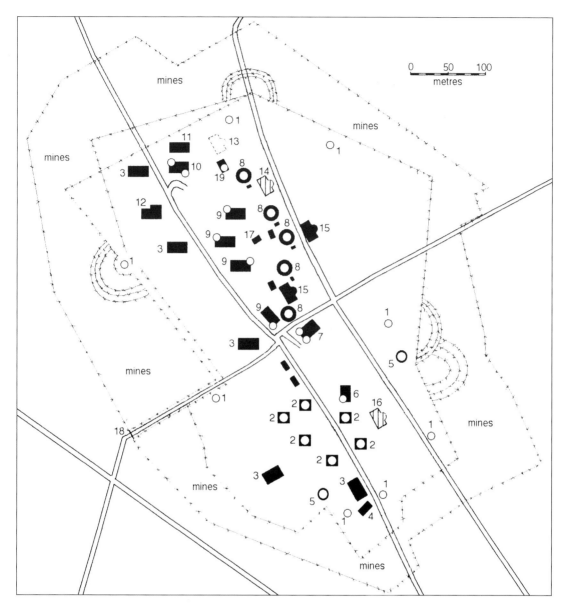

Saint-Marcouf battery. Key: 1 machine-gun position, 2 emplacement for 75 mm anti-aircraft gun, 3 personnel bunker, 4 rangefinder, 5 open emplacement for 20 mm anti-aircraft gun, 6 Azeville battery fire-control post with machine-gun tobruk, 7 Saint-Marcouf fire-control post with machine-gun tobruk and 20 mm anti-aircraft position, 8 open emplacement for 150 mm gun, 9 bunker with machine-gun tobruk, 10 bunker with two machine-gun tobruks, 11 ablutions, 12 supplies bunker, 13 projected casemate, 14 type 683 casemate under construction, 15 type 683 casemate, 16 type M272 casemate under construction, 17 water tank, 18 site entrance 19 machine-gun tobruk.

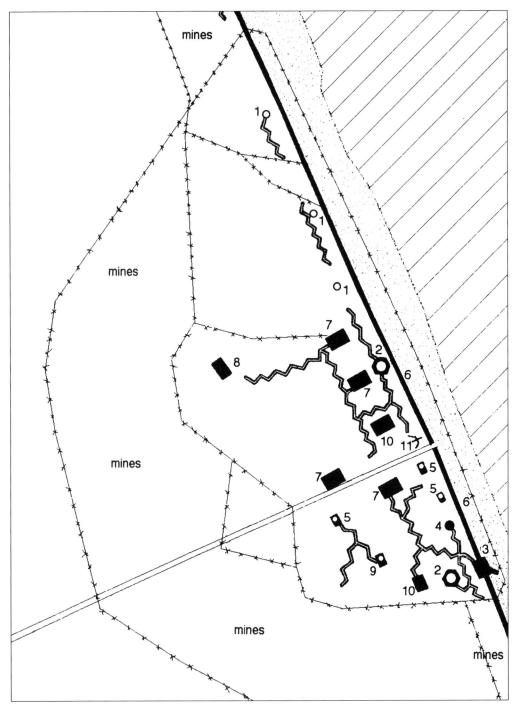

Wiederstandnest 5 at la Grande Dune (Exit 2 on Utah beach) showing trenches, barbed wire and minefields. Key: 1 machine-gun position, 2 open emplacement for 50 mm anti-tank gun, 3 type 667 casemate for 50 mm anti-tank gun, 4 tobruk with Renault tank turret, 5 machine-gun tobruk, 6 anti-tank wall, 7 type 702 personnel bunker, 8 type 501 personnel bunker, 9 tobruk for 50 mm mortar, 10 type 134 ammunition (type I) bunker, 11 47 mm anti-tank gun.

Circular platforms for guns long since removed, lying on the sand like giant wheels. (Jonathan Falconer)

This was a consequence of the constant drip of concerns about the availability of reserves on Hitler's mind from men like Guderian. It was not the result that he and others like him had wanted as it worsened a difficult situation rather than improved it. Local reserves were still available to be released without having to refer the matter to OKW but these were largely inconsequential because they were too small and lacked artillery and armour.

The origin of these categories lay in Führer Directive 40 as interpreted by Basic Order 7 issued by von Rundstedt at the end of May 1942. The second largest defence position was the strongpoint (*Stützpunkt*) and several of these could be grouped together to form a strongpoint group (*Stützpunktgruppe*). Such groups were usually located at the strategically important ports such as Dieppe. The strongpoint was the most common type of defence position within the Atlantic Wall and had been proposed as a defensive position back in December 1941 by OKW. It often consisted of several smaller positions, called resistance nests (*Wiederstandnester*, Wn), grouped to give each other supporting fire as well as to command a particular locality such as an exit off a beach, a part of the beach itself or a strategically important location further inland. If the strongpoint was made up of a number of Wiederstandnester the position usually incorporated a light or medium artillery battery for fire support. Most strongpoints were infantry positions but some were artillery batteries or anti-aircraft positions and these needed to be protected by infantry. The guns of artillery batteries were usually housed in casemates although many were still in open emplacements, some of the earliest structures built in the Atlantic Wall. Command and fire-control posts usually formed part of the artillery strongpoint. There were also light anti-aircraft weapons (20 mm cannon) and anti-tank gun and machine-gun positions for local defence. As with any fortification system, the outer perimeter was defined by field works manned by a platoon of infantry or even a company. All the positions within a strongpoint were well dispersed not only to increase the effectiveness of the defences but to minimize the effects of enemy attacks.

The arrangement of gun positions within a strongpoint varied according to the vulnerability and topography of the coast it was intended to protect. Gun positions were sited to allow fire to be directed in two directions and, if close to the shore, to allow a beach to be enfiladed. Usually, it was possible to establish a zone of crossfire with at least one other strongpoint. A strongpoint was intended to be able to defend itself against tanks, infantry and aircraft and was therefore appropriately equipped with anti-tank guns, mines, barbed wire and anti-aircraft guns, although there was no standardization of type or calibre of gun for these roles. Thus anti-tank weapons included 37 mm, 47 mm, 50 mm, 75 mm and 88 mm guns. There were also machine-gun and mortar positions. Anti-aircraft guns included single- and quadruple-barrelled 20 mm cannon. The 88 mm and larger calibre anti-aircraft guns tended to be used in dedicated anti-aircraft strongpoints rather than for the protection of artillery or infantry strongpoints. The types of structure built to house the weapons varied; no two strongpoints were identical. Artillery, irrespective of whether it was a field gun or an anti-tank gun, could be located to fire on a beach, inland or to give covering fire to a neighbouring strongpoint. Some strongpoints had a single function, like interdicting a beach, while others could have several functions that might include protection of a neighbouring strongpoint, interdiction of beach exits and protection of a strategically important site such as a radar station. The number and types of guns emplaced depended on such factors. There were also bunkers for personnel, ammunition storage and other purposes. To minimize the effects of shelling or bombing, the structures were dispersed but contained within a limited area that extended no more than about 400 m in any direction.

By the time that construction was brought to a premature conclusion by the Allied invasion in June 1944, more than 700 batteries had been built along the Atlantic Wall. A large proportion of these were in France. It is misleading to suggest that there was any uniformity although it has been claimed that they were all built according to a plan. Not only did the Heer artillery batteries differ from those of the Kriegsmarine but very few batteries belonging to either service were alike. This was not entirely due to different locations having different topographies. The differing philosophies of the Kriegsmarine and Heer toward the design of structures and the use and classification of guns ensured that their batteries were dissimilar in composition and layout. Nevertheless, because the basic requirement of all batteries was essentially the same – to engage the enemy – emplacements and casemates tended to be built in a line facing the sea.

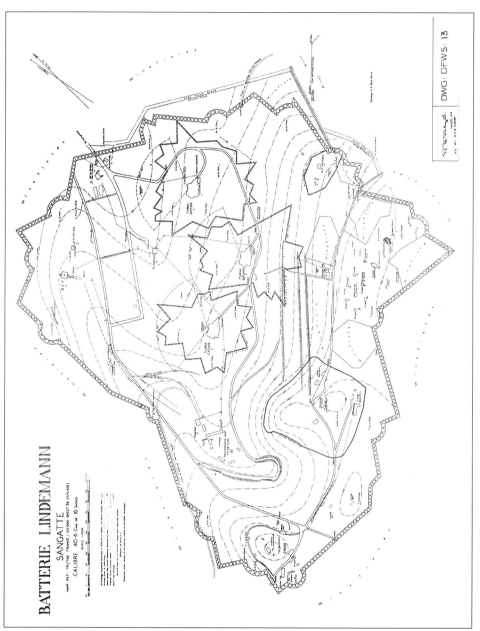

The plan of Lindemann battery as surveyed and drawn by the Royal Engineers in April 1945. The semi-circular bumps in the outer perimeter of barbed wire are adjacent to machine-gun tobruks. There were many other machine-gun posts on the site as well as anti-aircraft guns. The living quarters were sited at various locations on the periphery of the site about 300 m from the casemates. (Royal Engineers Library)

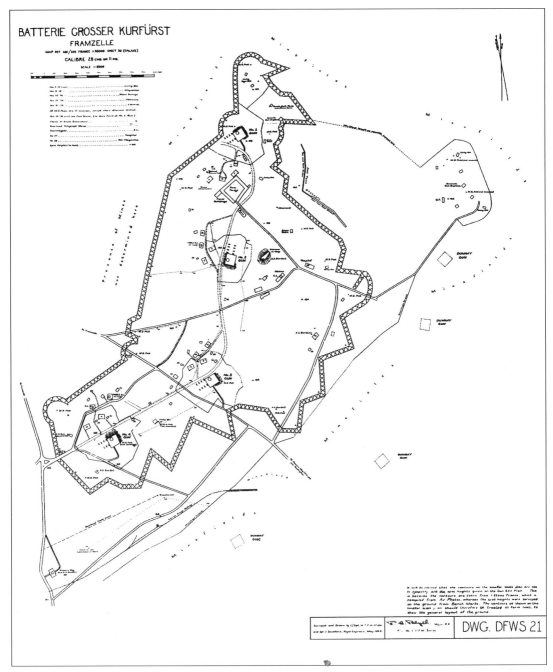

The Royal Engineers also surveyed Grosser Kurfürst and prepared drawings of the site, its casemates and other structures. Two personnel bunkers were located near each casemate, with magazines close by. There were also a kitchen, ablutions blocks and a medical bunker as well as numerous machine-gun posts and anti-aircraft guns. (Royal Engineers Library)

A fundamental difference between the two services was the way in which ammunition was stored at heavy gun sites, the Kriegsmarine preferring to keep everything under one roof, whereas the Heer opted for separate buildings. Separate positions within the battery site or neighbouring strongpoints or Wiederstandnester provided protection.

The Kriegsmarine's light batteries used simple bunkers and casemates. The design of medium batteries varied according to the date of their construction. The batteries constructed from late 1943 were often much simpler than earlier ones and were similar to army batteries. The guns were now in casemates rather than the open emplacements which had been constructed during 1942 and early 1943. The casemating of guns was a belated attempt at uniformity and simplicity to increase the speed of construction. The battery at Longues-sur-Mer in Normandy was a typical late-period medium battery with four casemates, a fire-control post and various other bunkers for self-defence. However, some medium batteries were adaptations of existing French batteries of an earlier age. Consequently, there was little uniformity between these batteries. The heavy batteries, such as those in the Pas-de-Calais, were all special constructions, although they followed the general layout of the medium batteries. These had their own screens of strongpoints for protection.

The Heer batteries differed according to whether they were coastal artillery units or divisional artillery that had been fixed at a given location. The latter were often very rudimentary sites with, from 1943, four casemates for field guns. These were basically roofed enclosures, albeit with very thick walls and ceilings. They mostly conformed to one of two designs both of which were much simpler than the designs used for Heeres Küsten Batterien. These used a wider range of casemate design. The choice depended to some extent on the guns to be housed in them. There were usually additional bunkers for the maintenance of the guns and equipment as well as medical and personnel bunkers at all Heer batteries but there were fewer than on a Kriegsmarine battery. Defence of Heer batteries was provided by a ring of machine-gun positions, many of which were tobruks, so-called after the town in Libya where they had been first used during the North African campaign. At its simplest, a tobruk was a concrete pit large enough for one man to stand in. Some were fitted with turrets taken from captured French tanks while others housed mortars.

Many army batteries were still equipped with open emplacements at the time of the invasion. It was not unusual for a battery to retain both even though the open emplacements had been made redundant. Smaller emplacements for anti-tank guns were still built on the flanks and at the rear of a position. There were usually a couple of positions for light Flak within the perimeter of the battery and these, too, were in open emplacements, sometimes on top of other bunkers. Heavy anti-aircraft batteries were established around ports and towns with the Kriegsmarine concentrating on the ports. Fewer gun positions were built for Kriegsmarine batteries than for those operated by the Luftwaffe. The Kriegsmarine usually had only four, whereas the Luftwaffe batteries sometimes had as many as eight.

A Ringstand for a tank turret at Saint-Malo. Note the gear teeth inside the rim. (Marcus Massing)

The Wiederstandnest was the smallest type of defence complex. It was self-contained and garrisoned by a squad or sometimes two squads. At the heart of each were one or more anti-tank guns supported by machine-guns and mortars, all of them in fortified positions which usually included bunkers. Some Wiederstandnester were no more than field works with added concrete fortifications. All the positions within a Wiederstandnest were interconnected by communications trenches and supported by fire trenches. In many ways, the resistance nest resembled a strongpoint of the First World War. The nest was surrounded by barbed wire and anti-tank and anti-personnel minefields. Such positions were intended to engage enemy infantry and armour once they started to come ashore. Wiederstandnester were often located on the flanks of a strong-point, to protect the artillery and anti-aircraft batteries as well as being put in forward positions such as among sand dunes. They were usually well camouflaged either by natural cover or by artificial means. Some nests were positioned to funnel

A Luftwaffe Flak observation post with glass-pannelled turret surmounting a bunker on the Channel coast, summer 1942. Both men are using binoculars. (282/1251/33a. Bundesarchiv)

The beach at Dieppe, September 1944, showing barbed wire, beach obstacles and the top of an anti-tank wall (running bottom left to top right). (Harold G. Aikman, National Archives of Canada PA183174)

attacks into killing zones. Often anti-tank ditches and other barriers, such as anti-tank walls and dragon's teeth (concrete tetrahedra), were constructed within both strongpoints and resistance nests as well as along the line of a beach and in beach exits.

Strongpoints and resistance nests were sometimes entirely independent of other similar sites and artillery batteries. When this was the case, the defensive capabilities of the strongpoint or resistance nest was increased to ensure that it could adequately defend itself from both infantry and tanks. Machine-gun and anti-tank gun bunkers were built in pairs to provide crossfire to make taking them by infantry assault more difficult.

Despite the importance given to concrete in fortifying a position and the fact that in 1943 Hitler forbade the construction of more field works, the infantry were under no illusion about the usefulness of rifle trenches and weapon pits for mortars and heavy machine-guns. Before any concrete buildings were constructed, a position was almost always first provided with rifle trenches and weapon pits so that some form of defensive capability was ready quickly. A well-prepared trench system was no walk-over for assaulting infantry or tanks and in recognition of this all categories of defensive position were provided with extensive field works. They were essential for local defence and intercommunication especially when concrete structures for these purposes had too low a priority for them to be built. Such works were positioned on

Loading a 240 mm Theodor Bruno railway gun in 1941. It is mounted on a turntable that enables it to be turned through 360°. These weapons were stationed to protect ports like Cherbourg and Saint-Nazaire. (69/2515/33. Bundesarchiv)

ridge crests, forward slopes, within sand dunes, locations that covered dead ground and approaches to resistance nests and where they could help funnel the enemy into killing zones. Sometimes, concrete bunkers were constructed at suitable places to allow the troops manning these trenches and weapons pits to shelter from air raids and shellfire.

A fifth category was later introduced, known as an Intermediate Position. This was no more than an isolated observation post, located in places where there were no defensive positions. They were merely intended to provide look-out posts on undefended sections of coast.

The composition of any position, large or small, varied according to a number of factors, not all of which were related to the strategic importance of a site. Availability of ordnance for artillery batteries affected how many guns and of which calibre were emplaced. Heer positions had to use a wide range of ordnance which meant that the casemates had to be adapted during construction to accommodate the guns. If the dimensions were wrong, the gun could not be installed. Some batteries, like the Merville battery, did not receive their ordnance before the invasion. Neither was the distribution of batteries and strongpoints regulated to provide maximum protection where it was most needed, although it was inevitable that most defences were located along the Channel coast. The Kriegsmarine endeavoured to provide two heavy batteries, two medium batteries and several light batteries for every major port it had to defend, and very nearly succeeded. The two ports which flanked the invasion beaches, le Havre and Cherbourg, did not get all their heavy guns before 6 June 1944. This was despite the fact that Hitler had identified Cherbourg as a likely Allied target should the invasion come in Normandy. In order to position enough heavy guns along the Channel coast, the Kriegsmarine removed a number of guns from its batteries along the North Sea coast of Germany and the Friesian islands, relocating them at Calais, Houlgate, Longues-sur-Mer and Saint-Marcouf. The Heer was not in a position to relocate guns in this way. However, it was able to make use of railway guns all of which fell within the heavy category. Many were placed in the Pas-de-Calais because they could hit southern England but others were positioned at ports such as Cherbourg.

The system of permanent defences was not much different from those developed by the Imperial German Army during the First World War. The forward defences were basically thinly manned outposts. Between about 1,000 m and 1,500 m further back was the main line of defence and beyond that a third line from which counterattacks could be launched if the main line was overrun, these lines being made up of batteries, strongpoints and resistance nests. The defences could be several kilometres in depth and it was this depth that Rommel objected to, believing

Firing the railway gun. Note the size of the crew, most of whom have their fingers in their ears.
(69/2516/5a. Bundesarchiv)

Beach obstacles made from tree trunks being inspected by Rommel. In the background are a few Belgian gates. Note that the obstacles point up the beach not out to sea. (719/243/33. Bundesarchiv)

that the invasion battle would be won or lost on the beaches because of Allied air superiority. When construction of the Atlantic Wall started in 1942, this concept of three lines or zones theoretically directed what was built and where. The proposal to make the coastline the main line had been made in December 1941 by OKW. However, coastline did not mean shoreline which was where Rommel wanted to make the main line. When Rommel took over control of the Atlantic Wall, he suspended work on what was the main line of defence and concentrated the building effort on the forward positions. Because of this change of approach, the depth of the defences varied from place to place according to what had been completed before Rommel took over and this depended on when the work in a particular area had been started. Such changes also meant that in some places the forward line was strong by the time of the invasion, although still only lightly manned, while at others, like Normandy, they were still in the process of being brought up to strength. Not only had Normandy been formerly considered a low-risk area so that fewer defences were constructed here but the forward defence or outpost line was in the process of being converted into the main line at the time of the invasion.

The forward line was, in effect, moved into the sea. Furthest out were deep minefields of sea mines. Between the high and low water marks, a wide variety of obstacles were used to prevent landing craft from getting inshore, from anti-tank mines strapped to tree trunks to tetrahedra made from steel beams and set in concrete bases. While the landing craft were negotiating their way through these obstacles, the batteries would destroy them before they reached the beach. The obstacles were extended up the beach which was sown with anti-tank and anti-personnel mines. An anti-tank wall was often built along the top of the beach and more mines and barbed wire either blocked exits off it or funnelled troops into killing zones. Just beyond the beaches were anti-tank ditches and yet more mines. Those troops who did manage to reach the shore and get off the beaches would be destroyed by the Wiederstandnester before they got inland. Impeding the enemy's exit from the beaches would allow mobile reserves time to mount a counterattack. At least, that was the theory. Although best known along the coast of Normandy, these inshore obstacles were widely distributed up and down the Channel and Atlantic coasts – everywhere, in fact, where there were beaches. They were used in considerable numbers as they were quick and cheap to make.

To augment the defence areas, a series of radar stations was built along the coast – although some of them had nothing to do with the Atlantic Wall and were part of the Reich's air defence system. The earliest had been built for the invasion of Britain. The stations were usually built in remote places where the reception was good, often promontories, headlands and cliff tops. Unfortunately, such locations were not necessarily the most advantageous from a defensive point of view. Stations operated by Luftwaffe personnel provided anti-aircraft batteries with air-raid warnings. The Luftwaffe signals regiments who manned the stations followed a well-established procedure for processing the radar information, passing it to Aircraft Reporting Centres which coordinated fighter defence and the anti-aircraft batteries. This was a

Tree-trunk stakes, some tipped with Teller anti-tank mines, along the beach at Dieppe. (Donald I. Grant, National Archives of Canada PA131224)

proven system used to defend Germany from RAF and USAAF bombing raids. Some Kriegsmarine batteries used radar for target acquisition and fire-control but the information was passed indirectly to the batteries in much the same way that the Luftwaffe stations passed on its radar information to the Aircraft Reporting Centres. This was not conducive to good fire-control as it was far too cumbersome.

German warships had used radar for gunnery control since before the war and its effectiveness and superiority over British gunnery radar was demonstrated during the Battle of the River Plate; the *Graf Spee* used a Seetakt set which had been installed as early as 1936, some two years before the Royal Navy fitted similar radars in its battleships. The Seetakt had a range of 25 km. It was sometimes used by Kriegsmarine shore batteries for the detection of ships and for rangefinding. The radar could measure the distance to a sea target and plot its bearing. The Kriegsmarine also relied on Freya sets (range 200 km), a large number of which it had lost to the Luftwaffe in early 1940 because it was really an aircraft detection radar although it was also used for sea targets. The Würzburg radar, with a range of 30 km, went into production in the spring of 1940 and the Kriegsmarine also used this for directing fire on sea targets from its shore batteries. However, it was not

The side of a bunker on the seafront somewhere on the Channel coast camouflaged with steps and a rail painted on it. There is an anti-tank gun on its roof and another bunker in the background. (293/1465/19. Bundesarchiv)

really suited to the job because its wavelength was too long. Although the Würzburg was improved during the war, its usefulness for fire direction was limited.

What was needed was radar of much shorter wavelength, known as centimetric radar. This was taking some time to develop, so Hitler halted all development on it in 1941. Hitler's short-sighted attitude arose from his inability to understand the technicalities of radar and his conviction that the war was going to be over quickly. He did not want research to be continued in any area if practical results were unlikely to be forthcoming within one year. Because of this embargo, the development of German centimetric radar fell way behind British work in the field. British bombers began using centimetric radar for target location and in 1943 a Lancaster fitted with one of these sets operating with a wavelength of only 9 cm crashed in Holland. The discovery of the radar set in the wreckage stunned Hitler into rescinding his earlier decision about the development of centimetric radar. It was too late to help the Kriegsmarine's shore batteries. The Germans remained at least two years behind the Allies in their development of centimetric radar and they were forced to devote all their efforts to developing radars to combat Allied aircraft.

CHAPTER 4

Designs on a Wall Theme

The West Wall along Germany's western border with France had been built in the late 1930s and its bunker designs formed the basis of the structures for the Atlantic Wall. Before the Atlantic Wall was conceived, the Kriegsmarine became involved in building concrete emplacements and bunkers on the French coast opposite southern England. These tended to be built according to their own designs although they were sometimes adaptations of the West Wall designs. As a consequence, there arose two independent design philosophies and two independent centres of expertise in reinforced-concrete structures: the Kriegsmarine and the Heer. Both services made use of their own fortress engineers to design and build their structures although the Organization Todt was usually the principal constructor. The Heer's fortress engineers were subordinate to the Army Ordnance Office which came under OKH. The fortress engineers were responsible for all aspects of the design and construction processes as well as the testing and proving of all designs. In theory, they chose the structures that were to be built in any given location but it is apparent that the Organization Todt often made these decisions without regard to service requirements.

Any design had two elements: the external and the internal. A design that externally resembled another often used a different arrangement of internal spaces. Approved designs (*Regelbau*) were given standard design numbers. Since all three services devised standard designs, those specific to one service were given a letter prefix to indicate its origin. Thus, L indicated the Luftwaffe and M the Kriegsmarine (from *Marine*), while H indicated Heer although army designs were usually just given a number. The Kriegsmarine was not content with just one prefix letter and used a variety according to the function of the structure concerned. Thus, FL signified Kriegsmarine Flak structures, while some Kriegsmarine designs had the suffix S (from *schwer* or heavy) which was applied to designs built at Kriegsmarine heavy batteries. The Kriegsmarine also used the prefix V (from *Versorgungsstände* – supply bunkers) for no good reason since its V structures were spread across most of the other categories.

By mid-1944, there were over 700 standard designs. Some of these dated back to the West Wall of the late 1930s and many designs had been superseded by later improvements so that at any one time only some of them were actually under construction. Nevertheless, such a large number of standard designs indicates a lack of confidence and an excess of bureaucracy. It is tempting to suggest that the existence of so many is indicative of a distinct lack of standardization. Few designs lasted more than about a year before being superseded by later improvements. It is questionable whether such changes were indeed improvements or whether they were simply changes for the sake of change although some of the later changes were introduced to simplify construction and to substitute concrete for steel. Some of the later designs may have been introduced due to a lack of awareness of existing designs that would have done the job just as well. The situation is further complicated by the fact that there were many non-standard designs that were not given numbers, some of them being unique to one location (such as some of the big-gun casemates in the Pas-de-Calais, for example). The total number of designs, therefore, far exceeded the 700 standard ones. Fewer than half of these were built in the Atlantic Wall. Some were much more common than others. Many standard designs appeared in adapted forms.

In all, around 250 standard designs along with countless other non-standard ones were used in the Atlantic Wall and most of these dated from 1942 and 1943. By comparison, the West Wall which was built over a similar timescale contained around 200 designs, few of which appeared in the Atlantic Wall. Moreover, the West Wall designs were 'new' in that there had been little previous design experience on which to draw. First World War experience was limited and did not include truly mobile warfare. This was not true of the Atlantic Wall. Not only was there the experience of designing and building the West Wall on which to draw but there was the practical military experience of taking modern concrete defences such as those at Eben Emael in Belgium in 1940. A smaller number of designs than were used in the West Wall ought to have been the logical outcome. In reality, the opposite was true.

However, experience was tempered by changes in approach to defence and the increasing reliance on fixed defences. Whereas the West Wall defences were intended to be part of the mobile counterattack doctrine, the Atlantic Wall was a mixture of different defence strategies that included holding ground at all costs, a Hitlerian approach that was a manifest failure in Russia but which was born of Hitler's inability to reconcile reality with desire. This suggests that the Atlantic Wall was designed and built on the fly and not according to some masterplan, and that designs were created as they were required without cross-checking with existing ones to see whether a new one was really needed or whether an existing design could be used or adapted instead. This did happen in some cases, suggesting that what was built was not decided according to standardization but according to the whim of the man in charge of a construction site. The argument that new designs were needed to accommodate captured weapons is implausible since they were mostly captured before the Atlantic Wall was conceived. Some of the design numbers have suffix letters. These were given to the improved designs that were altered too slightly to warrant giving them new numbers. A number with a prefix letter did not preclude that same number appearing with a different prefix (or without one) for an entirely unrelated design, although with and without a prefix the number could relate to similar designs used by different services. This was a bureaucratic system not an efficient one.

On the face of it, there appear to have been seven design series, namely the 100, 200, 300, 400, 500, 600 and 700 series; examples from all of them appeared in the

Atlantic Wall. A design was seemingly assigned a number in one of these series according to the service concerned and the year of its creation, although this rule does not seem to have been applied consistently. Designs belonging to both the Heer and the Kriegsmarine appear in the 100 series, for example, and many of those used in the Atlantic Wall dated from 1942. It has been argued that the designs of succeeding series were improvements over designs for structures of similar functions allocated to earlier series. This implies that the 600 and 700 series represented 'better' designs than the 100 or 500 series (all mostly related to the Heer) although 'better' is hard to define as it encompasses a wide range of criteria, some of which changed as the war progressed. For example, simplified designs that allowed for cheaper and faster methods of construction became important in late 1943 and early 1944 whereas in 1942 these criteria were not considered. The 200 and 300 series seem to have been used for Kriegsmarine designs irrespective of date although they were mostly from 1942 and 1943, while the 400 series appear to be almost exclusively Luftwaffe designs. On the other hand, the 500, 600 and 700 series seem to be almost exclusively Heer designs. Most designs used in the Atlantic Wall came from the 600 series (more than ninety) which was introduced in 1942. Fewest came from the 500 series (about seven, five of which dated from 1939). The concept of 'series' is probably false, however; numbers were simply assigned in the order in which designs were presented for acceptance and there is no significance to 699 and 700 other than the fact that 700 comes after 699. The dates of the designs tend to bear this out; the 100 series are older than the 600 series and the last of the 600 series appeared in 1944 when the 700 series appeared. And the fact that Kreigsmarine and Luftwaffe designs were prefixed by identifying letters meant that their numbering systems were different from the Heer's.

The system was further complicated by the use of suffix letters to signify the thickness of the concrete to be used. This was an unnecessary over-classification since the thickness of the walls and ceilings was a part of the design; their thickness was not decided on site. The suffix was not often used, however. The earliest designs, dating from the West Wall, had thinner walls and ceilings than the 100 series which superseded them. The 100 series introduced the thick wall which came in two thicknesses, classified as A and B, with walls and roofs 2 m and 3.5 m thick respectively. Standardization was most evident in the design of internal spaces once it was realized during the early construction of the West Wall that merely combining standard interior design features (based on what equipment was supposed to go in them) was not a recipe for uniformity or utility. In fact, the opposite turned out to be the case and resulted in some very poor interior designs that impeded the function of the structure. This learning process culminated in the 100 series.

Although the 400 and 500 series were supposed to supersede the 100 series, very few of the 500 series appeared in the Atlantic Wall and similar numbers of 100 and 400 series designs were used (fifty-one and fifty-eight respectively). Perversely, the 600 series reintroduced small, thin-walled structures that the 100 series had supplanted in the West Wall, with walls only about 1.5 m thick. One of these, a 50

A type 667 casemate housing an 88 mm anti-tank gun at Courseulles-sur-Mer, Normandy. This was the heart of Wiederstandnest 29 at the entrance to the harbour. The prefabricated blocks from which the casemate was constructed are clearly visible. (Ken Bell, National Archives of Canada PA140856)

mm anti-tank gun casemate (type 667), was built in large numbers, approximately 430 all along the French coast. Other designs in the 600 series introduced in 1944 had even thinner walls only 1 m thick; these were usually shelters and tobruks.

While the Heer preferred 2 m and 3.5 m walls, the Kriegsmarine adopted four different thicknesses for its standard designs, most of them less than the thinnest Heer wall: 1.2 m, 1.5 m, 1.7 m, and 2.2 m. A single structure could have walls of different thicknesses. The walls of its special structures were considerably thicker, however. Thus, not only did the shape of the Kriegsmarine structures differ from the Heer's but the different thicknesses ensured that their structures were not at all alike, a rather pointless divergence. On the other hand, the Luftwaffe was at least prepared to use Heer designs as the basis for its own but when it had the opportunity to collaborate with the Kriegsmarine, it failed to do so. Consequently, none of the Luftwaffe Flak emplacements were like the Kriegsmarine's. So much for interservice cooperation. It has been suggested that the superseding of designs by 'better' ones was the result of ongoing research and testing programmes to ensure that the 'best' designs were selected but there is little evidence to support this. On the contrary, it would appear that there was no real system for selection at all, only the appearance of one. The only clear case of 'better' designs superseding older, inadequate ones was when casemates replaced open emplacements. But in this instance, the criteria had changed.

The designs fell into several broad categories according to function, namely command posts (*Gefechtsstände*), communications posts (*Nachrichtensände*), observation posts (*Beobachtungstände*), gun emplacements (*Kampfstände*), bunkers

(*Unterstände*) and other types classified as '*Versorgungsstände*' which encompassed a range of functions from command post to storage bunker. Within these broad groupings there was a wide range of different types of structure, although it would appear that the terms were not consistently applied; often, different terms were used for the same sorts of structure. The term bunker (*Unterstand*) included troop quarters, ammunition magazines, emplacements for field guns, searchlight battery emplacements and storage facilities, hospital facilities and water storage facilities. Similarly, there were several types of gun emplacement for both field guns and pedestal-mounted guns as well as machine-guns, namely emplacements with turrets, casemates that faced seawards, casemates for enfilade fire, naval casemates, and open emplacements. Various terms were used to describe these, including *Unterstand* and *Stand* (bunker) while casemates

A view into a tobruk. (Neil Short)

were termed *Schartenstand*, rarely as *Kasematte*. The terms *Stellung* (position), *Bettung* (platform) and *Stand* were all applied to open emplacements. It is perhaps curious that field gun bunkers were categorized as shelters (*Unterstellraum*) rather than as weapon emplacements but such bunkers were often little more than reinforced-concrete garages to protect the guns from shelling or bombing, whereas weapon emplacements allowed the gun to be fired from within the structure. The gun shelters did not have the space to enable the trails of a field gun to be opened which would have meant that it was impossible to load and fire the gun while it was inside its shelter.

Bunkers (*Unterstände* or *Stände*) were the most commonly built structures in the Atlantic Wall, amounting to several thousand in all and constituting nearly half of all structures. There were twelve Heer designs, whereas there were only two Kriegsmarine and three Luftwaffe designs. The primary function of a bunker was protection for men, machinery, guns or ammunition from bombing and shelling. Bunkers for troops were often merely shelters but some of them were living quarters and self-contained. The first personnel bunkers were identical to those built in the West Wall and housed ten or twenty men (types 501 and 502 dating from 1939). Later army designs accommodated up to fifteen men (type 656 from 1943) and a Kriegsmarine design from 1942, type M151, accommodated twenty-eight. Personnel

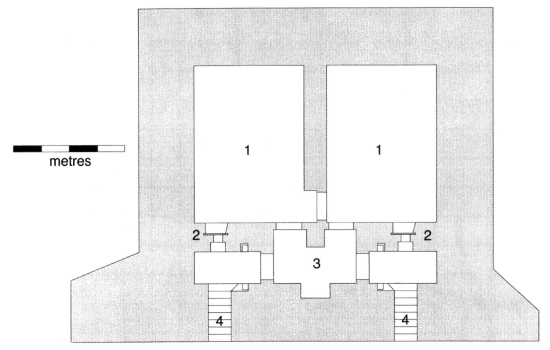

Plan view of a type 622 personnel bunker. Some had a tobruk. Key: 1 crew room, 2 steel embrasure plate, 3 gas lock, 4 entrance. (Ruud Pols)

bunkers were built in most coastal batteries and strongpoints. They were all essentially the same, differing only in detail and size, although some were built to include an ammunition store, such as type 655 from 1943, which was probably far from reassuring for the men sheltering in them during bombardments. Depending on their size, these bunkers were provided with one or two entrances but only one design seems to have been provided with a machine-gun embrasure (type L428 dating from 1942) to protect the bunker from assault; only a few of these seem to have been built. This was presumably because the designers assumed that during an attack the men would be manning their posts elsewhere. However, several of the designs included tobruks which could be armed with a machine-gun, for example, type 622 from 1942, types 655 and 656 from 1943, the latter having two, and type L435A from 1942 but the tobruk was not always built.

When field artillery was not housed in casemates, concrete shelters were usually built, of which there were eight designs (type 504 from 1939, types 601, 604, 605 and 629 from 1943, types 672 and 673 from 1943, and type 701 from 1944). Types 602 and 603 from 1942 were large enough for a tank to drive inside. Neither was built in large numbers, however. Some designs included separate rooms for the crew but many, especially those dating from 1943 and 1944, were no more than glorified garages (for example, types 672 and 701). Some were provided with armoured doors (for example, types 605 and 673). The crews were expected to shelter in slit trenches or in nearby personnel bunkers. Curiously, many of the designs seem to have been almost identical to each other; for example, types 601 and 629 anti-tank gun bunkers, and types 672, 673 and 701 gun bunkers.

Three types of ammunition bunker were built for artillery batteries according to the calibre of the ammunition they were intended to house. Type I was for light artillery, type II was for medium artillery while type III was for heavy artillery (types 143, 607 and 641 dating from 1942 and 1943). In 1943, another design was introduced, type 674, one of the so-called *Kleinstände* (small bunkers) designed to use less concrete than earlier structures. These had followed the Kriegsmarine gun classification despite the fact that most Kriegsmarine casemates were designed with ammunition storerooms and did not require separate bunkers except as main storage facilities. Such Kriegsmarine storage bunkers were different yet again for medium and heavy artillery ammunition, for example type S448a from 1942 and type M145 from 1943. None was built in large numbers. Different designs accommodated anti-aircraft ammunition. Once again, these differed according to the calibre of ammunition they were intended to house, such as type L407 for 88 mm ammunition and type L413 for 37 mm ammunition, both dating from 1942. Unlike most of the Heer and Kriegsmarine ammunition bunkers, some of the Luftwaffe bunkers were provided with machine-gun positions (for example, types L407A and L413A for light Flak ammunition, both dating from 1943). Altogether, there were fourteen designs.

A category of bunker that was only found in coastal and anti-aircraft batteries was the so-called machinery bunker of which there were twenty-one designs. Some of these sheltered searchlights (for example, type 606 from 1942 and type L411 from

A type 622 personnel bunker at Fort de la Varde, Saint-Malo. (Marcus Massing)

A shell-damaged type 622 quarters bunker at Carpiquet airfield, west of Caen, now in the service of the Canadian Army, July 1944. (Ken Bell, National Archives of Canada PA141708)

1942). Some included generators to power the searchlights (such as type FL277 from 1943). Where a generator room was not part of the design, a separate bunker was provided for the generator equipment (for example, type V192 from 1942). And, like other types of bunker, they ranged from the basic to the complex. The simpler designs tended to date from 1943 and 1944 while the complex ones dated from 1942. Some were provided with machine-gun embrasures (for example, type V192) but many were not. Other types of bunker housed kitchens (two designs, types 645 and 657 both from 1943) and water supplies (six designs, including types 646 and 658 from 1943). Such bunkers were usually built as part of self-contained strongpoints. Curiously, none date from before 1943, indicating that the nature of the strongpoints changed from their original conception. A less charitable interpretation is that when they started to build strongpoints no one gave any thought to how the garrison was supposed to sustain itself. Relatively few were built. Similarly, relatively few medical bunkers were built and most dated from 1942 and 1943 although one design was older and had been incorporated in the West Wall (for example, type 638 from

The battery at la Garde Guérin near Saint-Malo included a searchlight which was mounted in this emplacement, reached via a tunnel. (Marcus Massing)

1942 and type 118 from 1939). The designs dating from 1942 onwards were generally bigger but less complex than the 1939 design. Medical bunkers tended to be built at important sites, such as strongpoints that contained regimental headquarters and at the big-gun batteries.

There were several sorts of command post (*Befehlsstand* but the term *Kommandostand* was also sometimes used and the whole category was termed *Gefechtsstände*, which translates as battle headquarters). The smallest were intended as battle headquarters for a company commander (type 610 from 1942). Relatively few command posts for regimental and battalion commanders were built. There were eighteen designs of command post, two of them dating from the construction of the West Wall (types 117 and 119). Only one was a Kriegsmarine design (type M152 from 1942) and only five were Heer designs, the most common of which was type 608 dating from 1942. The majority of the rest were intended for anti-aircraft commanders and were some of the biggest structures in the Atlantic Wall. However, the majority of command posts erected along the French coast were for the army. All but two of the designs incorporated at least one machine-gun embrasure (type Fl354a from 1943 and ⁱʳ L417). Most were single-storey buildings but a couple had two storeys, while a couple of anti-aircraft command posts had substantial rectangular

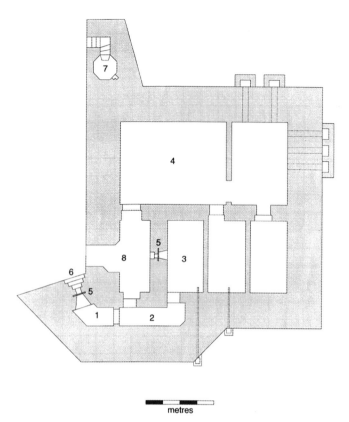

Plan view of a type M183 machinery bunker. Key: 1 gun room, 2 gas lock, 3 ventilation equipment room, 4 machine room, 5 steel embrasure plate, 6 embrasure, 7 observation post (tobruk), 8 entrance. (Ruud Pols)

metres

observation towers (for example, type Fl250 from 1942 and type Fl354a). Because of their function, command posts were usually built in the centres of batteries and strongpoints so that they were protected by outlying bunkers and gun sites, but sometimes they were some distance away on a separate site.

The coastal batteries also made use of fire-control posts, a form of combined command and observation post. These were referred to as *Leitstände* (control posts). Those used by the Heer were very different from those used by the Kriegsmarine because the two services used different rangefinding equipment. Some of the Kriegsmarine designs were very large and complex but the two Heer designs were smaller and simpler, type 636a dating from 1944, an improvement of the 1942 version, type 636. However, only a few of the later design were built; the earlier version was much more common. Like the Kriegsmarine designs, these included both an observation room and a room for a rangefinder. Eleven Kriegsmarine designs were used in France, some of them resembling the superstructures of warships; some had high towers surmounted by the rangefinder (such as types M157 and S414 from 1942). Whether this was deliberate or purely coincidental is difficult to tell although separate observation rooms, one above another, were necessary for the different instruments used for directing fire on sea targets. Some enclosed the rangefinder in a

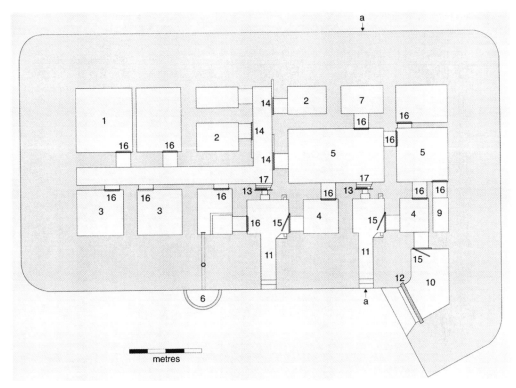

Plan view of a type 117 battalion and regimental battle headquarters. Key: 1 officers' room, 2 NCOs' room, 3 radio room, 4 gas lock, 5 other ranks' room, 6 emergency exit, 7 wireless officer's room, 8 antenna duct, 9 store room, 10 gun room, 11 entrance, 12 steel plate, 13 steel embrasure plate, 14 sliding steel door, 15 steel barn door, 17 embrasure. (Ruud Pols)

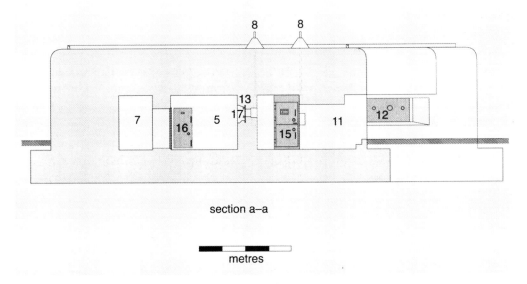

Elevation of a type 117 battle headquarters. (Ruud Pols)

53

A fire-control post built in 1942 into the side of the cliff at la Garde Guérin, a narrow finger of land to the west of Dinard. The battery's three casemates were similarly built into the cliffs along the two sides of the promontory and were all reached by tunnels bored through the rock. (Marcus Massing)

steel cupola (for example, types S100 and S446 from 1942 and 1943 respectively). Many, like the two army designs, were provided with machine-gun embrasures but none of the navy designs were very alike (there were five or six distinct subgroups). Many had two or even three floors, such as type M120 (1942), type M132 (1943) and type M157. The construction of the later designs (none dates from before 1942) was usually simplified to incorporate concrete components that had formally been made from steel, such as in canopies covering observation platforms in which steel ceiling plates had previously been used. None of these designs was built in large numbers.

Besides these large structures, a number of smaller, simpler so-called measuring posts (*Messstellen*) were also built to house equipment used for targeting ships. These were mostly used by army shore batteries. There were three designs, namely types S449 and 637 from 1942 and type 697 from 1944.

All anti-aircraft batteries made use of fire-control posts. The designs used by the Luftwaffe differed from those used by the Kriegsmarine. While the former incorporated square instrument rooms in its earliest designs, which by 1943 had become octagonal and incorporated an extension, the Kriegsmarine instrument rooms tended to be circular. There appears to be no sound reason for such differences. In all, there were seventeen designs, some for heavy batteries, others for light batteries. The Luftwaffe subdivided its designs into two types, B1 and B2,

The machine-gun embrasure, set in an angled wall, protecting the entrance to a bunker on the high ground west of Dieppe. (Ken Bell, National Archives of Canada PA183165)

corresponding to two types of rangefinder. There were four designs of each type (B1: L404, L404A, L424 and L424A. B2: L403, L403A, L425 and L425A.) Generally, both types were included on a site, unless the guns were directed by radar, in which case only one type of fire-control post was built. Almost without exception, the bulk of these structures was below ground with only the roofless instrument room being exposed. Some had machine-gun embrasures.

Very few observation posts were constructed. Their purpose was mostly to provide remote sections of coastline with some sort of military presence. They were built to three designs, all of which included a steel turret (type 143 from 1942, and types 665

A type 120 artillery observation bunker with steel turret at Fort de la Varde, Saint-Malo. (Marcus Massing)

and 666 from 1943). They were relatively small and invariably manned by infantry. Artillery batteries also made use of observation posts but their function was rather different from merely watching remote sections of coast. These were manned by artillerymen to spot targets and the fall of shot, being placed at elevated sites from which it was possible to see the battery's fire zones. These locations were inevitably some distance from command posts and batteries. Some were built close to the edge of the coast and acted as command posts. Artillery observation posts were generally more complex than the infantry posts and incorporated a machine-gun embrasure. The two earliest designs, types 120 and 121, dated from 1939. Type 121 was unusual in having Category A walls 3.5 m thick. Types 120 and 121 and two from 1942 (types 613 and 614 which was on two floors) made use of steel turrets but a further two designs (types 615 and 627) dispensed with the turret and substituted a canopied roof over a forward-looking slot in the concrete structure.

The use of steel observation turrets was much more common in the earliest Atlantic Wall structures than in the later ones. Shortage of steel meant that by 1944 alternative designs had superseded the steel turret. What this came down to in practice was the slit created by building a cantilevered roof over an observation room. This was commonly used in the design of command and fire-control bunkers, for example, type M178 from 1943 and type 636a. The size of such openings was kept to a minimum, partly because they represented a structural weak point, but because of the thickness of the concrete the observers were almost as safe as if there was no opening. In some instances, the slits seem to have been enclosed by glass panels. Observation for reasons of self-defence was a military necessity and many structures

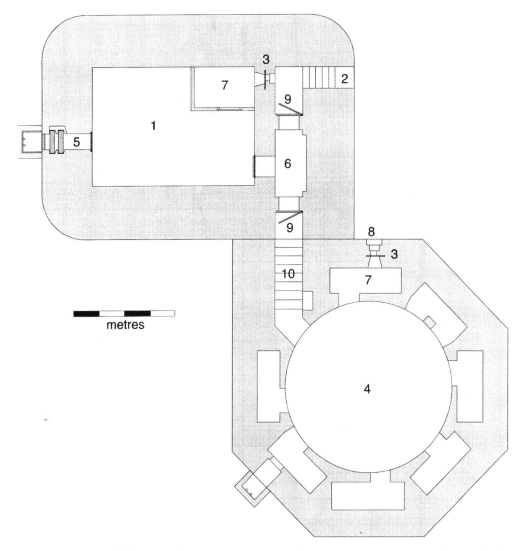

Plan view of a type Fl249 heavy Flak emplacement. Type Fl243 was a mirror image, while type Fl243a had no crew shelter (which was below ground). Key: 1 crew room, 2 entrance, 3 steel embrasure plate, 4 Flak position, 5 emergency exit, 6 gas lock, 7 gun room, 8 embrasure, 9 steel door, 10 access to flak position. (Ruud Pols)

incorporated tobruks which were often little more than concrete foxholes grafted on to the side of a building. The tobruk was isolated from the rest of the building so that the observer had to leave the safety of his bunker and use a stairway in the extension to reach his observation post. The tobruk could also be used as a machine-gun position.

It is not surprising that a large proportion of the structures built along the coast were for guns, amounting to about a third of everything built. Without these, there would have been little point in most of the other structures. There were several types according

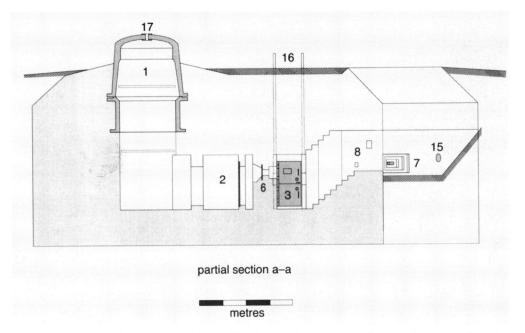

partial section a–a

metres

Elevation of a type 644 machine-gun bunker. Key: 1 six-embrasure turret, 2 ammunition room, 3 steel door, 4 ventilation equipment room, 5 gun room, 6 steel embrasure plate, 7 embrasure, 8 entrance, 9 gas lock, 10 emergency exit crawlway, 11 observation post (tobruk), 12 brick screen, 13 brick partitions, 14 crew room, 15 ventilation port, 16 antennae ducts, 17 periscope port. (Ruud Pols)

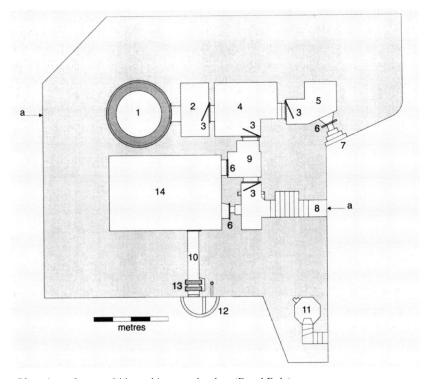

metres

Plan view of a type 644 machine-gun bunker. (Ruud Pols)

Two Canadian officers examine a damaged Renault turret in a tobruk above a beach at Dieppe, 1944. The beach has at least three types of obstacle. (Ken Bell, National Archives of Canada PA134448)

to function and the sort of weapon they were to house: turreted machine-gun emplacements, turreted mortar emplacements, Kriegsmarine emplacements for turreted naval guns, casemates for indirect fire, casemates for enfilade fire, and open emplacements. One distinction drawn by the Heer was whether the gun was intended to provide direct or indirect fire. In the latter case, the guns were generally located some distance inland, whereas the direct-fire guns tended to be sited to enfilade a beach. The requirements of the two functions were not the same and consequently the designs were different. Luftwaffe anti-aircraft gun emplacements were inevitably of the open type but they differed from Heer open emplacements because the requirements were different.

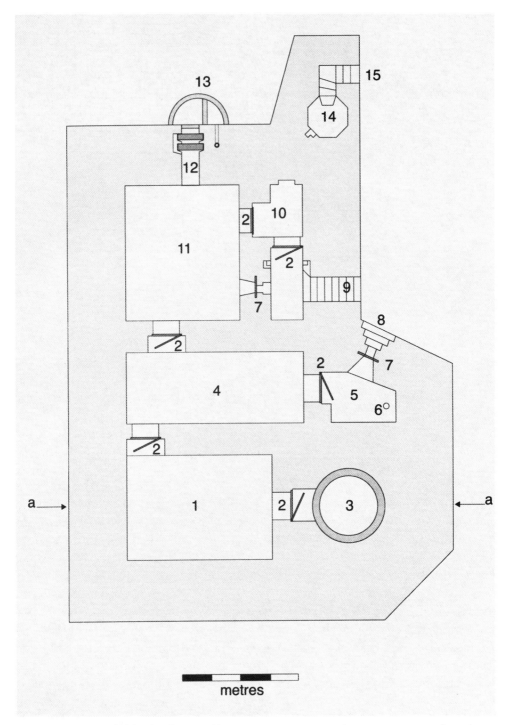

Plan view of a type 633 bunker for an M19 automatic mortar. Key: 1 ammunition room, 2 steel door, 3 mortar turret, 4 ventilation equipment room, 5 gun room, 6 periscope, 7 steel embrasure plate, 8 embrasure, 9 entrance, 10 gas lock, 11 crew room, 12 emergency exit, 13 brick screen, 14 observation post (tobruk), 15 tobruk access, 16 exhaust flue. (Ruud Pols)

Elevation of a type 633 bunker.
(Ruud Pols)

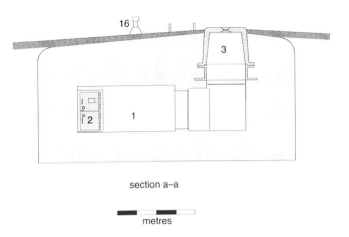

section a–a

metres

There was a plethora of designs. There were fourteen bunkers with armoured turrets with machine-gun embrasures, seventeen casemates for indirect-fire guns, thirty-four enfilade gun casemates, seven naval turret designs (not including the casemates built in the Pas-de-Calais which were one-off specials) although the majority were not built in France, four open emplace-ments for enfilade guns, and twenty-one Flak emplacement designs.

The bunkers incorporating armoured turrets with machine-gun embrasures came in a variety of forms, developed from designs like type 112 used in the West Wall. Turrets with one, three or six embrasures were used (for example, types 647, 632 and 644, respectively), the embrasures often being fitted with ball mountings to allow the gun to be traversed and elevated. An aperture for a periscope was often provided in the roof of the turret. Most bunker designs also included an embrasure in the rear wall to protect the entrance. Types 135 and 633 were for the 50 mm automatic mortar which fired through a closable aperture in the turret roof; around forty of the type 633 were built in France. (The automatic mortar was an ingenious design, breech loaded using a magazine of six rounds.) Type 664 was for a short-barrelled 105 mm Howitzer but only about half a dozen of these seem to have been built. Bunkers and tobruks (also called *Ringstände*) housing turrets taken from French tanks were used all along the Atlantic Wall (the First World War vintage Renault FT 17 turret which mounted a machine-gun, and the Renault R 35 turret which mounted a 37 mm gun were typical).

Casemates for guns intended for indirect fire were built exclusively in coastal batteries some distance from the shoreline. Four designs included rooms for the crew and a self-defence machine-gun embrasure at the rear, while seven merely housed the gun and required separate bunkers for the crew. Heer designs were mostly for pedestal-mounted guns and allowed for 90° or 120° traverse and high-angle elevation (for example, types 649, 651 and 670, and types 650, 652 and 671, respectively). Type 611 was one of three Heer designs intended to house a field gun; about 100 were built in France from its

Fitting a 105 mm gun into a type 671 casemate using wooden blocks and levers. (294/1531/14. Bundesarchiv)

The rear of a type 611 casemate showing the access to the gun room (left) and the entrance next to the self-defence machine-gun embrasure. This one is at Fort de la Varde. (Marcus Massing)

Canadian officers examine French 75 mm ammunition laid out in the embrasure of a type 612 casemate at Dieppe after the port's capture in September 1944. Note the camouflage netting with branches attached to it in a half-hearted attempt at concealment. (Ken Bell, National Archives of Canada PA183098)

introduction in 1942. Guns of 170 mm, 194 mm, 210 mm had casemate designs specific to those calibres but very few were constructed (for example, types 688, 686 and 683, respectively). None of these had crew rooms. The 170 mm was a well-designed and well-engineered Krupp gun with a range of 18.5 miles but a slow rate of fire. Inexplicably, ammunition for it was scarce. The 210 mm was an equally good design from Skoda. All these casemates included magazines but this did not preclude the construction of separate

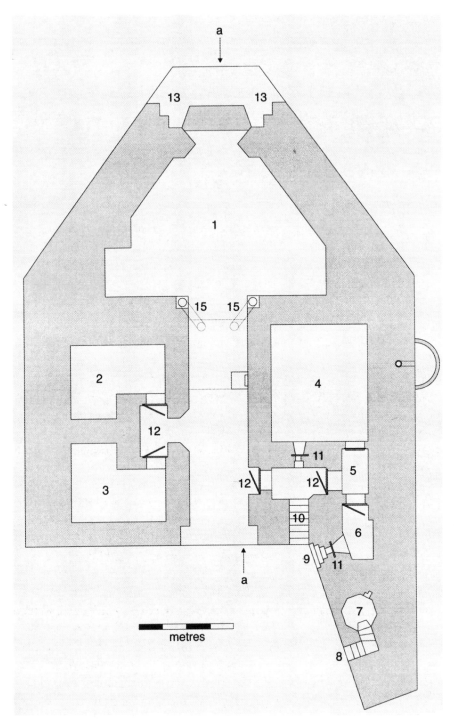

Plan view of a type 611 casemate. Key: 1 gun room, 2 shell room, 3 cartridge room, 4 crew room, 5 gas lock, 6 machine-gun room, 7 observation post (tobruk), 8 tobruk access, 9 embrasure, 10 entrance, 11 steel embrasure plate, 12 steel door, 13 stepped embrasure wall, 14 stepped embrasure roof, 15 spent case shut, 16 spent case dump. (Ruud Pols)

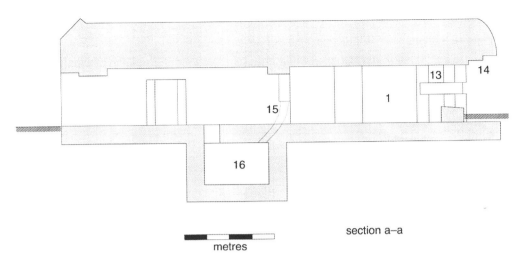

section a–a

metres

Elevation of a type 611 casemate. (Ruud Pols)

magazine bunkers as well. The most common design, type 671, was introduced in 1943 and was one of the simplest and smallest; around 220 were built along the Atlantic and Channel coasts. The Kriegsmarine made use of five casemate designs, three of them incorporating machine-gun embrasures for self-defence but none had crew rooms. The most common appears to have been type M270, around forty-six being built along the French coast. Like the Heer designs, they allowed either 90° or 120° traverse. There was not a lot of difference between the Heer and Kriegsmarine designs or indeed between any of the designs, which begs the questions, why there were so many and why the Heer and Kriegsmarine did not use the same ones rather than adopt their own.

The fact that the Heer had to use such a wide variety of guns in its casemates militated against standardization of designs. This was a problem when it came to the embrasure which tended to be large to accommodate all types of gun. The opening had to be closed in some way otherwise the benefits of encasing the weapon in thick concrete would be negated because the gun and its crew would be unprotected from shrapnel and small arms fire. An armoured gun shield was intended to cover the opening but few casemates seem to have been fitted with them by the time of the invasion. The size and shape of the embrasure was inevitably dictated by the gun that was housed in the casemate. It had to allow sufficient elevation and traverse to enable the gun to engage targets in its predetermined fire zone. The embrasure opened like a V-shaped notch when looking at it from above, the angle of the opening determining the range of traverse. Resembling stairways tilted on their edges, the sides of the V were stepped rather than smooth to prevent shells ricocheting into the opening. The roof of a casemate was usually extended beyond the embrasure in a smooth or angular arc over the gun barrel. Its lower surface was also stepped inwards. The angle of the opening determined the maximum angle of elevation. The casemate was also protected against the mining effects of shells that

A Ringstand for a 50 mm anti-tank gun in 1943. This one has a 'roof' to help conceal it from aircraft. Camouflage netting could also be attached to it. Note the squiggle-pattern camouflage. (293/1453/31. Bundesarchiv)

penetrated the ground immediately in front of the embrasure before exploding. This was done by extending an apron of concrete in front of the casemate that could be as thick as the external walls.

Casemates that were intended to provide enfilading fire were distinctly different from other casemates and usually incorporated a flanking wall that shielded the gun barrel from the seaward side. These casemates were usually placed sideways to a beach and some were incorporated into anti-tank walls. The designs were exclusively Heer, some of them having been used in the West Wall (for example, types 105 and 515). These flanking casemates were meant to house a machine-gun, anti-tank gun or field gun. Only a couple seem to have been armed with a pedestal-mounted gun, types 703 and 704 from 1944. Some were very simple designs, like types 700 and 703 which were not much more than rectangular boxes with an embrasure and no flanking wall, while others incorporated a machine-gun embrasure to defend the entrance, crew rooms and variety of other rooms for machinery and storage (for example, type 633A). Armour plate was often built into the structure as a gun shield (for 37 mm anti-tank guns and machine-guns), the barrel protruding through it via a ball joint, and the roof was often extended over the barrel towards the flanking wall in a triangular fillet. Some designs of enfilade-fire casemates were rarely built while others were built in their hundreds, for example, types 612, 667 and 669. Types 612 and 669 housed field guns.

Originally, the Heer put all its guns in open emplacements, for which there were several similar designs; but none seems to have been given a Regelbau number.

An artillery battery on the Channel coast housed in open emplacements. Note the rudimentary turntable on which the gun is mounted and the rooms off the platform area. (291/1242/27. Bundesarchiv)

Many of these still existed at the time of the invasion although not all were occupied as from 1943 they were in the process of being replaced by casemates. The Heer appears to have had only one design of open emplacement that came within the standard series, the type 600. This was for the 50 mm anti-tank gun and was fairly widespread. The Kriegsmarine made use of several designs but few seem to have been part of the Atlantic Wall by mid-1944 (for example, types M158 and M180), having been replaced by casemates. By 1944, the majority of open emplacements were for Flak; there were twenty-one designs. Some of these included an underground bunker for the crew or an underground command post for commanders of small Flak units, for example types Fl242 and L410A. The diversity of designs is hard to explain since there were only a limited number of anti-aircraft gun types (20 mm, 37 mm, 40 mm, 88 mm, 105 mm and 128 mm) but there were, for example, at least eight designs for 37 mm emplacements.

Communications centres, signal posts and radar stations were built in far fewer numbers than other structures. The Heer had two designs for bunkers in which accumulators were charged (types 142 and 660), a design for a switchboard bunker (type 616) and three signals centres for commanders, one of which was specifically for radio communications (types 617, 618 and 691, respectively). The Kriegsmarine had at least three designs for radar bunkers (for example, type V143 for the Mammut radar) as well as designs for related bunkers and signals posts (for example, type V142). Many of these were fairly large structures and were provided with machine-gun embrasures for defence. The Luftwaffe had at least five designs for radar bunkers (for example, type L480 for the Wassermann radar). Since the radars used by the Kriegsmarine and the Luftwaffe were essentially the same, it is difficult to understand why they did not use the same or similar designs. The Kriegsmarine design for its Mammut radar was completely different from the Luftwaffe design (type L485) which post-dated the Kriegsmarine's. The Luftwaffe also used several designs of communications bunker, some of them quite small. There were also a number of designs of bunker for directing nightfighters but these were nothing to do with the Atlantic Wall and everything to do with defence of the Reich.

Manuals containing the specifications of these designs were compiled for each service. A manual contained not only a detailed engineering drawing of each design but its material requirements and an illustration of how earth should be banked against the structure to help blend it into the landscape. In addition, there were technical data on weapons, fields of fire and ranges. These manuals were the guides from which the construction engineers worked. In view of the number of new designs that appeared at different times, these manuals must have been thick and heavy – provided they were kept up to date by whoever was responsible for this tedious job. The structures erected at any given site were inevitably derived from what was in the manual currently being used by the constructors. It is likely that differences between manuals accounted for some of the differences between similar types of site. In other words, everyone was working from different manuals.

The requirements that any design had to fulfil clearly differed according to its function, although some aspects of all structures were the same. The primary function of all structures was the protection of the occupants from bombs, shells and small arms fire. This obviously extended to the protection of the equipment housed in the structure. Consequently, certain features of the structures were much the same, such as the thickness of the walls and ceilings which were built to withstand direct hits from high-explosive ordnance. To make the structures more bombproof and shellproof, earth was usually banked against the walls so that little of the concrete was exposed. Earth helped to absorb and dissipate the shock waves from an explosion. Earth and steel-reinforced concrete formed a composite structure that was an extremely effective armour. Although damage could be inflicted on the bunkers, they could take a tremendous amount of punishment and still protect their occupants from serious physical harm – although the psychological harm might well have been intensified by a sense of being trapped within a tomb-like bunker during prolonged heavy bombardments. The occupants were sometimes stupefied by noise and vibration.

CHAPTER 5

Concrete Ideas

Concrete tends to disintegrate under impact, including when struck by the shock waves of an explosion. This is because, although strong under compression, concrete is weak under tension such as bending and shearing. Concrete's poor tensile strength led to the development of steel-reinforced concrete as a structural building material by Hennebique in France in the late nineteenth century (steel-reinforced concrete as a non-structural material was invented in 1867). The nature of the reinforcement itself makes a difference to the strength of the material. In modern reinforced concrete, bars of cold-worked mild steel joined by soft mild steel links are used to form a three-dimensional lattice into which the concrete is poured. The cold working increases the tensile strength while soft mild steel is malleable and less prone to breaking under tension, bending instead. The idea is for the steel to carry the tensile loads while the concrete takes the compressive loads. This makes reinforced concrete a very strong material. Modern concrete is usually made up of about 20 per cent cement and 80 per cent graded aggregate which contains about three parts sand to two parts gravel which is graded according to size (the ratio of cement to sand to gravel is about 1:2:3). The water which is added to the mix reacts with the cement in a complex series of chemical processes that release a large amount of heat and leads to the material setting rock hard, irreversibly binding all the elements together. In theory, the structures built in the Atlantic Wall from about mid-1942 were supposed to use a concrete that contained aggregate consisting of about two parts sand to one part gravel. The proportion of cement in the concrete was higher than in modern concretes to reduce the setting time and speed up the construction process. It also tended to produce a harder concrete.

The fact that concrete is pourable before it sets makes it an ideal material for building complex engineering structures, especially bombproof and shellproof casemates and bunkers. However, the Germans encountered unexpected problems when building such large structures: the large quantity of heat produced by the setting concrete, and shrinkage. During the building of the West Wall, similar problems had been countered with quick-drying cement. Many of the Atlantic Wall structures were many times bigger than those in the West Wall and the problems were correspondingly bigger. With the Atlantic Wall, however, they abandoned quick-drying formulas which took longer to make than ordinary Portland cement, leading to delays. Portland cement is so-called because of its resemblance to Portland stone when set. It is usually a mixture of 75 per cent limestone (calcium carbonate) and 25 per cent clay which is mainly alumino-

Tying together the components of the reinforcement lattice. The bunker's turret has already been lowered in place. It has a tobruk on the left. (295/1586/31a. Bundesarchiv)

silicate but also contains some iron oxide. These are ground together and fired at 1500 °C and the resulting clinker is mixed with 3–5 per cent gypsum. This is then ground and the result is cement. The size of its particles is directly related to the setting time – smaller particles make faster setting times. Shrinkage could be minimized by keeping the concrete damp while it set but this slowed the production rate.

The steel reinforcement rods used in the structures of the Atlantic Wall were 12 mm in diameter and spaced at 20–25 cm. The ends of these rods were hooked to increase the reinforcing effect, a technique that had been used in the First World War. The ends of the vertical bars often extended beyond the upper surface so that camouflage netting could be attached to the hooked ends. The three-dimensional mesh of reinforcement bars was constructed by first prefabricating the vertical components as two-dimensional nets that could be fixed in place. Then, the horizontal rods were laboriously inserted through the vertical nets and tied to them with 2 mm steel wire. Sometimes horizontal bars 22 mm in diameter were used in roofs and ceilings instead of the 12 mm rods.

There was a wider range in cement quality than the Germans would have liked but the pressure of time meant that compromises had to be made. In the early days of the

Atlantic Wall, German cement rather than local French cement was used for the concrete but by 1944 French cement was more commonly used. This was partly to obviate the growing problem of transportation under increasing Allied air attacks; by May 1944, it was estimated that only 20 per cent of cement supplies were reaching their destination. By spring 1943, this had already led to a need to allocate cement according to strict priorities. Casemates for Heeres Küsten Batterien received one of the highest priorities, with support bunkers following behind. Luftwaffe and Kriegsmarine positions were given lower priorities. As far as the Kriegsmarine was concerned, this was largely because the majority of its gun emplacements had already been built, whereas the army had few casemates for its guns. These priorities, drawn up at the beginning of 1943, were based on the tactical requirements at that time, to ensure that there were adequate supplies of cement where they were needed most. Curiously, the Atlantic Wall as a whole did not seem to have been given the highest priority for cement until November 1943.

Although it has been suggested that sabotage played a part in the poor quality of some of the concrete, the more likely cause was poor cement and a lack of coarse aggregate. The resulting mix would have been considerably weaker than concrete made from good quality Portland cement combined with sufficient coarse aggregate; lack of coarse material led to voids being formed in the concrete which acted as stress concentrators, weakening the material. This quality shortfall was probably due to hasty methods of aggregate screening with an over-reliance on local sources of sand and gravel, which was often insufficiently coarse. Another factor may have been the weather. The concrete of structures built in the winter months may have been adversely affected by low temperatures. A low temperature when the concrete is poured tends to reduce tensile strength because the heat produced during the setting process is insufficient to allow this process to proceed properly. Usually, large structures like those of the Atlantic Wall would not be constructed in the winter months for this reason. However, the Germans did not have the luxury of being able to wait until the spring; although it may be significant that less concrete was consumed in the winters 1942/43 and 1943/44 than in spring and summer of 1943 and 1944. To compensate for the lower temperatures the Germans may have added calcium chloride to the mixture to accelerate setting and increase the amount of heat produced in the process. They certainly used seawater on occasions to add up to about 3 per cent salt; sea salt contains calcium chloride. The amount of water added to the mixture had a direct affect on the tensile strength of the set concrete. The less water added to the mixture, the stronger the concrete but the more difficult it was to pour. The Organization Todt established a range of ratios of water to cement that would not compromise strength while keeping construction at an optimum speed.

The Todt tested the strength of the concrete after it had set. It is not clear quite what they would have done had some of the concrete been found to be substandard. Substandard concrete must have been knowingly used from time to time and once the structure had been built there was very little that could be done about it.

The structure could hardly be torn down and rebuilt. It is likely that such buildings would not have been drawn to anyone's attention since someone would have been made accountable. An advantage of a convoluted bureaucracy was that accountability could be swamped in a welter of forms and circular procedures that then disappeared up a hidden cul-de-sac. Because concrete continues to harden for some time after it has set, the Todt tested it 28 days after it was laid, by which time a 20 cm cube had to withstand a compressive force of 350 kg/m². In February 1945, the US Corps of Engineers completed a survey of the Atlantic Wall defences in Normandy and concluded that the 'standards of construction were not as high as those normally found in the United States'. This was attributed to the Organization Todt's use of forced labour. According to the Corps of Engineers, the way the concrete was made resulted in it containing an excessive amount of fine aggregate, producing a weaker concrete than one made with coarser aggregate. Their tests indicated an average strength of 3,600 lb/in² (253 kg/cm²).

From May 1942 when von Rundstedt issued Basic Order No 7, the Heer fortress engineers stipulated that every cubic metre of concrete should have 60 kg of steel reinforcement. At the same time, four construction categories were established, defining the thickness of the external walls but these were already well-established ideas. Not surprisingly, the most important structures were allocated the thickest walls. Hitler's headquarters bunkers, underground factories and the V-weapon sites were all designated Category E, the heaviest category, with walls 5 m thick. This thickness seems to have been arrived at by Hitler himself who demanded that the walls and ceilings of his bunkers should be capable of withstanding the largest Allied bombs. The same criteria were subsequently applied to other important buildings. Surprisingly, perhaps, the submarine pens were designated Category A, the next category down, with walls 3.5 m thick. Heavy-gun casemates and radar bunkers were also designated Category A. Next came Category B with walls 2 m thick. Most of the structures in the Atlantic Wall were Category B; 2 m was stipulated as the minimum thickness of external walls of fortifications that housed military personnel but this was undermined by the fourth and lowest category. Category B1 structures had walls only 1–1.2 m thick. So-called improvised structures and field defences were designated B1. Considerable numbers of Category B1 structures had been erected prior to May 1942; these were in effect strengthened field works. On Hitler's orders, no more were to be built as they were not capable of withstanding heavy bombardment. Nevertheless, by the beginning of 1944, similarly thin-walled bunkers and shelters were being erected in increasing numbers because of a shortage of materials.

A Royal Navy report written after the effects of the pre-invasion bombardment had been assessed made it plain that even 15 in naval shells had been unable to penetrate the thick carapaces of the Category B structures. None of them were destroyed although many were damaged to some degree. The report suggested that the concussions from the shells may have incapacitated the occupants but the evidence of D-Day did not support this view as many of the defenders had still manned their

The remains of a type M162a fire-control post on the island of Grand Bé off Saint-Malo, showing how reinforcement bars were arranged at a corner. (Marcus Massing)

guns after the bombardment had lifted. It is unlikely that a longer bombardment would have made much difference. This failure by the Allied warships and bombers to neutralize the shore batteries and strongpoints was not so much an operational failure as a technological one. The Allies lacked weapons capable of destroying thick-walled steel-reinforced concrete structures. In the Gulf War of 1991, it took smart munitions, with heavier payloads than Second World War bombs and naval shells, aimed at the weakest points in the bunkers, to kill the occupants – but these, too, failed to destroy the bunkers. Bunkers are notoriously difficult to destroy even with carefully placed demolition charges in peacetime. In the Second World War, Allied infantrymen, engineers and armour had to kill the occupants because they could not destroy the bunkers. By dropping demolition charges or hand grenades into one or more of a structure's apertures or squirting a flamethrower at the embrasure or entrance, the defenders could be killed or persuaded to surrender. But it could be a painfully slow process.

Some of the weakest points on any bunker were its corners where walls met and where the roof joined the walls. Square joints and edges tend to focus stresses which

The entrance to a type 105 machine-gun bunker in the Citadel at Saint-Malo showing the self-defence
machine-gun position. Rather than a concrete embrasure, this had a steel plate with an aperture for the
gun with a vision aperture (right). There was a similar plate at the front for another machine-gun.
(Marcus Massing)

weakens the structure. To counter this, the corners and leading edges of the walls were often rounded on the exterior face rather than left square (although the corresponding internal edge or corner was). The radius of curvature was either 0.5 m or 1 m. Rounding the corners and edges not only helped to reduce the effects of direct hits on these areas but encouraged the deflection of shells.

The ceilings of Category B structures were originally reinforced with a steel liner on the inner face which also helped to prevent spalling. Spalling was more of a problem for the roof than the walls simply because the walls were vertical and usually had a mass of earth against them, whereas the roof, even if covered by a thick layer of earth, could still receive direct hits because it was horizontal. To simplify construction, the liner formed part of the shuttering, a practice well known in civil engineering when live loads have to be carried by a structure. (A live load is something that moves over a structure and exerts a variable force by virtue of moving, such as traffic over a bridge, rather than a dead weight, such as the weight of the structure itself.) The liner was made up of several plates that rested on the lower flanges of a series of spaced rolled-steel I-beams (also known as RSJs) that spanned the ceiling. These were either 30 cm or 45 cm apart. The liner plates were held in place by the sheer weight of the concrete above them. This form of construction was continued up stairways, the ceilings of

A light Flak position of twin MG 34s at Dieppe, August 1942. This is a wood-lined tobruk. (291/1223/28. Bundesarchiv)

which mirrored the steps beneath. As steel became scarcer for construction work, preformed concrete beams were used instead of steel ones and the liner plates were dispensed with. Sometimes, timber beams were used.

Category A structures, like the big casemates at Sangatte near Calais, for example, used a more complex system of reinforcement in the ceilings because the weight of concrete was enormous, far greater than anything in the category B structures, and the span of the ceilings was greater than those in Category B buildings. The I-beams were closer together, spaced only 25 cm apart, and a second set rested on the lower flanges of the first set and between these were placed sheets of corrugated steel, the permanent shuttering.

The internal walls did not need to be anything like as thick as the external ones as they performed the same functions as internal walls in any building. They held up

Mortar tobruk. This one is at Fort de la Varde at Saint-Malo. (Marcus Massing)

ceilings and roofs and divided up the internal space although they also had the additional function of confining explosions to minimize casualties. All internal spaces were designed according to their function, using the minimum necessary for the efficient execution of that function. The dimensions of these spaces conformed to multiples of 10 cm, a measurement probably chosen for convenience. The thickness of the internal walls varied according to where they were within the structure and were 25 cm, 50 cm, 80 cm or 100 cm thick. The thickest walls faced the entrances which were normal door width, 80 cm. Internal doors were located in walls that were at least 50 cm thick. The height of each internal space was either 2 m or 2.2 m which did not allow much headroom but helped to reduce the overall size of the structure. Corridors were often 1.2 m, 1.4 m or 1.5 m wide. Ceilings in single-storey structures were 80 cm thick although for short spans in relatively safe locations within the structure this was sometimes reduced to only 20 cm. It has been suggested that the geometrical relationship between the internal spaces implies an architectural form. It is more likely that function and building materials dictated their size and shape so that the structures inevitably bear a resemblance in the same way that all tanks tend to look alike.

It was certainly function that determined how many entrances were built into a structure and the fact that entrances were at the back and did not lead directly into the heart of the building. Even the simplest bunker required anyone entering it to make a 90° turn into a small room that acted as a gas lock before entering the main part of the interior, although this was not always the case with casemates. This precaution ensured that assaulting infantry could not simply blow in the door to get at the occupants but had to fight their way inside through a series of rooms and corridors all sealed by armoured steel doors that isolated the heart of the structure. In theory, an enemy could penetrate the building but be unable to prevent the occupants from continuing to fight. The internal wall facing the entrance was often provided with an armoured embrasure for a machine-gun. In addition to this, some structures were provided with an extension at the back to house a machine-gun room to cover the entrance. The external wall of this extension was set at 60° to the back wall and the machine-gun fired through an armoured embrasure set into it. The roof often had a triangular extension from this gun room to the entrance to provide further protection.

The incorporation of a gas lock followed the mistaken belief that gas warfare was inevitable, although by the middle of the war it should have become apparent that neither side had the stomach for it. Nevertheless, it remained a feature of many designs. The gas lock was designed to keep all contaminants out of the working areas of the bunker which were supplied with clean filtered air.

In the event that a bunker was destroyed or taken by the enemy, an emergency exit was provided to enable the crew to escape. This was merely a narrow crawl shaft, 60 cm by 80 cm, through an external wall to a shielded ladder on the outside, consisting of steel rungs embedded in the outer face, up which the escaper could climb to ground level and open a trap door in the surface. The crawl shaft was normally sealed on the inside by a steel door 80 cm by 80 cm and, about halfway along, by two brick partitions supported in recesses in the shaft and by short steel beams that were removable. After the beams were taken out, the partitions could be demolished to allow the occupants to escape.

According to Dorsch, by the time of the invasion, in excess of 6,500 bunkers and casemates of standard designs had been built from the Spanish frontier to the Belgian border. About 42 per cent of the structures were bunkers of various sorts for personnel and equipment while about 39 per cent were casemates and gun emplacements (2,759 and 2,546 structures respectively). There were also a considerable number of non-standard structures. These included more than 2,800 tobruks, over 400 open anti-tank gun emplacements and nearly 200 non-standard anti-tank bunkers. In addition, there were 283 non-standard gun emplacements including sixteen for guns of 220 mm and 240 mm as well as casemates for guns as big as 300 mm and 406 mm. Altogether, there were about 5,000 non-standard structures. Thus more than 11,500 Atlantic Wall structures were built along the French coast. So much for standardization: 43 per cent of everything built in the Atlantic Wall was of a non-standard design. There were, of course, at the time of the invasion a large number of structures still in the process of construction. It has been estimated that there were approximately the same number under construction as had been completed so that in total there were in the region of 23,000 Atlantic Wall structures in France, either completed or in the process of construction.

Approximately 6,900,000 m³ of concrete were used in building these structures, consuming some 2,600,000 tonnes of cement along with 455,000 tonnes of reinforcement steel, the bulk of which was consumed between spring 1942 and summer 1944.

A propaganda shot of the rear of casemate No. 1 at the Todt battery. This is now a museum. The lettering has long since vanished. (73/35/5. Bundesarchiv)

CHAPTER 6

Workers on the Atlantic Wall

Organization Todt, named after its founder, Fritz Todt, came into existence in early 1938 for the specific purpose of constructing the West Wall. It was formed from the workers who had been involved in the construction of the Autobahnen under Todt's direction since 1933. Prior to its inception, the Heer's own fortress engineers had been entrusted with the project but they did not have the manpower or resources to complete the work in the time demanded by Hitler. They had already spent two years building the West Wall when the Todt took over. Organization Todt remained outside all ministry, military and party control throughout its existence even though it was an agency of the Armaments Ministry. This did not change with Todt's death in 1942. Although Albert Speer was now nominally head of Organization Todt, it was run by Xaver Dorsch, his deputy.

With the Fall of France in 1940, Organization Todt acquired a military-style hieriachical structure. Those of its units that were involved in building work for the Heer were classed as army auxiliaries and came under military control. At about the same time, Todt personnel were kitted out in military-style uniforms (which have been variously described as olive-green, khaki and brown) and had to wear an armband on the left arm that bore a swastika and the legend 'Organization Todt' although there appear to have been a number of variations on this theme (including 'Org. Todt' over 'Deutsche Wehrmacht' with a circled German eagle). It had become a quasi-military organization. It would appear that lorry drivers were equipped with pistols or sub-machine-guns for self-defence. During the raid on Dieppe in 1942, a number of bunkers were under construction and Organization Todt personnel were caught up in the fighting. Because of their uniforms some of them were mistaken for Wehrmacht soldiers and killed by the Canadians. Surprisingly, when Hitler was informed of their deaths by Dorsch, he was persuaded by Jodl's argument that it had happened because OKW had failed to let the Allies know via Switzerland that Todt personnel wore uniforms; Hitler refrained from ordering the reprisals that Jodl had anticipated. This may have been partly due to Hitler's exhilaration at his enemy getting such a bloody nose which reinforced his belief that a strongly defended coastline could not be breached. In May 1943, rank badges were introduced and by the autumn of 1944 Organization Todt had become a fully fledged paramilitary unit, armed for the defence of Germany, and was renamed Front-OT.

Before December 1941, most of the Organization Todt's work along the French coast had been for the Kriegsmarine. This had been undertaken by its Special Projects Group which had worked with the navy's fortress engineers. Because of the

An obviously posed photograph of a member of the Organization Todt instructing a worker in 1942. Note his two armbands. (MW 2355/10. Bundesarchiv)

lack of a coordinated building plan before the beginning of 1942, the Todt construction units acted as independent building contractors and there was little overall control within the Todt. This was exacerbated by building firms seeking separate contracts with the service concerned. There was little communication between the building groups or with the services, a situation that frustrated von Rundstedt when he took command of Army Group West. He complained that Organization Todt should come under his command but it availed him nothing and the Todt remained independent throughout the war.

After Speer took over the Armaments Ministry, he introduced a number of reforms to improve the efficiency of the Todt including a centralized administration. At the same time, to prevent competition and increase coordination, he simplified the way in which civilian building firms were contracted. The Central Office was run by Dorsch without reference to Speer and it was from here that orders went out for the construction work. It decided what was built and where although, in theory, this was now in cooperation with the armed services. The new administration created Einsatzgruppe West which was responsible for all building work from Holland to the Spanish frontier as well as that in the South of France to the Italian border. Its headquarters were in the Champs Elysées, Paris and was headed by Oberbaudirektor

Karl Weis (*Oberbaudirektor* was a rank created especially for Organization Todt which had a rank structure much like any of the armed services). He had joined the Todt in 1938 and had already overseen the construction of the batteries in the Pas-de-Calais as well as some of the work on the U-boat pens. As Oberbaudirektor Einsatzgruppe West, Weis was also Chief Engineer to Army Group West.

In practice, the new streamlined system did not work quite as planned because of the military-style chain of command that was now in operation. Einsatzgruppe West was divided into Einsatz Atlantic and Einsatz Mediterranean and each of these was subdivided into Oberbauleitungen. The Oberbauleitungen under Einsatz Atlantic concerned with the construction of the Atlantic Wall in France included Northwest, Cherbourg (which included Alderney but not the other Channel Islands), Rouen, Saint-Malo, North (Brest), Middle (Lorient), South (Saint-Nazaire), Paula (la Rochelle) and Bordeaux, the last four of which were principally but not exclusively concerned with the U-boat pens. There were others unconnected with the construction of the Atlantic Wall. Each of these Oberbauleitungen were further subdivided into *Baustellen* or construction sites. These all had staffs that mimicked military staffs. Only seven Oberbauleitungen existed in 1942 but by 1944 there were nineteen, including the Mediterranean areas and the Channel Islands. Later the system changed and Normandy became an Einsatz with three Oberbauleitungen, Cherbourg, Saint-Malo and North (Brest). Cherbourg was later upgraded to an Einsatz and was responsible for the construction of fortifications from Trouville, just west of the Seine estuary, to Granville on the Atlantic coast below the Cotentin peninsula.

In each Oberbauleitung there was a Technical Section responsible for surveying sites, drawing up plans, testing building materials, assigning building firms to particular sites and directing operations on each site. The supply of labour was controlled by a different department, while another was concerned with supervising the contracted building firms; its head was often the managing director of one of the firms involved. Many building contractors, engineering firms and other specialist suppliers were German but some were local French firms. To ensure that no building site was run by a Frenchman, a distinct possibility as more and more French firms became involved, steps were taken to ensure that German staff outnumbered foreigners and that the head was always German. There was always the underlying fear that, no matter how close the collaboration between French and German staff, foreign workers would take every opportunity to sabotage construction which French supervisors might tacitly sanction if they themselves were not supervised. Such sabotage might entail little more than poor workmanship, corner cutting and slowness. Until 1944, French firms were not trusted enough to be under direct contract to the Todt but were permitted to be subcontractors to German firms, although this was a fine distinction that had less to do with reliability than it had to do with political manoeuvring by those in the Nazi heirarchy. There were constant arguments between Speer and the Gauleiters of the regions where industry was based about the forced removal of labour to work in German factories, including skilled workers from French firms involved in the Atlantic Wall. By an irony, such forced labour could still end up working on the Atlantic Wall but in an unskilled capacity.

Before Organization Todt became heavily involved in the construction of the Atlantic Wall, it had relied on its own labour force which was largely made up of conscripted Germans, reinforced by the construction companies of the fortress engineers. After early 1942, however, other sources of labour were needed because of the magnitude of the project. Forced foreign labour became essential. The management of the labour supply became a major undertaking for the Todt. Unskilled labour was supplied by the Reich Labour Service (*Reichsarbeitsdienst –* RAD) which conscripted men between the ages of nineteen and twenty-five for six months service prior to being drafted into the armed services. The RAD had existed since 1935 as a Nazi organization and in 1940 it was reorganized into regiment-like Groups to cope with the exigencies of war. A RAD Group now comprised between four and six companies of 200 men who were armed. By the beginning of 1943, there were thirty-nine RAD Groups in France with a total of 32,000 men but not all of these were involved with the construction of the Atlantic Wall. The numbers declined during 1943 and 1944 as they were withdrawn to Germany to help repair bomb damage as well as man searchlight and anti-aircraft batteries as the RAF and USAAF increased their bombing of the Reich.

Army construction companies worked only on army sites and were probably more involved in the Atlantic Wall than those of the other services, the navy's tending to work independently of the Todt. About 20,000 army personnel were building the Atlantic Wall by the autumn of 1943, made up from fourteen Fortress Engineer Construction Battalions, four Pioneer Construction Battalions and five Rock Drilling Companies. These units were directed by the Todt on site but remained independent of it. This only served to complicate matters since, in effect, each site had two labour forces, each under independent control by organizations that did not always see eye to eye. Perversely, the fortress engineers were directed by the Todt because it was in charge of construction, whereas the army was in no position to issue orders to the Todt about what it wanted built. The situation was further complicated by the paramilitary nature of the Todt's organizational structure which categorized and divided up workers as though they were soldiers. With this came implied Wehrmacht control of their activities, suggesting that army commanders could issue orders to the Todt construction units. They could not. Dorsch ensured that there were no infringements of his authority by the Wehrmacht. Curiously, RAD personnel were usually under Wehrmacht jurisdiction. Although construction was the responsibility of the Todt, supply and installation of weapons and armour plates and turrets was the responsibility of the Heer fortress engineers. This convoluted control system was typical of the Nazi state.

Even with the RAD personnel and the fortress engineers, there were simply not enough workers to undertake the project in the timescale demanded by Hitler.

Although some skilled labour was recruited locally, the only solution was forced labour, the need for which grew as the war progressed and more RAD units were withdrawn to Germany. The use of forced labour was not, of course, confined to the building of the Atlantic Wall. It was widely used throughout German industry. It was drawn from concentration camps, foreign nationals from all the occupied territories, Soviet prisoners of war and other POWs. Their treatment varied widely according to who they were – which, in turn, often decided for whom they worked. Without the use of this unwilling labour force, the Atlantic Wall would not have been built as there were simply too few Germans and willing foreigners to build it unaided. Although willing foreign recruits had swelled the ranks of the Todt's construction workers in the early years of the war, these were now too few to make much impact on the speed with which it was necessary to build the Atlantic Wall following Hitler's demands in 1942. The Todt, like so many German firms, resorted to forced labour, a system that was helped by the Armaments Ministry and Albert Speer.

In May 1943, there were 260,000 workers in France involved in the construction of the Atlantic Wall and special projects such as the U-boat pens and V-weapon sites. Only about 26,000 were German, most of whom were supervisors. In June 1944, this figure had risen to 286,000 workers of which only 15,000 were German. Of the remaining 271,000, 85,000 were French, 25,000 were from French North Africa and French Indochina, another 20,000 were Italian, 15,000 were Spanish and 25,000 were Poles. An additional 15,000 were classified as Ostarbeiter, the term used for men from Russia and Poland and Slavs. It is unclear why there should have been this apparent overlap in classification but there was probably some perverse logic. There were 10,000 Dutch, 10,000 Belgians, 10,000 Czechs, 1,000 Norwegians and Danes, and 5,000 from the Baltic states. As many as 50,000 were from concentration camps. Only these, however, were listed as forced labour, whereas in reality most if not all of the 271,000 probably had no choice in whether they worked for the Germans. That was certainly true of the Ostarbeiter who, along with the men from concentration camps, received the worst treatment and were worked the hardest. It is probable that some of the 271,000 were indeed volunteers but there were degrees of volunteering which depended on the nature of the alternative. If you were French, staying in France to work on the Atlantic Wall so that you avoided being transported to Germany to work in an armaments factory was probably a sufficiently attractive alternative to encourage you to volunteer. Nevertheless, it is difficult to determine how many of the 85,000 French workers were volunteers.

By the end of June 1944, the number of workers had fallen to 160,000 with some 18,000 Germans. It is not surprising that there should have been fewer workers following the Normandy invasion but an increase in the number of Germans when Organization Todt was withdrawing from France seems a little suspect. It is extremely unlikely that the number of Germans working with the Todt in France would have increased after the invasion. Neither is it credible that during the height

The worker on the roof of the bunker in the foreground is applying pitch to waterproof the structure ready for covering with earth. In the background is what appears to be a command post or a fire-control post camouflaged with painted-on windows and door. (291/1213/22. Bundesarchiv)

of the building programme in France, May 1943, there were fewer workers than in June 1944 when work had tailed off sharply to about one-fifth of the spring 1943 output. By 18 June, all Todt workers had been withdrawn from construction work and were involved in road repair and the clearing of rubble to aid the movement of reinforcements.

The diversity of nationalities meant that there was a language problem although everyone was expected to respond to German instructions. The opportunities for misunderstandings may not have been as great as might be imagined, however, since most of the work conformed to repetitions of standard procedures. All the workers had to do was learn the procedures and a smattering of appropriate German words and phrases; a full understanding of foreign languages was unnecessary for the majority of workers.

CHAPTER 7

How to Build a Wall

O nce a location had been chosen, it had to be surveyed before work could commence. After this was completed and the site of each structure had been laid out, the next step was excavation. This was a major undertaking that required adequate shoring of the sides of the deep holes to prevent collapse and often water had to be pumped out because of rain or the level of the water table. The excavated earth had to be removed and dumped. The sites would have been little different from any civilian building project but for one significant difference. Because of the size of such sites, they were easily discernible from the air and something had to be done to conceal the activities from Allied reconnaissance aircraft. Consequently, attempts were made to camouflage as much as possible, including spoil heaps, throughout the period of construction. This was not easy as everything on a site was constantly changing as the structures took shape. Netting and local vegetation were used to conceal plant and dumps of building materials as well as the heaps of excavated earth. Something in the region of 28,000,000 m³ of earth had been excavated by June 1944. Despite extensive use of camouflage, by the end of 1943, Allied air attacks were severely disrupting progress.

Once a hole had been dug to the required depth the foundations were laid. These consisted of a 10 cm concrete layer laid directly on the earth. The structure's floor of 80 cm thick concrete was laid on top of this, into which drainage gullies and pipes were set. These led to a gravel-filled sump outside what would eventually be the entrance from where it was piped away. A good drainage system was not only important to ensure that ground water was kept out of the building but, depending on the type of structure, the occupants were provided with lavatories and washrooms all of which needed drainage. The floor was provided with anchor bars along the lines of the walls so that the walls could be tied to the floor; otherwise the joint between the floor and the walls would have been a weak link in the structure since the floor set hard before the wall concrete was poured.

Before this could be undertaken, the reinforcement had to be constructed and fitted. This consumed a considerable amount of steel. A type 671 casemate needed 14 tonnes of reinforcement bars while a type 611 casemate needed 63 tonnes. In addition, the steel plates in the ceilings took another 15.6 tonnes and 3 tonnes, respectively. Once the reinforcement lattice had been completed, the internal shuttering was built followed by the external shuttering. This defined the shape of the structure and the thickness of the walls, both internal and external, as well as the thickness of the roof. Constructing shuttering was a fairly lengthy process and a skilled job because the shapes were often complex. Mostly, wood was used until it became scarce later in the war and preformed concrete shuttering became

The wooden shuttering for an open emplacement under construction on the edge of a beach in the summer of 1942. (291/1213/20. Bundesarchiv)

widespread. This had the advantage that it could be left in place, unlike wooden shuttering which had to be removed once the concrete had set. Wood grain and the shape of the planking leaves a distinctive impression in concrete and this is evident in many of the structures. Originally, the Organization Todt wanted to use steel shuttering because it would have been quicker and easier to dismantle and reuse but the steel was not available. To increase the speed of building wooden shuttering, panels of as large an area as possible were always used on flat surfaces. On curves, it was necessary to use smaller planks to achieve the necessary curvature.

Once the walls had been cast, the guns of some casemates were installed before the roof was cast because it would have been impossible to get the gun into the casemate afterwards. The method of constructing horizontal spans followed a slightly different procedure from that used for the construction of the vertical components. If the structure was not intended to house a gun or if the gun could be fitted after the roof had been cast, the reinforcement for the ceiling and roof was installed before the walls were cast so that a complete lattice of metalwork was created but the roof reinforcement could only be constructed after the internal shuttering had been built. The steel I-beams were installed along with the liner plates, all of this being supported by timber props, before the reinforcement mesh was installed. This was set in precast concrete spreaders to maintain the shape of the three-dimensional mesh, ensuring that none of the reinforcement bars were out of alignment when the concrete was poured. The external shuttering was then

The labour-intensive process of constructing a bunker. The concrete is being helped down the improvised wooden chute by men with spades. Note the latticework of reinforcement and the hooked ends on the rods. (359/2031/10a. Bundesarchiv)

constructed using timber bracing and props to ensure that the vertical surfaces remained vertical under the weight of concrete.

The internal walls were cast first. The concrete was poured in 25 cm layers each of which was compacted by vibrating the shuttering before the next layer was poured. After all the concrete had been poured, it was kept damp for seven days while it set before removing the shuttering. This was to reduce shrinkage. According to Dorsch, it took 70 man-hours to lay 1 m³ of concrete. It is not clear whether this figure took into account the time taken to dig the hole and disperse the spoil. On this basis, a type 611 casemate which contained 1,330 m³ of concrete took 93,100 man-hours to build and a type 671 casemate which contained only 300 m³ took 21,000 man-hours; some 200 of the type 671 were built, which amounted to about 420,000 man-hours.

If steel turrets were part of the design, they were fitted before the concrete was poured. The turrets were provided with wide rims near their bases to help anchor them in the concrete. The turret sat on a separate steel base and the two were bolted together with massive bolts that passed through the turret rim, through the rim of the base and were embedded in concrete beneath. The turret had several large projections round its circumference about halfway up. These were lifting points; the steel cables from a crane were passed round them. The turrets were cast in one piece

A steel turret is lowered on to its supporting base with a crane. This was a laborious process that involved raising and lowering the turret several times before the bolt holes in the turret married with those in the base. Note the projections on the side of the turret being used to lift it. (295/86/22. Bundesarchiv)

in a variety of thicknesses, the thinnest being no more than 4 mm which was just enough to stop small arms fire. The thickest was 650 mm but this was not common; 350 mm was more usual although most were 250 mm or 300 mm. However, the turret walls were not of uniform thickness. The roof was thickest while the walls were thinnest at the bottom. These thicknesses of armour compared with those used in the glacis plates of the later German tanks. The thickest armour on the Panther D, for example, was a mere 80 mm (the glacis plate at 35°), while the thickest on the much less common Tiger II was 180 mm (the front of the turret at 80°) and its 50° glacis plate was 150 mm thick, enough to stop most Allied anti-tank rounds at point-blank range. The slope of the glacis plate effectively doubled the thickness of the armour horizontally, so that the Panther's hull front was effectively 160 mm thick while the Tiger's was 300 mm. However, the concept of sloped armour post-dated the design of the bunker turrets so they had to rely on sheer thickness to prevent penetration. There were, however, some turrets with a conical cross-section in which the upper part was, indeed, sloped but whether this was done to increase the effective depth of the armour or for some other reason is unclear.

The turrets ranged in size according to their function, those with six embrasures and fitted with two machine-guns tending to be the largest at 3.68 m in height with an

One of several steel turrets outside the walls of the Saint-Malo Citadel. They were reached by underground passages. (Marcus Massing)

external diameter of 3.13 m, while a one-man observation turret was only 1.6 m high with an external diameter at the base of 1.04 m. Most of the height of a turret was embedded in concrete but the largest, armed with two machine-guns, still stood about 1.5 m above ground level, while observation turrets usually stood less than half a metre above ground level; those that used a centrally mounted periscope for observation were often nearly flush with the ground. The periscope could be rotated through 360° and retracted when not in use. Alternatively, a rangefinder could be fitted and an azimuth scale on the ceiling, encircling the instrument, could be used to plot targets or the fall of shot. These turrets ranged in weight from 2 tonnes to 6 tonnes, which amounted to a lot of steel. There were a wide range of designs, including six patterns of observation turret, some of which were for infantry use while others were for artillery observers. Each observation embrasure was fitted with an armoured hinged cover plate that completely sealed the opening when closed. Additional armoured slits were sometimes provided for observation when the embrasures were sealed and the periscope retracted so that the occupants were not blind.

There were at least four designs of turret with three embrasures and at least five designs with six embrasures, based on the thickness of the armour; externally they were very similar. Two of the six embrasures were fitted with machine-guns using

89

A one-man observation turret being examined by a Canadian soldier. Dieppe is in the background. Although the earth cover on the bunker has long gone, the bunker and turret are still there. (Ken Bell, National Archives of Canada PA131232)

ball joints similar to the machine-gun mounted in a tank's front plate, the guns being fixed to pintle mountings attached to the corrugated steel floor. Some observation embrasures were fitted with a pintle to mount a machine-gun to add extra firepower. All turrets were entered through the floor via closable doors that were reached from beneath by means of a steel ladder. Ventilation systems to provide the turrets with fresh air were essential to allow the occupants to remain alert.

Most of the structures within the Atlantic Wall were buried. Even those structures that needed to have one face exposed, such as casemates and command posts, often had the rest of the structure buried with banked earth so that the exposed wall was like

The effects of anti-tank rounds on a steel turret. The American gunners had aimed at the machine-gun embrasures. More than one gun was firing at this turret. Some rounds have penetrated but others have glanced off leaving deep gouges. This is in the Citadel at Saint-Malo. (Marcus Massing)

A partly built bunker on the opposite side of the control post shown on page 84, showing what appears to be the entrance with a machine-gun embrasure for self-defence. Note the exposed hooked ends of the reinforcement bars. (291/1213/24. Bundesarchiv)

a cliff face. This not only increased the physical protection of the structure but reduced its silhouette by blending it into the surrounding topography. All surfaces that were to be covered with earth were first painted with pitch to waterproof them. The infilled and banked earth was then covered with turf and vegetation to help the new surface become indistinguishable from the natural landscape. The roof of some buried structures was sometimes provided with a raised lip that ran round its perimeter to prevent the earth from being washed off in the rain. Despite all this effort to camouflage the structures, aerial reconnaissance could still locate them, partly because the arrangement of bunkers within a location tended to form a distinctive pattern that could still be discerned from high up and partly because of trackways leading to the individual bunkers and casemates. While the bunkers and casemates were under construction a further complication was the rail tracks that were laid up to the building under construction, along which trucks of cement were pushed.

Some of the exposed concrete surfaces were roughened in an attempt to simulate natural rock. This texturing was achieved in a number of ways during construction,

A bunker in front of the east headland at Dieppe. It has a multi-colour pattern of camouflage reminiscent of First World War patterns. The entrance in the extension on the right is the access to a tobruk. (Ken Bell, National Archives of Canada PA183166)

including the random insertion of timber blocks through the shuttering so that the concrete flowed round them to produce indentations. Similarly, wads of waste material or paper were attached randomly to the inner face of the shuttering to produce indentations. Random raised lumps were also applied to exposed surfaces by embedding pieces of rock or concrete rubble in a coat of cement applied to the surface after the concrete had hardened. Sometimes, bump-shaped wire formers were applied to the surface and coated in cement to create a lumpy surface. This left an air space beneath the bump which it has been suggested provided additional armouring because it acted like spaced armour which was widely applied to German tanks to defeat shaped-charges and anti-tank rounds. However, the outer surface of the bump would have been too close to the main concrete layer to have much of an effect in dissipating an explosion. In any case, the sheer thickness of the walls and roof was sufficient to defeat direct hits from the biggest ordnance. The trouble with these textures, of which there was a wide variety – in effect, each was unique – was that they did nothing to break up the basic shape of the underlying structure. However, when combined with camouflage paint, the result could be quite effective.

All bunkers and casemates were painted with appropriate colours to help them blend into the background. As static objects, camouflage paint was an ideal method of concealing them as there was no danger of their revealing themselves by

It is difficult to tell whether this is intended to be imitation stonework or a dazzle pattern. The last soldier of the trio is carrying a Hotchkiss machine-gun. (719/210/6a. Bundesarchiv)

movement and unnatural shadows. A wide variety of schemes were used, including splinter patterns, patterns of squiggles or mottles over a background colour, and bold asymmetrically curving bands over a background colour. These resembled the patterns applied to the upper surfaces of Luftwaffe aircraft. Camouflage netting was often draped over the painted structures, using the exposed hooked ends of the reinforcement bars as attachment points. Some painted patterns were designed to resemble stonework or brickwork. In addition, some structures were painted to resemble local buildings with timber frames like those in Norman houses, windows with shutters and curtains, and doors. To support the illusion, false roofs were often built on top. This deception was more frequently applied to casemates than to other structures. Some command and observation bunkers were made to look like church towers.

Although steel became scarce, armoured embrasures remained a feature of many of the structures. There were three types: flat armoured plates that closed a large opening in the exterior wall of a machine-gun room, smaller plates that were embedded and bolted inside the interior recess of a small stepped embrasure like those provided for self-defence machine-guns, and plates that fitted inside stepped embrasures to mount a 47 mm anti-tank gun. A common machine-gun embrasure

A fire-control post disguised as the Strand Café with a convincing fake roof but rather less convincing painted-on windows, early 1944. (298/1785/21. Bundesarchiv)

plate was 40 mm thick, 60 cm long and 40 cm wide but they came in a variety of sizes and thicknesses. Some were fitted with a ball joint like those used in turrets. Most machine-guns were mounted on pintles fixed to a raised platform or plinth. Several types of machine-gun were used in bunkers. The MG 08 and MG 08/15 Maxims, the latter being an MG 08 fitted with a wooden stock and a pistol grip, were of First World War vintage and needed a different sort of mount from the MG 34 and MG 42 which could use standard pintles like those fitted to tanks. Other machine-guns included the MG 26(t), the Czech ZB 26 (on which the Bren was based) and the MG 37(t). Similar plates were fitted inside recessed apertures in internal walls such as the one facing the entrance but the gun apertures in these were no more than rectangular slots. The aperture could be closed with a sliding shutter that ran in channels although some of the larger armoured plates were fitted with hinged covers similar to those used in turrets.

About nine bunker designs used a large armoured plate in the exterior wall of a machine-gun room. Apart from the gun aperture, the plate also had an observation aperture for the gunner. Typically, this plate was 2 m tall by 2.8 m long and 60 mm thick but there were other sizes and thicknesses. It was embedded in concrete to a depth of about 30 cm all the way round the edges which were also secured in place

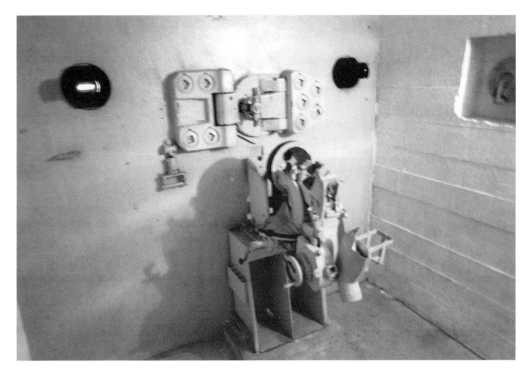

The interior of a machine-gun bunker. The wall is a steel plate with a hinged aperture cover, below which is the machine-gun mounting, the gun barrel passing through a ball joint. (Marcus Massing)

with bolts between about 65 cm and 1 m in length. It is not altogether clear why such plates were used, since the concrete was probably better protection than the steel which would spall under bullet impacts. Smaller plates would have served the same purpose but this approach does not appear to have been adopted.

It has been suggested that two 10 cm plates were used back to back instead of a single plate of 20 cm. There seems little reason for the Germans to have done this since two plates do not double resistance to penetration. In fact, they are only marginally better than one of the plates on its own. The only way that two plates offer an advantage over one is when they are separated by a substantial air gap, a phenomenon that was well known; spaced armour was commonly applied to German tanks by early 1943 (for example, the side skirts attached to the hull and to the turret of the Panzer Mk IV, and the shields on anti-tank guns were often spaced armour). Spaced armour does not appear to have been used in any of the bunkers in the Atlantic Wall and there appears to be no evidence that they ever used two plates back to back.

The armoured plates used for 47 mm Pak 36 (t) Skoda anti-tank guns were rather more complex than these machine-gun plates. The plates were fitted in concrete embrasures and consisted of a steel lining plate that followed the contours of the stepped embrasure, an inner plate that contained a ball joint which took the barrel of

The steel embrasure plate next to the entrance of a type 112 bunker, showing the stepped embrasure, vision aperture and triangular roof extension. (Marcus Massing)

the gun, its ranging coaxial machine-gun and sighting aperture, and an exterior shield that could be lowered or raised from inside the bunker by a pulley system and a hand-operated winch, the shield resting in a slot within the exterior wall when the embrasure was open. The gun was mounted on a semicircular track to allow it to traverse through 45° (although some tracks allowed only half this amount of traverse), the mount being pivoted to allow the gun to be elevated 12° or depressed 20°. The larger-calibre anti-tank guns (50 mm, 75 mm and 88 mm) fired from their embrasures without additional steel shields, relying on those already fitted to the gun.

Some pedestal-mounted 155 mm Heer artillery pieces housed in casemates were provided with armoured semi-circular shields that enclosed the casemate opening and revolved with the gun through 120° to keep the opening sealed. A vertical slot allowed the gun to be elevated 35° and depressed by 5°. It is not clear how thick the shield was but it appears to have been in the region of 30 mm. Some of the casemated guns of 150 mm and above had shields like field artillery while some of the biggest guns were housed in turrets like those on a ship. Sometimes the turret was enclosed in a casemate. These were all Kriegsmarine guns. Pedestal-mounted Heer artillery often had no shielding and fired from an open embrasure; field guns had their own shields but these still meant that the embrasure was a large unprotected space into which flat-trajectory, high-velocity guns could fire armour-piercing rounds although they were

The gun room of an anti-tank gun bunker showing the breech of a 47 mm Skoda and the embrasure plate. There were six bunker designs for this sort of mounting. The man on the right is not staring at a blank wall but is looking through an observation slit (the light rectangle). (291/1213/27. Bundesarchiv)

relatively safe from naval and field artillery because of the high angles of trajectory of these weapons. Heavy steel chains were sometimes suspended over the embrasure as a form of spaced armour. This had the advantage of only slightly impeding lines of sight while increasing the protection of the casemate. The idea was that artillery shells or the 3-inch 60 lb semi-armour-piercing rockets fired by ground-attack aircraft such as Typhoons would hit the chains and explode outside the casemate.

All the doors within a bunker were armoured. A rubber seal went all the way round the edge of the door to ensure a gas-tight and watertight seal when the door was closed and bolted. External doors and those leading to gun rooms were of the stable-door type and 40 mm thick. In theory, being able to open the top half when the bottom half was jammed by rubble or some other obstacle meant that the bunker's occupants could still escape should they not fancy crawling along the escape duct or were unable to remove the brick partitions that blocked it. Internal doors were usually one piece and thinner than external ones. Some were mounted on hinges while others were slidable on rails. Most doors had a narrow viewing slit with thick glass or a larger square aperture for shooting through, with a sliding cover plate on the inner face.

All these sealed rooms, designed to cope with gas attacks which never came, meant that a free flow of air was impossible and all but the simplest casemates that

A close-up of Caesar at Lindemann battery. Note the chains hanging over the embrasure. (Donald I. Grant, National Archives of Canada PA133142)

were open at the front and back needed a ventilation system to enable the occupants to breathe. This constituted a major piece of engineering since it entailed penetrating walls with air ducting and vents, installing pumps and fans (capable of moving air at a rate of 1.2 m³/min or 2.4 m³/min, the simplest being driven by a hand pump) in a separate room which needed to be designed into the building in the first place, as well as fitting removable filters at inlets, and puncturing exterior walls for air intakes and exhaust outlets, the size of which was dictated by the volume of air that had to be circulated. The size and positioning of inlets and outlets represented a serious weakness in the overall strength of a bunker. The bunker could stand or fall according to how well these features were designed because they were potential entry points for hostile munitions, the sort of points which in a later age would be targeted by bunker-busting smart munitions. Such munitions had already been invented. The US radio-guided 1,000 lb AZON bomb, for example, was little

The armoured steel stable door,
showing locking mechanisms.
Note the aperture with sliding
plate in the lower section.
(Marcus Massing)

different from the smart bombs used in Vietnam and the Gulf, although much less sophisticated than the later weapons. It could have been guided on to bunkers, possibly on to their weak spots. It had been used successfully as early as February 1944 against an Italian viaduct and against locks on the River Danube. The AZON and the later more sophisticated RAZON were successfully used against Burmese bridges. And iron bombs such as Barnes Wallis's 12,000 lb Tallboy and 20,000 lb Grand Slam were successfully used in 1945 to penetrate the roofs of U-boat pens which were up to 10 m thick. The Royal Navy developed a rocket-assisted bomb to do the same job. None of these weapons were used against the bunkers in the Atlantic Wall largely because it was believed that conventional weapons would destroy them.

To minimize the weaknesses of ventilation openings in exterior walls, they were located in a rear wall that could be defended along with the entrance by a machine-gun firing from an embrasure. The oval openings were covered by angled-louvre grills that lay flush with the wall which prevented anything being tossed into the ducts. Other potential weak spots were created wherever something punctured an exterior wall or the roof, including stove exhaust flues and radio aerials. Stoves and radios were not installed in all bunkers, however. Radio was not the principal means of communication between bunkers, being reserved for the more important buildings within a strongpoint or battery. They were more often used by the Kriegsmarine than the Heer. Radios needed external aerials because the steel lattice of the reinforcement acted as a Faraday cage which blocked radio signals. An aerial had to be passed up a 150 mm diameter shaft through the roof, set into the bunker when it was being constructed. The aerials were telescopic and only extended when required. It would appear that radio equipment and aerial were sometimes set up outside and taken back inside after use but clearly this was not feasible under battle conditions. Communication between bunkers and casemates within a strongpoint or battery was usually by telephone which required the laying of cables about 2 m down when the structures were built, deep enough not to be cut by artillery fire or bombing. The system was based on the field telephone, operated by cranking a handle; large switchboard systems used batteries. The cables were connected to junctions that allowed communication between all the main structures in a strongpoint. Communication between rooms in the same bunker or casemate was made possible by voice tubes like those used on ships.

The gun crews of casemates faced a problem that the occupants of other bunkers did not, namely the fumes and noise from their own gun. In addition, when the gun was fired, the air pressure in the gun room suddenly increased because of the confined space. This had the potential to rupture eardrums and concuss. The solution was the blast valve in which a shutter in a duct leading to another part of the casemate was automatically opened by the increased pressure to release the overpressure. An extractor duct was installed near the breech of the gun to remove cordite fumes which were exhausted via a grilled opening in the back wall of the casemate. As far as noise was concerned, the only solution was for the crew to stick their fingers in their ears and open their mouths to equalize the pressure each time the gun was fired.

CHAPTER 8

Atlantic Wall Locations and Fighting

DUNKIRK

Dunkirk is best known in Britain as the place from where the BEF was evacuated in the dark days of 1940 rather than for any association with the Atlantic Wall. The sandy beaches stretching east of the port towards Belgium that facilitated the escape of the British Army became the focus of anti-invasion defences when OKW recognized that these same beaches were ideal for landings from the sea. With the flat open country that extends from the dunes beyond the beaches, the area was seen as the sort of location the Allies might choose for an invasion, especially as the crossing would be short and the port of Dunkirk was nearby. A large number of gun emplacements and bunkers were built in this region.

The beach at Bray-Dunes, just across the Franco-Belgian border, is typical. Here, the Germans built several gun emplacements and bunkers in the dunes as part of resistance nest Adolf. These include a type 637 fire-control post, two type 501 and two type 502 quarters bunkers, a type 645 kitchen bunker and two type 680 casemates each housing a 75 mm anti-tank gun to enfilade the beach. They still exist in drunken postures as they slide down the beach and sink into the sand. A short way along the coast at Zuydcoote is a Kriegsmarine battery built on a French battery that predated the First World War. Four type 671 casemates for 105 mm guns and one for a 150 mm gun were built in a line along the foot of the dunes. The Germans made use of an existing French fire-control post but also built a type M162a post of their own above the dunes.

A large number of strongpoints and batteries were built around the landward side of Dunkirk which was designated a fortress by Hitler on 4 September 1944 when the German army was in retreat. The same directive designated Boulogne and Calais as fortresses. Dunkirk's defences extended from Bray-Dunes in the north to Bergues, about 6 miles inland to the southeast of Dunkirk, and down to Loon-Plage, about 3 miles down the coast, west of Dunkirk. There were sixteen batteries in this defence perimeter, including those located in the town. Only four had guns in casemates, all the others having open emplacements. Few of the inland bunkers and gun positions now survive and most of those within Dunkirk have long since disappeared under postwar development projects to rebuild the town which was badly damaged during the war. One of the few bunkers to survive in the town is located at the start of the east jetty, part of the outer harbour. This is a type 631 anti-tank gun bunker with the 47 mm gun still in

A French Somua S-35 tank used as a pill-box near the Franco-Belgian border. In the background is a command post flying the tricolour following its capture in September 1944. (Ken Bell, National Archives of Canada PA143908)

The same tank (previous picture) from another angle. Note the steel tetrahedra obstacles on the beach. (Ken Bell, National Archives of Canada PA143907)

position. A battery of four 155 mm guns was built just south the town at Fort Castelnau (now in a leisure area). About half a mile to the east of there, near Lebecque's Farm, there are the remains of an army coastal battery, the type 671 casemates having been built with false roofs to disguise them as houses. This type of casemate was common in coastal batteries. Both locations have various support bunkers still in evidence.

About half a mile to the northwest of Loon-Plage, west of Dunkirk, was a battery of four casemated 155 mm guns. These type 699 casemates were disguised as houses like those at Lebecque's Farm. Dunkirk's defences extended even further west to Gravelines and Fort Phillipe and beyond to Marck, almost to Calais. Gravelines was the site of a battery of two 280 mm guns, called Kurze Bruno (Little Bruno). A single type 669 casemate sits in splendid isolation about a quarter of a mile from Mottes's Farm to the southwest of Gravelines. It once housed a 76.2 mm gun. Along the beaches on both sides of the channel that leads to Gravelines are a large number of bunkers of various types, including enfilade-fire bunkers (for example, types 612 and 680). On the beach in front of Grand Fort Philippe is a type 633 bunker that once housed a M19 automatic mortar in its steel turret. There were also two radar stations in Petit Fort Philippe which directed the fire of a Kriegsmarine battery at Masson's Farm which has long since vanished. At les Huttes d'Oye, west of Grand Fort Philippe, is the leaning tower of a fire-control post which the constructors had attempted to disguise as a church tower. It leans because its foundations were dynamited after the war.

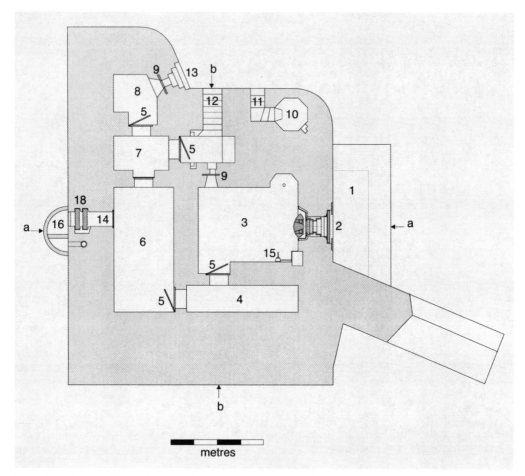

Plan view of a type 631 bunker for 47 mm anti-tank gun. Key: 1 spent case dump, 2 embrasure, 3 gun room, 4 ammunition room, 5 steel door, 6 crew room, 7 gas lock, 8 machine-gun room, 9 steel embrasure plate, 10 observation post (tobruk), 11 tobruk access, 12 entrance, 13 embrasure, 14 emergency exit crawlway, 15 winch, 16 emergency exit, 17 spent case chute, 18 brick partitions. (Ruud Pols)

Besides the artillery batteries, Dunkirk was ringed by Flak batteries ranging in calibre from 20 mm to 88 mm. One such battery was at Petit Synthe, the southern suburb of the town. Six 88 mm gun emplacements were constructed in a line and the battery included a large Flak command post on top of which was a fire-control radar. Inside this building, which still stands, is a wall painting of a gauntletted fist, the badge of Flakabteilung 252 to which this battery belonged. There were, of course, several other Flak units in the area.

It fell to the 2nd Canadian Infantry Division to assault the fortress of Dunkirk at the beginning of September 1944. Within the defence perimeter was the 18th Luftwaffe Feld Division, commanded by General von Tresckow, which included three infantry regiments and an artillery regiment. A battalion of the 82nd Fortress

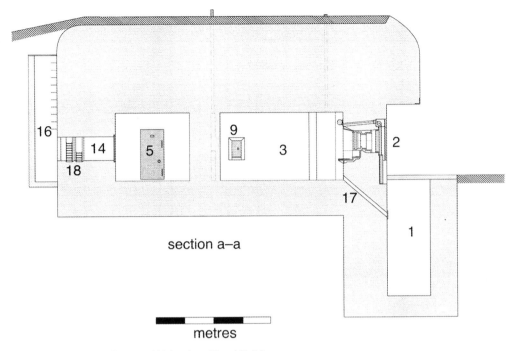

section a–a

metres

Sectional elevation of a type 631 bunker. (Ruud Pols)

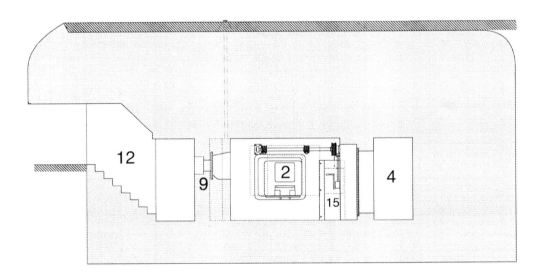

section b–b

metres

Sectional elevation of a type 631 bunker. (Ruud Pols)

Infantry, a low-standard static unit, and Heeres Küsten Artillerie Abteilung 1244 provided five batteries of artillery. There were also various naval units and three Flak groups, Leichtflak 415 and 765 and Flakabteilung 252. These already considerable defences were reinforced by elements of the retreating Fifteenth Army so that the defenders numbered 12,000 by the time the Canadians attacked.

On 5 September, Dunkirk's defences were found to be too strong to be taken as easily as Dieppe which had fallen unopposed to the Canadians a few days earlier. Although the garrison was not first-line quality and was composed of a wide variety of units, it could nevertheless put down a considerable curtain of fire on the attacking Canadians. Loon-Plage was taken on 9 September after heavy fighting. By 14 September, Montgomery issued orders that Dunkirk was to be contained and dealt with later. It never was because it became unnecessary. Although earlier he had been keen to take one or more of the Channel ports to facilitate a drive into Germany and to Berlin, the emphasis had changed. It had become more important that the seaward approaches along the Scheldt to the port of Antwerp were taken to allow the port's facilities to be used. This would shorten the overextended supply lines that still went all the way back to the surviving artificial harbour at Arromanches in Normandy. It was partly because of Hitler's appreciation that the Allies needed port facilities that the Führer designated the Channel ports as fortresses. Of these, only Dunkirk held out until the end of the war. On 16 September, the containment of the fortress of Dunkirk was taken over by the 4th Special Service Brigade which had been moved from le Havre following the port's recent capture.

CALAIS

Like Dunkirk, Calais was heavily defended by strongpoints and artillery and Flak batteries as well as minefields. To the east of Calais, Waldam battery was a Kriegsmarine battery built on top of the dunes. It consisted of two 150 mm guns in type M270 casemates but also included an unusual concrete turret that housed another 150 mm gun. A reinforced-concrete turret had been proposed by the Kriegsmarine towards the end of 1942 because of the shortage of steel for such things and the knowledge that open emplacements left the gun and its crew too exposed to air attacks. A prototype was demonstrated to Rommel in April 1944 in Paris but concrete turrets were beset with problems and few were built. The one at Waldam was only experimental. It rotated on rollers on a specially constructed platform but firing the gun tended to jam the turret which was a massive dead weight. The only other concrete turrets were used a short way down the coast at Cap Blanc Nez for 170 mm guns. Waldam's concrete turret is still there among the dunes along with a fire-control post dating from 1940 which was part of another battery, Oldenburg. Waldam is not easy to reach as there is no road, only a track that leads to it.

Oldenburg was another Kriegsmarine battery, located in the dunes just beyond the eastern edge of the town. It was constructed in 1940 to house two 240 mm guns with

The fire-control post at the Waldam battery. (Joe Kaufmann)

Another view of the fire-control post at the Waldam battery with part of the concrete turret on the right. (Joe Kaufmann)

Observation post at Fort Lapin. (Joe Kaufmann)

integral shields that had formerly been emplaced on the island of Borkum, the first German island in the Friesian chain along the coasts of Holland and Germany. These guns had a range of 16.5 miles and were initially in open emplacements but in 1941 they were converted to massive casemates which still survive. Each casemate contained magazines next to the gun room which was located in the centre. A machine-gun bunker was built on top of the western one. Two smaller bunkers of type 612, one at each end of the site, housed 76 mm guns to protect the approaches to the site along with four bunkers housing 50 mm anti-tank guns. Flak protection came in the form of four 75 mm anti-aircraft guns and a number of 20 mm and 40 mm guns distributed about the site. There were also personnel bunkers, a large medical bunker and a fire-control post. There are several wall paintings inside the accommodation bunkers and one in the medical bunker. Both Waldam and Oldenburg were flanked by a large number of bunkers along the dunes to protect them from assault from the beaches in the event of landings there and many of these are still in evidence today.

A number of old French forts on the west of Calais were converted into defensive positions by the Germans, including Bastion II, the Citadel (a sixteenth-century fortification) and Fort Lapin and Fort Nieulay dating from the seventeenth century. Nothing now remains of Bastion II where the Kriegsmarine installed three 194 mm

A 280 mm railway gun of Eisenbahn Batterie 713 emerging from its protective 'Dombunker' in Hydrequent. Note the sliding steel doors. (227/274/15a. Bundesarchiv)

guns in type M270 casemates. The remains of Fort Lapin are on the northwest edge of the town right up against the shore line and about half a mile from the site of Bastion II to the east. Another Kriegsmarine battery was installed here. This had two type M270 casemates housing 164 mm guns and two open emplacements for two more, along with three 76 mm guns for self-defence. Fort Nieulay is on the western tip of the town. Calais was also protected by positions at Coquelles a few miles to the west of the town. And there were also a number of railway guns to the west but most evidence of their existence has disappeared under the Channel Tunnel rail terminal. A so-called cathedral bunker, a long, arched bunker that resembles an airship hanger, into which one of the rail guns used to disappear for protection, still stands to the east of Fort Nieulay. There were also a number of railway guns in the Cap Gris Nez area, including the marble quarry in Hydrequent, about 7 miles due east. When the Canadians overran this area on 5 September, they discovered that the two 280 mm guns and the single 210 mm gun had gone. Its 75 m long bunker still remains, however. The 280 mm guns could fire a 250 kg shell 38 miles at 54° elevation.

On 5 September 1944, the Canadian 7th Infantry Brigade and 7th Reconnaissance Regiment began the investment of the Calais defence area and the big-gun batteries on Cap Gris Nez, a frontage of about 20 miles. By the time the 3rd Canadian Division supported by the 2nd Canadian Armoured Brigade and specialist armour from the British 31st Tank Brigade of the 79th Armoured Division was ready to attack Calais on 25 September, much of the countryside to the south and west of the town had been inundated by the garrison breaching many of the ditches that criss-cross the area. The defences to the west were considered to be strong although much of the higher ground

The rear of a personnel bunker in the area of Calais, October 1944. The number on the side is the sector code. (Donald I. Grant, National Archives of Canada PA133948)

was not defended. Only the high ground at Vieux Coquelles (just below Coquelles, now almost swamped by the Channel Tunnel rail terminal) had been developed into a strongpoint. The Calais defence perimeter was defended by about 8,000 men led by Oberstleutnant Schröder but only about 2,500 were infantry. They were not prime troops and he referred to them as 'mere rubbish'. They were subsequently described by the Canadians as old, ill and of low morale with little will to fight. Only the Flak crews were young and prepared to put up much resistance.

The RAF carried out a number of heavy raids on Calais to destroy the defences. More than 600 heavy bombers dropped 3,000 tonnes of bombs on the town's defences on 20 September. On the afternoon of the 24th, 126 heavy bombers again attacked targets in Calais but due to a mix-up the Flak batteries were not shelled in advance and eight bombers were shot down. The next morning, 300 RAF bombers dropped another 1,300 tonnes of bombs but this raid like the others failed to destroy many of the concrete defences. The Canadians attacked as soon as the raid ended at 1015 hrs. This included an assault on the Lindemann battery. There was heavy fighting around the Coquelles defences which were eventually overcome the next day with the support of the 6th Armoured Regiment and further raids by the Second Tactical Air Force. Calais was again bombed the following day by 342 Lancasters which dropped more than 1,700 tonnes of bombs. After more heavy fighting the Canadians took Fort Lapin and Fort Nieulay and reached the outskirts of Calais.

Schröder then sought a ceasefire to allow the evacuation of civilians but when the fighting restarted 24 hours later German resistance began to collapse. The Canadians then took Bastion II and the Citadel and entered the town. By 1 October, Calais had been cleared of Germans. For fewer than 300 casualties, the Canadians took about 7,500 prisoners. Their readiness to surrender has been attributed to the bombing of the town by RAF heavies but the quality of the troops and their lack of training for this sort of fighting must have been significant factors.

CAP BLANC NEZ AND CAP GRIS NEZ

This region of the Pas-de-Calais is the closest part of continental Europe to southern England and it was here that the Germans placed some of their biggest guns. They were capable of bombarding not only British shipping in the Channel but also English soil. Nine coastal batteries were set up here in 1940 for the proposed invasion of England, including 170 mm guns in fixed positions and 280 mm railway guns. The biggest batteries were not built until 1942 and 1943, however. These were Lindemann at Sangatte near Cap Blanc Nez, Grosser Kurfürst at Framzelle and Todt at Haringzelles in the Cap Gris Nez, and Friedrich August at la Trésorerie close to

The Lindemann battery under construction in 1942. The turret is in place and the casemate is being constructed round it. (363/2267/19. Bundesarchiv)

Boulogne. Albert Speer once had a demonstration of one of the big guns at Cap Gris Nez and was told by the commander that it had fired at Dover but was disappointed to learn afterwards that it had only fired into the sea.

The biggest guns were at the Lindemann battery, three 406 mm naval guns which could hurl a 600 kg shell 29 miles. The range could be extended to 34 miles by using extra propellant. With these shells, the guns were capable of hitting English targets up to about 7 miles inland and up to about 12 miles inland if extra propellant was used. An even heavier shell weighing 1 tonne could also be fired from the guns but it had a shorter range and was not capable of hitting targets in southern England. These were used to shell shipping. The guns could be traversed through 120° enabling the Lindemann guns to range between Hythe and Broadstairs. They had a maximum elevation of 55°. The guns were mounted in steel turrets similar to those on a ship and these were enclosed by massive casemates with walls and roofs 3.5 m thick, each casemate consuming 14,400 m³ of concrete. Organization Todt evidently took only ten weeks to construct the battery. The battery had originally been called Schleswig-Holstein but this was later changed to Gross Deutschland. With the loss of the *Bismarck* in May 1941, the battery was renamed yet again in honour of the battleship's captain. The three casemated guns were also named: Anton, Bruno and Caesar. The battery was one of seven that came under the command of Naval Artillery Battalion 244 (*Marine Artillerie Abteilung* or MAA) which also included Oldenburg battery with its 240 mm guns and those at Bastion II and Fort Lapin in which its headquarters were located.

The Lindemann battery was built in 1942 about a mile south of the village of Sangatte just below the Noires Mottes ridgeline. Evidently, the Kriegsmarine wanted to allow the guns to traverse through 360°, like the Grosser Kurfürst battery near Framzelle, which would have meant that no overhead protection would have been possible but Hitler interfered and insisted that such protection was provided and hence the guns only had 120° of traverse. This battery was entirely offensive in purpose and the fact that it was placed so close to the coastline that it could be quickly overrun by a determined enemy landing nearby or, indeed, attacking from the landward side, cut no ice with the navy. However, defensive measures were taken and the whole site was turned into a strongpoint to protect the big guns.

Each of the three casemates was massive. The circular concrete base of the gun room, on which the turret turned, was about 18 m in diameter. A large part of the bulk of each casemate was below ground. The gun platform was at ground level while there were three stories behind it, two of them below ground. The gun was in a steel turret that was 15 m long, 3.5 m wide and 5.5 m tall, weighing approximately 50 tonnes. Each casemate was about 35 m by 30 m and about 12 m tall above ground. The two upper floors were quarters for the crew (the battery was served by 99 men). They had all the creature comforts including showers, lavatories and a recreation room built into

(Opposite) *Another view of Lindemann under construction. The crane is being used to lift a steel component of the roof (in front of the crew). A similar component is already in place over the turret.* (363/2268/30. Bundesarchiv)

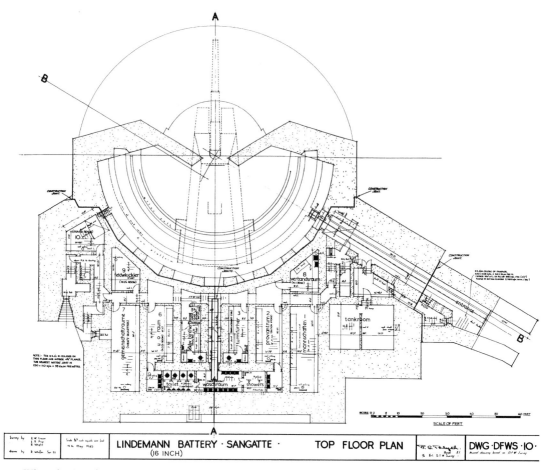

When the Royal Engineers examined Lindemann battery they surveyed the casemates and prepared detailed drawings, dated May 1945. (Royal Engineers Library)

each casemate. As with most Kriegsmarine casemates, each one was provided with magazines for shells and propellant which came in metre-long brass cases. The magazines were on the lowest floor and had space for 250 shells and 100 cases.

The site included a medical bunker on two floors equipped with four wards to accommodate 35 patients and an operating theatre. The lower floor contained the machinery to run the hospital. The bunker, a variation of type 118, was located on the left-hand side of the site and about 230 m from the third casemate (Caesar), buried in the side of the escarpment. It was 22 m long and nearly 13 m wide with walls and roof 2 m thick. About another 100 m to the left of the hospital was the first of two reserve magazines, which were buried side by side in an adjacent escarpment. The battery's 12 m long fire-control post was located at the front of the site, lower down the slope. This was a variation on type S100 and included a Würzburg Riese radar dish and a rangefinder housed in a steel cupola. One of the interior walls was adorned by a painting of a Spanish galleon on the high seas, possibly evoking the

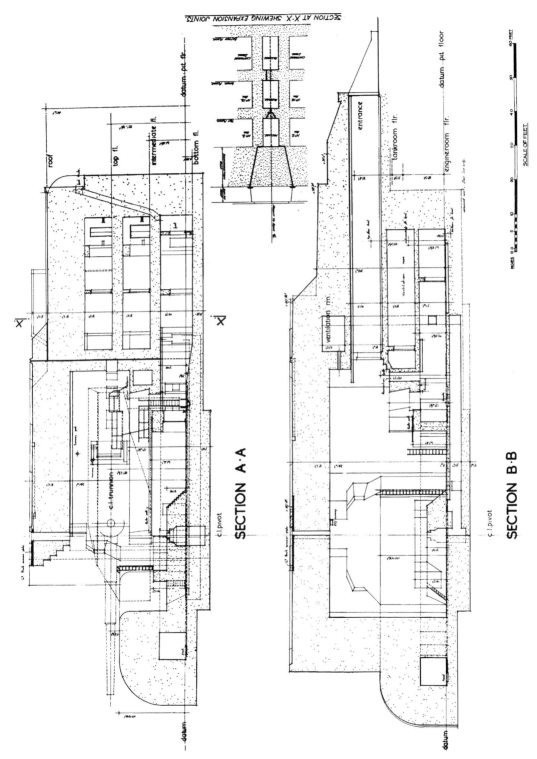

SECTION AT X-X SHEWING EXPANSION JOINTS.

roof

top fl.

intermediate fl.

bottom fl.

datum

datum - pit. flr.

c.l.trunnion

c.l.pivot

X

SECTION A·A

entrance

tankroom flr.

engineroom flr.

datum - pit floor

ventilation rm.

datum

c.l.pivot

SECTION B·B

SCALE OF FEET

Cross-sections through a Lindemann casemate, showing its three floors. (Royal Engineers Library)

Spanish Armada, a rather unwise association. Nine 20 mm Flak positions were located at the front and back of the site and a dummy Flak position was built a few hundred metres outside the southeast corner. Eighteen machine-gun positions were dotted over the position, some in isolated tobruks, others next to gun pits for anti-tank guns and light field guns which were housed in bunkers and open emplacements. The site was self-contained and included separate living quarters for the support troops as well as bunkered reservoirs, pumphouses and kitchens. Each casemate was surrounded by electrified wire in a random starburst pattern and the whole site was enclosed by a belt of barbed wire reinforced in places with a line of steel obstacles known as Belgian gates in a similar pattern. These steel-framed structures resembled gates and were mounted on rollers. Also known as element C, they were 2 m high, 2.75 m wide and weighed 1.5 tonnes and were widely used as beach obstacles. There were also minefields inside and outside the wire and an antitank ditch with a vertical wall of concrete about 3 m high along the eastern edge of the wire. The whole site was about 1.5 km across.

Between 1942 and September 1944, Lindemann divided its time between shelling British shipping, the port of Dover and the British long-range batteries in Kent. Between the beginning of November 1942 and the end of March 1944, Caesar fired 84 rounds, as recorded on the wall of the turret. It is believed to have fired 130 before Lindemann was taken by the Canadians in September 1944. Similar records were kept for the other guns but these had been removed by the time the Canadians occupied the site. Assuming the three guns fired similar numbers of rounds, the total comes to about 390. The battery had many more rounds in its magazines when it was captured. Caesar's record was subsequently removed and presented to Dover in 1954 where it was displayed on the esplanade.

When the German garrison at Boulogne was threatened by the advancing Canadians at the beginning of September 1944, the town's commander decided to evacuate unnecessary personnel by sea. To cover this, the Lindemann battery, along with the Grosser Kurfürst and Todt batteries further down the coast, fired at the guns at South Foreland (four 9.2 in guns) and Wanstone Farm (two 15 in guns called Clem and Jane), both manned by 540 Coast Regiment Royal Artillery, late on the evening of 1 September to prevent the British guns shooting at the German ships. However, the attack on the British guns did not prevent them from shooting at the ships nor returning fire on the German batteries. Little damage seems to have been inflicted on the batteries on either side of the Channel. Following a day of quiet, Lindemann and other batteries started shelling Dover on the afternoon of the 3rd. The Kentish guns returned fire but failed to damage the German batteries, while the battery at Wanstone was hit several times by 380 mm shells from the Todt battery, causing casualties. The Wanstone battery evened the score on the night of 4/5 September when one of its 15 in shells hit Bruno at Lindemann. This knocked out Bruno's power system so that it could no longer operate. Bruno's barrel was severely damaged by a shell exploding prematurely although it is unclear whether this was a result of the Wanstone hit. This was the only occasion during the war when a shell fired by a cross-Channel gun succeeded in disabling a gun in an enemy battery.

The smoke on the horizon is a bombing raid on the Cap Gris Nez batteries on 26 September 1944. The man in the foreground is filming it. He appears to be standing at the edge of a bunker. Note the anti-glider stakes in the middle distance. (Donald I. Grant, National Archives of Canada PA133144)

(Left to right) Lieutenant H.A. Staples and Major O.L. Corbett of the North Shore Regiment and Lieutenant J. Wareing, Royal Armoured Corps, pose in front of Bruno. (Donald I. Grant, National Archives of Canada PA133140)

Lindemann's two remaining guns along with the Todt and Grosser Kurfürst guns kept up a desultory bombardment of the Kentish towns for the next two weeks. Most of the damage done to Dover and nearby towns by cross-Channel bombardment between autumn 1940 and autumn 1944 was done during the first three weeks of September 1944 when the German batteries destroyed 239 houses and damaged a further 1,936. The randomness of the shelling betrayed its lack of purpose. The only reason for it was to expend ammunition as it was clear that it would not be long before the batteries were overrun by the advancing Canadians. Cap Gris Nez and Cap Blanc Nez and their batteries had been cut off from Boulogne and Calais since the beginning of September. As part of the assault on Boulogne on 17 September, the 7th Infantry Brigade, 6th Armoured Regiment and the 12th Field Artillery Regiment and 3rd Medium Artillery Regiment were ordered to take Lindemann. The Wanstone guns were requested to help silence Lindemann. For this, the British battery was helped by AOP Austers from No. 660 Squadron which were in direct communication with the battery. The Wanstone guns started firing at Lindemann just after 0900 hrs on the 17th. Over a period of 2½ hours, the battery fired 60 rounds at Lindemann, which fired back.

Mid-afternoon and the guns were again in action against Lindemann, this time joined by the two 14 in guns at St Margaret's at Cliff (known as Winnie and Pooh) manned by the Royal Marine Siege Regiment. The barrels of the Wanstone guns were by now so badly worn that the shells fell short and the guns stopped firing, leaving only Winnie and Pooh in action. These repeatedly hit Caesar but failed to put it out of action. The two British guns fired 114 rounds at Lindemann and other targets in the area, including field artillery positions and Flak emplacements. The Canadians failed to take the battery and most of the attackers were subsequently withdrawn for the assault on Calais. On 20 September, 5,600 500 lb and 1,000 lb bombs were dropped on Lindemann, 350 of which fell within 90 m radii of each casemate; 23 hit the casemates, 13 fell on Caesar, four on Bruno and six on Anton. The casemates and their guns survived.

One of the guns of Lindemann battery being examined by men of the North Shore Regiment, September 1944. Note the open door on the side of the turret. (Donald I. Grant, National Archives of Canada PA133143)

The North Shore Regiment advances on Bruno of Lindemann battery, 26 September 1944. They have just passed through gates in the casemate's barbed-wire perimeter. A bomb crater is clearly visible on the left. Note the painting of a gun on the side of the casemate. (Donald I. Grant, National Archives of Canada PA133139)

On 25 September, the 8th Canadian Infantry Brigade supported by Shermans and Crabs from the 79th Armoured Division attacked the battery. The Crabs flailed paths through the minefields for the infantry who were then fired on by the Grosser Kurfürst battery. Crocodiles and AVREs flamed and blasted the outlying bunkers and gun positions. The AVRE, a modified Churchill, was essential for the destruction of bunkers. It was armed with a 290 mm spigot mortar which could fire a 18 kg bomb

The Noires Mottes ridge with Caesar of Lindemann battery in the centre of the picture, Anton to its right. The figures are men of the North Shore Regiment. The effect of the heavy bombing raid on 20 September 1944 can be seen. (Donald I. Grant, National Archives of Canada PA133137)

(known as the Flying Dustbin) 75 m. It had been specifically designed for blasting bunkers. Night brought a pause in the assault but the next morning the battle was over as 285 Lindemann defenders involuntarily surrendered, having got roaring drunk during the night.

After the war, Royal Engineers attempted to blow up the casemates but despite using 7,000 lb of explosives on Anton all they succeeded in doing was partially dropping the roof, sending a crack through one of the walls; 2,000 lb of plastic explosive was detonated on Bruno's roof with a similarly inconclusive effect. Today, the Channel tunnel has nearly obliterated the heavily cratered Lindemann site and the casemates have disappeared under the spoil but the fire-control post at the front of the site is still visible as are some of the outlying bunkers including those at the cliff edge.

The Grosser Kurfürst battery was built in the spring of 1943 on the Cap Gris Nez headland just east of the village of Framzelles and straddled the hamlet of Floringzelle, the northern tip of the elongated site being only a couple of hundred metres from the cliffs. About the time of its inauguration, Hitler visited the battery. It replaced an earlier battery of two 280 mm guns called the Prinz Heinrich battery,

Private C.D. Walker of the North Shore Regiment inside Caesar's 406 mm muzzle at Lindemann while Lieutenant M.G. Aubut looks on. (Donald I. Grant, National Archives of Canada PA133141)

built near Sangatte in late 1940. Prinz Heinrich's guns were evidently moved to the Leningrad area when the new battery was built. Grosser Kurfürst, or Great Elector, was named after the heroic Friedrich Wilhelm (1620–88) whose reforms following the end of the Thirty Years War (1618–48) laid the foundations of the future Prussia. The battery comprised four 280 mm guns in steel turrets measuring 11 m by 6.5 m and weighing 57 tonnes. These were not enclosed in casemates and consequently the turrets could rotate through 360°. They were set in rectangular concrete bunkers of type S412 that were partially buried. Each bunker was about 27 m by 29 m and more than 5 m high and contained magazines that held 210 shells and 250 cases of propellant. The turret bunkers only had accommodation for six. Like the Lindemann guns, Grosser Kurfürst's were capable of firing several different types of shell. A typical high-explosive shell was 1.3 m long and weighed 284 kg. The charged brass cases each weighed 65 kg and were a metre long. Cloth bags of propellant were also used with the cases, each of which weighed 34 kg. The guns had a range of 23 miles and could easily reach southern England.

The site was about 1,000 m across and 500 m wide, the four guns being set in an approximately north–south line at intervals of about 250 m. The guns were mirrored

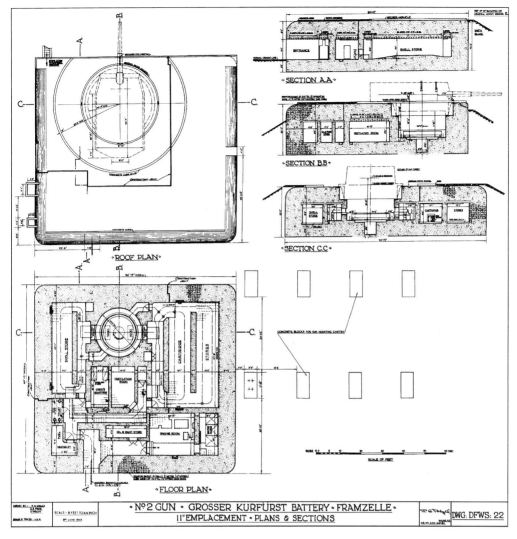

Drawings of No. 2 casemate at Grosser Kürfurst prepared by Royal Engineers. This is a type S412 design. (Royal Engineers Library)

by a set of dummy guns outside the perimeter of barbed wire, Belgian gates and minefields. These dummies had wooden barrels and a system to mimic muzzle flash. Like the Lindemann site, there were numerous machine-gun and anti-tank tobruks and Flak positions dotted about the site. It also had its own medical bunker (type 118b) but, along with the command post and a fire-control post fitted with Würzburg Riese radar and a rangefinder, it was located outside the main site, in a sub-site on top of the cliffs at the tip of Cap Gris Nez. This was surrounded by wire and protected by a Flak battery and machine-gun posts some of which were concrete tobruks.

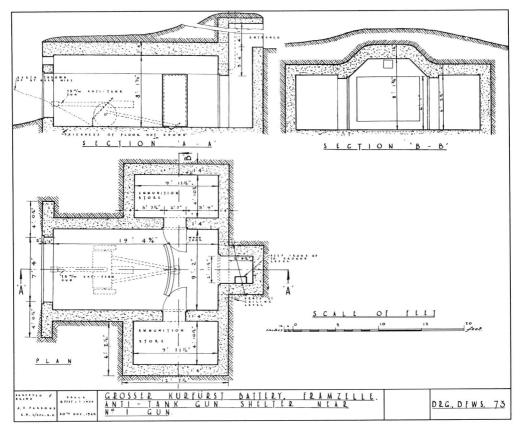

A bunker for a 75 mm anti-tank gun on the Grosser Kürfurst site, near No. 1 casemate. (Royal Engineers Library)

The battery fired more than 400 shells at Kent between 1943 and June 1944. When Grosser Kurfürst fired at the Kent batteries during the evacuation of Boulogne, Winnie and Pooh both returned fire with ten rounds. A couple of days later on 3 September, Grosser Kurfürst and the other big guns again fired at Dover and the Royal Marine guns again returned fire, shooting seven rounds at the battery before changing targets and shelling the Todt battery which returned fire, causing casualties among the Royal Marines and a lot of damage. On the 19th, the Royal Marine guns again fired at Grosser Kurfürst, shooting 60 rounds on to the target after six ranging shots, but the accuracy of the British guns had deteriorated due to barrel wear and little damage was inflicted. The battery was heavily bombed several times during September, receiving an even higher tonnage than Lindemann, but, as with the raids on Lindemann, little damage was done to the concrete structures although the site was severely cratered and all the four gun bunkers received several hits. One bomb even exploded on one of the turrets. This merely dented the 100 mm armour, however, shearing its 5 cm bolts. Many of the support bunkers were damaged but the raids were surprisingly ineffective.

The Kriegsmarine batteries Grosser Kurfürst and Todt (about a mile south of the Great Elector) were assaulted by the Canadian 9th Infantry Brigade on 29 September with support from the specialist armour of the 79th Armoured Division. The armour destroyed casemates and bunkers as the infantry advanced and the crew of one of the AVREs dismounted and placed a demolition charge on the turret of No. 4 gun, the southernmost of the four. This led to the surrender of the battery but the command post site continued to resist and was subjected to 90 minutes of shelling by assorted tanks and self-propelled artillery, aided by Crocodile flamethrowing tanks and AVREs before the battery commander eventually gave up.

In 1946, the Royal Engineers had a field day demolishing the gun bunkers. These were all blown up to leave only heaps of concrete blocks and rubble which subsequently became heavily overgrown. The approximate area of the site has become wooded, while the surrounding land has been returned to agriculture. The command post was partially demolished after the war using an unexploded 1,000 lb bomb that had lodged beneath the structure. A modern radar scanner was built on top of its remains in 1979. Slightly east of Waringzelle, about half a mile south of Framzelle, there are the remains of Würzburg and Mammut radar posts (the latter a type V143) along with two type M176 casemates that once housed 150 mm guns and two type 622 personnel bunkers.

Unlike Lindemann and Grosser Kurfürst, the Todt battery at Haringzelles just southwest of Audinghen and about a mile south of the Great Elector still exists. The

The rear of one of the Todt battery casemates with a 280 mm railway gun. (Joe Kaufmann)

battery was similar to Lindemann in that it comprised steel turreted guns enclosed in concrete casemates but, unlike Lindemann, Todt had four guns. Each casemate was about 25 m across and about 15 m high at the back but only 8 m at the front because of the banked earth. The battery was named after Fritz Todt and had formerly been called Siegfried battery. It was officially opened by Grossadmiral Raeder and Admiral Dönitz in February 1942 but construction was not completed until November the same year. These were 380 mm weapons. Each barrel was 19.6 m long, weighed 104 tonnes and could be elevated 45°. One of these guns could shoot a 495 kg shell 34.6 miles and a 800 kg shell 33 miles (each shell was 1.65 m long). These guns were claimed to be very accurate but there is no reason to suppose they were any more so than any of the big guns on either side of the Channel. The casemates were on two floors with the magazines on the upper floor along with the gun room, while the lower floor containing the crew accommodation was below ground level. The site was smaller than Lindemann or Grosser Kurfürst but like them was protected by anti-tank guns, machine-gun posts and Flak. Similarly, it had its own medical bunker (of a non-standard design), located behind casemate No. 2. The fire-control post was located three-quarters of a mile southwest of the main site.

The Grosser Kurfürst and Todt batteries came under the command of MAA 242 which also included two smaller calibre batteries, one of 150 mm guns at Wissant (M3 battery, on the bluffs at the east of the town), the other of 170 mm guns on the

One of the casemates at Friedrich August battery at la Trésorerie after its capture by the Canadians, September 1944. The barrel of the 305 mm gun is just visible, parallel with the ground. (Donald I. Grant, National Archives of Canada PA167980)

Another of the Friedrich August casemates. Heavy chains have been suspended over the embrasure as extra protection. Battle damage is clearly visible. (Donald I. Grant, National Archives of Canada PA174409)

Cap Gris Nez, nothing much of either of which now remains. When the Canadians attacked these batteries at 0600 hrs on 29 September, only the defenders of M3 put up a serious fight, knocking out all the supporting tanks before the infantry succeeded in crushing the defenders. At Todt, two of the 79th Armoured's Crocodiles were disabled but the remaining flamethrower tank clearly scared the gun crews and they quickly surrendered. By mid-morning, the fighting was over and the Canadians had taken 1,600 prisoners. Kent was never shelled again. For some reason, unlike the other big-gun batteries, Todt was never bombed.

The four casemates of the Todt battery now sit in woodland that has grown up round them since the end of the war. The No. 1 casemate at the top of the site was bought in 1970 by a hotel owner from Wissant who turned it into a museum, the Musée du Mur d'Atlantique. It opened in 1971. During the year-long clear-up operation to remove rubble and sludge from the interior and pump out the 3.5 m of water that had flooded the lower level, a shell case was found which is now on display along with a 380 mm shell and other weapons and equipment. This casemate is intact and in good condition with access to all its rooms. One of the walls bears the rhyming slogan *In Einigkeit mit Emsigkeit, zum kampfe für Gerechtigkeit, Wuchst du empor dem feind zum trutz, Deutsche Wehr für Deutschlands Nutz* (In unity with zeal, to do battle for justice, you grew in defiance of the foe, German [weapon of] defence for Germany's good); while on the wall of the shell magazine of No. 4 are the words *Einer muss zerbrechen und das wird niemals Deutschland sein!* (One [of us, i.e. Germany or England] has got to break and it will never be Germany!). Todt battery's reserve magazine was at a tiny place called Breslau, half a mile southeast of Onglevert. The bunkers are still there.

The other casemates are privately owned but are open to the public. These are not in such good condition and one is badly damaged due an accident soon after the capture of the site. Two French workers decided to explore the interior of casemate No. 3, removed a couple of lengths of cordite from one of the shell cases and lit them to use as torches. This proved to be reckless in the extreme and it seems that the naked flames set off a huge explosion that ruptured the casemate, blowing out the front and the roof, doing as much damage as any systematic demolition programme could have done, completely obliterating one man and blowing the legs off the other who was found some distance away.

The Friedrich August battery of three casemated 305 mm guns was near the village of la Trésorerie, about 3 miles north of Boulogne but was not part of Fortress Boulogne. Although the gun rooms of each of its three casemates were essentially the same, the casemates were not identical in design. There seems to have been no sound reason why they should have been dissimilar. They were similar to the casemates of Oldenburg battery at Calais. Like the other big-gun batteries, Friedrich August was entirely offensive in purpose and it played no role in the defence of Boulogne, although its outlying defences did. The site was protected with anti-tank guns in bunkers, machine-gun positions and Flak, as well barbed wire and minefields. Despite the fact that the distance to Dover from here is 27.5 miles, these guns were still able to bombard the port with 250 kg shells. The battery was under the command of MAA 240 which included batteries in Festung Boulogne. As part of the preliminary to the attack on Boulogne, RAF mediums bombed the battery on 14 September. The attack on Boulogne began on 17 September and included an assault by the 8th Canadian Infantry Brigade on Friedrich August. They were supported by Crab flail Shermans of the 1st Lothian and Border Yeomanry, AVREs of 81st Assault Squadron, Royal Engineers and Crocodiles of 141st RAC. The battery fell on the 19th.

Today, only one of the casemates still exists, although it is not intact, one has been demolished to make way for industrial development, and little remains of the third.

FORTRESS BOULOGNE

Boulogne was one of the first ports to be designated a fortress by Hitler. The town was ringed by a chain of strongpoints, batteries and resistance nests, most of which were sited on high ground. They included Saint-Etienne-au-Mont to the south of the town, the location of an infantry strongpoint, a battery of 155 mm artillery and a Flak battery, and Mont Lambert to the east, where there were two strongpoints and another 155 mm battery. There were several strongpoints immediately south of Boulogne around le Portel, including a 94 mm battery to its south and a 138 mm

Bunkers on Mont Lambert, part of Festung Boulogne, after their capture by North Nova Scotia Highlanders, 18 September 1944. Note the preformed concrete blocks lying around. These would have been used to build more bunkers. (Donald I. Grant, National Archives of Canada PA176968)

battery at Mont de Couppe as well as an 88 mm Flak battery at Mont Soleil. North of Boulogne at la Crèche there were three artillery batteries, Crèche I, II and III, arranged in a triangle, III and I forming the west–east base with II at the apex. Southeast of la Crèche was another group of strongpoints and a Flak battery. There was another group of strongpoints southeast of Boulogne at Herquelingue. Within this defensive ring there were eighteen Flak batteries, nine artillery batteries and many more infantry strongpoints and resistance nests.

The guns of most of the artillery batteries were in casemates. Two coastal batteries had type 671 casemates but they were not identical; the four 105 mm guns of Crèche II and the four 94 mm guns of the coastal battery at le Portel were in slightly different versions of this type. The three 138 mm guns in the Kriegsmarine battery located in the old French fort at Mont de Couppe, however, were of type M270. The artillery batteries for the landward defence of Boulogne had a wider range of casemate types. A typical battery was the one at Herquelingue. Here there were two type 611 casemates and two type 669, one of the commonest types, for the 155 mm field guns of the 7/147 Artillerie Regiment which used a type 626 command post. The casemates were aligned across the brow of the high ground, facing northwest. The battery had a type 114 bunker with a six-embrasured steel turret for self-defence and a type 641 ammunition bunker at the rear of the site. It was protected by two 20 mm anti-aircraft guns. The 4/147 Artillerie Regiment battery on Mont Lambert also had two type 611 and two type 669 casemates but for self-defence had a type 630 bunker. The guns of the 5/147 Artillerie Regiment

A Somua S-35 tank turret, armed with a 47 mm gun, mounted on a tobruk in the street in front of the Grand Commerce hotel, Boulogne in 1942. (618/2618/15. Bundesarchiv)

battery at Equihen just south of Saint-Etienne-au-Mont were in open emplacements as were the guns of 6/147 Artillerie Regiment battery southeast of Mont Soleil.

Infantry strongpoints followed no general pattern in their use of bunkers. Their positioning depended on the topography and direction of a likely attack. Strongpoint 240, near the column commemorating Napoleon's Grande Armée at the northern tip of Boulogne, dispersed its bunkers along the edge of the high ground in a U-shape. There were five tobruks and twelve bunkers in two main groups, plus an isolated group of two and one on its own. There were seven different types of bunker, including two type 630 machine-gun bunkers with two embrasures (one was the bunker on its own), and a type 626 and a type 680 for 75 mm anti-tank guns. The latter was a simpler design that dated from 1943, whereas the former dated from 1942. As the type 680 was with a type 621 personnel bunker, also dating from 1943, and both were apart from the other bunkers, it is possible that these were later additions to an existing strongpoint. There was a single type 634 with a single machine-gun embrasure and a turret with three embrasures. At least one other type 621 bunker and a similar type 622 personnel bunker were in one of the main groups. The strongpoint also include a Flak position.

The strongpoint astride Fringhen Farm at Saint-Etienne-au-Mont, south of Boulogne, StP 269, known as Heliotrope by the Germans, had a similar number of bunkers as StP 240. Here there were two type 630s, a type 105 machine-gun bunker and a type 505 bunker for a 37 mm anti-tank gun. The strongpoint was the headquarters of 1/104 Infanterieregiment and therefore had a command post in the shape of a type 117 bunker as well as a medical bunker of type 118. Adjacent to this strongpoint on the high ground to its southeast was an artillery battery which had to make do with open emplacements.

Photographed during Operation Wellhit, the assault on Boulogne by the Canadian Army at the end of September 1944, this shows the back of a badly damaged light Flak bunker. The wooden stairs on the outside reach to the gun position on the top. Note the craters and battle damage. (Donald I. Grant, National Archives of Canada PA167979)

Boulogne was defended by as many as 10,000 men. Most infantry were from two fortress battalions and a fortress machine-gun battalion, none first-rate units, but there were also engineers and artillerymen from the 64th Infanterie Division within the defence perimeter. The garrison was under the command of Generalleutnant Heim who had served as Guderian's chief of staff in Poland in 1939 and later in Russia. Although the 3rd Canadian Infantry Division arrived at Boulogne on 5 September, nothing could be done to capture the port until le Havre had been taken as the necessary specialized armour was fully occupied there, as was the RAF. During 11–13 September, Heim evacuated 8,000 civilians from the town with the cooperation of the Canadian commander. To soften up Boulogne's garrison before the Canadian assault, the strongpoints and artillery batteries were subjected to forty-nine air raids by the Second Tactical Air Force, including sorties by rocket-firing Typhoons and medium bombers. At 0825 hrs on 17 September, Lancasters and Halifaxes bombed the strongpoints and batteries on the high ground from north of Boulogne to below Mont Lambert. This was the opening of Operation Wellhit which started on the same day as Operation Market Garden. Boulogne's southern defences were subjected to a similar raid in the afternoon. The heavies flew 688 sorties against the defences that day and dropped 3,445 tonnes on them.

While the raids were in progress, fifteen Canadian and British artillery regiments and two heavy anti-aircraft regiments shelled the German positions with 328 guns.

It had not been possible to engage in a counter-battery shoot before the start date because of an ammunition shortage. The morning bombardment and air raid lasted about 90 minutes at the end of which the 3rd Canadian Infantry Division began their assault with armoured support from the Fort Gary Horse (10th Armoured Regiment) and the AVREs, Crabs and Crocodiles of the 79th Armoured Division. Unfortunately, the concrete casemates and bunkers were hardly affected by the bombardment and as soon as it ended the German guns began shelling the Canadians. Their progress was further slowed by the minefields and barbed wire that formed integral parts of the batteries and strongpoints. Paths through minefields often had to be cleared by the Crabs under German shellfire. Although some progress was made, few of the first day's objectives were reached. The defenders fought tenaciously and only grudgingly gave ground. It took the specialized bunker-busting armour to break the defenders.

Heim claimed that casualties from the air raids were negligible although the British thought that the raids and the shelling had effectively reduced the defenders' ability to fight. There is no doubt that German communications were seriously disrupted and the bombardment had a negative psychological effect on the defenders. However, all agreed that neither the air raids nor the shelling had much effect on the concrete fortifications and few were destroyed. It was estimated in an after-action study that a battery of six emplaced 88s in Henriville was hit by 5,700 artillery rounds that fell within a 140 m radius and yet managed to return fire with 2,000 rounds. Allied intelligence had identified what it thought were the defensive positions before the battle but it later transpired that as many as eight strongpoints had not been detected,

A view from the strongpoint at le Portel towards the town after the battle for Boulogne was over.
(Donald I. Grant, National Archives of Canada PA177043)

testament to the effectiveness of camouflage. On the other hand, several dummy positions were identified as real ones and wastefully bombarded.

The strongpoints and battery on Mont Lambert were taken the next day and the strongpoints in the region of Saint-Etienne surrendered on the 20th. Mont Lambert had been Heim's headquarters and with its loss he moved it to le Portel. On the evening of the 21st, the strongpoints and batteries of la Crèche were bombed by seventy-five mediums which dropped 400 bombs on the positions. They surrendered the next morning. The batteries and strongpoints in the region of le Portel surrendered in the afternoon and the battle for Boulogne was over. In the meantime, the Canadians had forced their way into the port, taking the Citadel on the 18th along with 200 prisoners, helped by a local who showed the Canadians a secret tunnel into the Citadel. The harbour was taken on the 21st. The crew of an 88 on the end of the breakwater were the last of the garrison to surrender on the 22nd following Heim's instruction to capitulate. It had taken six days to capture the port and the British and Canadians suffered 634 casualties. They took 9,517 prisoners. But Heim had destroyed the harbour facilities and had sunk ships across its mouth before he surrendered. It took until 12 October before the port was working again.

Many of the casemates and bunkers of Boulogne's defences still exist, including many of the casemates of la Crèche, particularly the type 671s along the shoreline and a fire-control post for Crèche II as well as other bunkers. There are also several along the coast below le Portel. In the region of Mont Lambert, there are a number of bunkers that were part of a strongpoint, an artillery battery and a Flak battery but some are in ruins. A rare example of a type 664 bunker that had a turret for a 105 mm howitzer is in a copse on the south slope of Mont Lambert. There are also bunkers and casemates on the high ground to the south of Saint-Etienne, remains of the three strongpoints in the area, including Heliotrope around Fringhen Farm. On the Herquelingue hill there are several bunkers of various types and casemates, as well as six bunkers (types 630, 623 and 505) along the road from Herquelingue to Isques. Nothing much remains of the strongpoint near the monument to the Grande Armée, nor is there much left in Boulogne itself.

About 3 miles north of Boulogne is the town of Wimereux. It was here that Hitler had a headquarters bunker constructed for his personal use during Operation Sealion. When this fell through, it became the headquarters of the Boulogne Coastal Defence Sector. It was sited on the left bank of the River Wimereux and camouflaged to look like a house.

BOULOGNE TO LE TRÉPORT

Between Boulogne and le Tréport the coast is open with wide sandy beaches backed by broad dunes. The few towns and villages along this stretch of coast became the focus of strongpoints and artillery batteries. There were, for example, six strongpoints and batteries in the region of Hardelot-Plage, including one to the south of Hardelot in which two groups of emplacements were constructed parallel with the beach, the

Artillerymen of the 3/1245 Heeres Küsten Artillerie Regiment loading a 155 mm gun in an open emplacement at le Touquet, 1944. Note the wooden frame carrying camouflage netting and the wooden platform between the trails. The gun has been adapted to traverse on a fixed mounting. (299/1825/21. Bundesarchiv)

An open emplacement for a 75 mm field gun at le Touquet. This one is built with a seaward protective wall to allow the gun to enfilade the beach. Behind the camera is a concrete shelter for the gun. Note the wooden platform and the beach obstacles in the sea. (299/1825/61. Bundesarchiv)

emplacements and bunkers in each group being connected by concrete tunnels beneath the dunes. The forward group included two 50 mm anti-tank gun emplacements and one for a 75 mm gun as well as a machine-gun tobruk and a mortar tobruk. The rear position had two emplaced 50 mm anti-tank guns and two mortar tobruks. In addition, there was a separate 47 mm anti-tank gun in a bunker in the first line and a second emplaced 75 mm gun in the second line. Both of these had tunnels linked to other bunkers.

Mont Saint-Frieux and the surrounding hills to the south of Hardelot dominate the beach at Dannes. These became the site for the several interlocking strongpoints that included a Flak battery, a couple of artillery batteries and infantry positions. In all, there are about fifty bunkers, casemates and emplacements of various types in the area. Further down the coast at Sainte-Cecile, the beach was defended by four anti-tank bunkers (one each of types 612, 640, 680 and 506, each housing a different sort of anti-tank gun) and two machine-gun bunkers of type 515.

Just south of Sainte-Cecile is the mouth of the River Canche which was protected by four artillery batteries, one north of the river at Saint-Gabriel beach, a second one in the now wooded area above Etaples, a third along the beach south of le Touquet and the fourth at Stella Plage. The first battery consisted of six emplaced 155 mm French guns and a fire-control post of type 119 which was protected by two type 680 casemates, each housing a 75 mm anti-tank gun, plus a type 680 machine-gun bunker. The second battery consisted of three 170 mm guns housed in type 688 casemates. The third one consisted of six emplaced 155 mm guns. This battery was

Steel hedgehog beach defences in the sea at le Tréport. (297/1719/26. Bundesarchiv)

protected by several enfilade-fire casemates and machine-gun bunkers along the beach. The fourth was a Kriegsmarine battery under the command of MAA 240 based at Boulogne. It consisted of four 105 mm guns in type 671 casemates. A large anti-tank wall barred access into the countryside beyond. All these batteries had various other bunkers including fire-control posts.

Coastal batteries were also established further down the same expanse of beach and dunes at Merlimont (including one on rudimentary wooden platforms and protected with sandbags) and Berck-Plage, the market town of Fort Mahon on the other side of Authie Bay and at Saint-Quentin to defend the mouth of the River Somme. This was also defended by a battery across the estuary at Saint-Valéry-sur-Somme as well as one on the Pointe du Hourdel at the western tip of the estuary. Several more batteries were established at la Mollière, Cayeux and around Ault. In the area of le Tréport there were several batteries and strongpoints, including three at Mers-les-Bains and four at Mesnil-Val. Le Tréport was captured by the 3rd Canadian Infantry Division in early September without much of a fight. The division reached le Touquet by the 4th and Boulogne by the following day. These strongpoints and batteries played no part in delaying the Allied advance.

DIEPPE

When on 19 August 1942, the Canadians and British mounted a raid on the town of Dieppe and the two coastal batteries that flanked it, the defences encountered by the attackers were nothing like those that the Allies faced less than two years later in Normandy. The batteries flanking the town in 1942, one at Berneval-le-Grand, about 4 miles east of Dieppe, the other at Varengeville-sur-Mer, about 4 miles to the west, were not casemated. The guns were in open emplacements. During the attack by members of No. 4 Commando on the battery at Varengeville, a sniper was able to kill some of the gun crew and pin down the others which prevented the guns from being fired. This battery was subsequently strafed by Spitfire Mk Vs armed with cannon before being blown up by the Commandos under the supervision of Major Patrick Porteous, Royal Artillery. For his bravery and leadership during the action, including a bayonet charge on the battery after he had been wounded, Porteous won the VC.

Little remains of these batteries. Most of the surviving structures were built after the raid when the defensive capabilities of the area were significantly increased because it was thought that Dieppe could become the site of a future Allied invasion. By 1944, there were 24 strongpoints, artillery and Flak batteries in the region of Dieppe, including some on the landward side. However, Dieppe was never designated a fortress and remained a strongpoint group which included an artillery regiment and two infantry regiments in its garrison. There were 20 bunkers and emplacements within Dieppe itself. Mont Robin, to the west of the town was the site of one of the strongpoints, and in excess of 50 bunkers are still there, including the remains of a Flak battery and a bunker of type L485 for a Mammut radar.

An old buttressed wall in Dieppe into which an embrasure for a 47 mm Skoda anti-tank gun was built (the dark rectangle next to the far right buttress). There appears to be a bunker in front of the wall. (Ken Bell, National Archives of Canada PA183102)

In September 1944, Dieppe was captured by the 2nd Canadian Infantry Division without a fight because the Germans abandoned the place before they arrived. Dieppe's harbour was undamaged and the first British ship started unloading supplies on 7 September. By the beginning of October, Dieppe was unloading more than 3,000 tonnes a day.

DIEPPE TO LE HAVRE

The cliffs along this section of the Channel coast, combined with the lack of a significant port until le Havre, made the likelihood of an Allied landing anywhere here seem very unlikely. Radar stations were set up at Saint-Valéry-en-Caux,

Dieppe, September 1944. This shows the camouflaged entrance to an abandoned bunker. (Ken Bell, National Archives of Canada PA183099)

Looking across the beach at Dieppe from the rear of a command bunker on the cliff to the west of the town. (Ken Bell, National Archives of Canada PA183168)

An anti-tank barrier in a Dieppe street. The despatch rider is Canadian. (Ken Bell, National Archives of Canada PA161887)

Fécamp and Cap d'Antifer, about 10 miles west of Etretat. Established in August 1940 by the Kriegsmarine, the Cap d'Antifer station was one of the first to be built in France by the Germans. The Saint-Valéry station was located near Manneville-és-Plains to the southeast and comprised two Freya sets and two Würzburg Riese sets. At Fécamp, there were two complementary stations established near each other, one on the north side of the harbour near the Notre-Dame-du-Salut church, the other a little further up the coast. This was the earlier of the two and consisted of two Seetakt sets, while the later station, established in front of the church, comprised a See Riese set and a Mammut set. The radar stations were defended by their own Flak batteries. These radars were for the detection of ships, unlike the station just down the coast at Bruneval, the location of an aircraft detection Würzburg set, which was raided by British paratroopers on the night of 27/28 February 1942, the raiders making off with the vital equipment by sea. The stations had been discovered by aerial reconnaissance in late 1941. No bunkers had been detected but, by the time of the raid, several were under construction. In 1944, there were two groups of radars at Cap d'Antifer, one group of two Kriegsmarine sets and another group of three Luftwaffe sets. The latter group near la Poterie was surrounded by an anti-tank ditch.

Although there were a number of isolated batteries and observation posts on the coast between Dieppe and Fécamp, there were no major defence works until Fécamp which had twenty-nine strongpoints and resistance nests to defend it and the surrounding area including Yport to the west. A strongpoint adjacent to the north side

The observation slit of a bunker on the high ground above Dieppe, September 1944. (Ken Bell, National Archives of Canada PA183169)

of the harbour included a couple of casemates for 75 mm guns, two anti-tank gun bunkers and several tobruks for machine-guns and mortars. One of the casemates was entered by a 185 m tunnel bored through the cliffs, the entrance to which was via a cellar in one of the houses. This was constructed in 1942, its creators leaving their signature on the tunnel wall '*Gesteins Bohr Komp* 88 1942' (bored by Company 88). A second battery was near the village of Criqueboeuf-en-Caux about a mile to the southwest of Fécamp. This consisted of six 155 mm guns in open emplacements. Another similar battery was at Yport.

The next major area of defence works was around the fishing port of Etretat, another 8 miles down the coast. Here there were thirteen strongpoints, four of them artillery batteries of 75 mm guns, along the neighbouring coast and inland. Little remains of any of them today. The garrison infantry were from two fortress companies stiffened by the 3rd Battalion of the 34th Infanterieregiment, while the artillery came from the 17th Artillerie Regiment.

As the British and Canadians reached these strongpoints and batteries along this part of the coast, they found that many of them had been abandoned. The 1st Polish Armoured Division of the II Canadian Corps took le Tréport in early September while the 51st Highland Division of the British I Corps entered Saint-Valéry-en-Caux unopposed because the Germans had left.

LE HAVRE

Le Havre at the mouth of the River Seine was the second most important port in France and was consequently designated a fortress. All fortresses were supposed to have two heavy naval batteries but le Havre's were incomplete at the time of the invasion. Nevertheless, it was one of the most heavily defended ports in the Atlantic Wall. It was protected by eight Kriegsmarine batteries and four Heer batteries as well as three Luftwaffe Flak batteries with numerous other light Flak units. The infantry contingent consisted of three battalions of the 33rd Infantrieregiment and a battalion of fortress infantry. In addition, there was an anti-tank company from the 17th Luftwaffe Feld Division. In all, there were about 12,000 men in the defences of le Havre under the command of Oberst Wildermuth while the naval contingent was under the command of Admiral Treschow.

Kriegsmarine batteries were located at Brière a little south of Octeville-sur-Mer (four 155 mm guns of 2/MAA 266), at la Corvée near Clos des Ronces, (1/MAA 266) and on the seafront along the Albert I Boulevard at le Nice Havrais (3/MAA 266). This consisted of four 150 mm guns in type M176 and M272 casemates. Another battery of two 75 mm guns was located at the end of the north jetty (4/MAA 266), one of whose casemates still exists, while two more batteries were on the south jetty (5/MAA 266 on its northern end, 6/MAA 266 in the middle). These were to protect the S-boat and T-boat flotillas that were based at le Havre as well as the mouth of the Seine. Yet another battery was on the end of the south quay of the harbour (8/MAA 266) while 7/MAA 266 was sited at the tip of the southern jetty of what is now called the Môle Centrale.

The battery near Clos des Ronces (also known as the la Corvée battery) was only built in 1944. It was here that the sole heavy naval gun was placed, a 380 mm weapon with a maximum range of 34 miles which meant that it was capable of hitting the British invasion beaches – the mouth of the River Orne was only about 17 miles away. It was mounted in a steel turret which could traverse three-quarters of the Seine estuary. The turret sat on a type S536 casemate that had not been completed by the time of the invasion. Two additional emplacements were also under construction as the battery was supposed to have three 380 mm guns. Rather ignominiously, the remains of the battery are now a rubbish tip.

One Heer coastal battery was located on the top of the cliffs at Clos des Ronces (3/HKAR 1254) about 150 m in front of the 380 mm Kriegsmarine gun. Two of its three 170 mm guns were in type 688 casemates but the third was in an open emplacement. These guns had a range of nearly 17 miles and commanded the approaches to le Havre. A variety of bunkers were also built on the site for personnel and ammunition. Ecqueville was the location of another battery (1/HKAR 1254). This was well beyond the main line of defence and was intended to be part of another defence line that was never completed. The battery consisted of four type 621 casemates for 105 mm guns and had a trapezoid-shaped fire-control post. A third battery (2/HKAR 1254) was in the old French fort of Sainte-Adresse where three type 671 casemates and an open emplacement accommodated four 105 mm guns with a range of 12.5 miles. Two of the casemates were in the fort's southwest bastion along with a fire-control post, while the third was outside the walls on an embankment opposite the entrance. In addition to these, there were six gun emplacements, two inside the entrance, the others in the bastions. A searchlight was housed in a bunker beyond the outer ditch, opposite the southwest bastion. The fourth (4/HKAR 1254) was on the Cap de la Hève with four 105 mm guns in type 671 casemates. Due to erosion, these have fallen to the foot of the cliffs. Not far away, the Kriegsmarine had a Seetakt radar, the bunker for which is still there.

To protect the landward side of the port, six other batteries covered the northern and eastern flanks of the city, one at Bléville on the northwest side with four 150 mm guns, another at Févretot north of the city and to the west of Bléville wood (also known as Montgeon forest) with another four 150 mm guns, with a third nearby at les Mont Trottin with four 155 mm guns in type 669 casemates. Another group of batteries was sited at Rouelles to the east of the wood, another at the Montgeon Château further to the east, with a third east of the city at Graville with a total of twelve 155 mm guns. In addition to these, about forty strongpoints were established on the high ground from the north side of the town to the east with an anti-tank wall along the north running from the coast, below Octeville, to southwest of Montivilliers and northeast of Fontaine-la-Mallet, where the defence line turned south and followed the Lézarde valley down to Harfleur. Another anti-tank ditch ran from southeast of Octeville up to the coast at Ecqueville. In front of part of the anti-tank wall was a minefield that started just below Octeville and ran eastwards to just below Fréville. The isolated battery at Ecqueville was surrounded on three sides by minefields with the cliffs on the fourth side.

At the end of August 1944, the British I Corps crossed the Seine and on 1 September it wheeled left and headed for le Havre, sending the 51st Highland Division on to Saint-Valéry-en-Caux. On 4 September, the division joined the 49th Division and invested le Havre. The German commander was asked to surrender but he declined. The softening up bombardment began on the 5th with the monitor HMS *Erebus* firing its 15 in guns at the Clos des Ronces battery which returned fire. *Erebus* was hit and withdrew. On the 6th, the southeastern defences were bombed and on the 8th it was the turn of the northwestern area of the port. In all, about 4,000 tonnes of bombs were dropped. Bad weather then postponed operations until the 10th when sixty heavy bombers raided the Clos des Ronces battery. This was followed by another bombardment by *Erebus* which had been repaired. She was joined by the battleship HMS *Warspite* adding its four 15 in guns to the bombardment (one turret had been out of action since being hit by a glider bomb off Salerno in September 1943). The battery was silenced. That day, a thousand bombers in two raids dropped 4,950 tonnes of bombs on le Havre's defences.

While this was happening, the divisional artillery and two heavy and six medium artillery regiments shelled the landward batteries. Immediately the last air raid ended, the assault on the town began. The 49th Division attacked with the 34th Tank Brigade from the northeast towards the high ground east of Fontaine-la-Mallet using flails to breach the minefields. In the dark and in sodden conditions, the German anti-tank guns knocked out 34 flails and two command tanks. The subsequent assault on the strongpoints resulted in the loss of six AVREs. By the 11th, the division had reached Harfleur with the aid of rocket-firing Typhoons, which were very effective as bunker busters, and turned west to le Havre.

The 51st Division attacked from the north with the 33rd Armoured Brigade using searchlight beams reflected off the clouds to illuminate their way. They advanced through the Montgeon forest, took Octeville and were approaching the Sainte-Adresse fort on the evening of the 11th. By late afternoon on the 12th, the battle was over and le Havre was in Allied hands along with 11,300 prisoners but the Germans had destroyed the harbour. It did not become usable again until 9 October.

Le Havre was badly damaged in the fighting. After the war, the port was rebuilt and expanded and in the process most of the concrete structures built by the Germans were demolished.

LOWER NORMANDY

In late 1943, the Kriegsmarine built a battery of four 150 mm guns at Vasouy, a short way up the coast from Honfleur at the mouth of the Seine. The guns were sited to protect the landward side of le Havre and were unable to engage the Allied armada

A view across the dunes and obstacle-strewn beach at Deauville, Normandy, garrisoned by the 744th Infantrieregiment on D-Day. On the left is a 50 mm anti-tank gun with a 'roof' in an open emplacement. Note the wall on its seaward side. The entrance to the bunker is on the right. (Thompson, National Archives of Canada PA129168)

The rear of a bunker on Juno photographed on 10 June 1944. (Frank L. Dubervill, National Archives of Canada PA133739)

on D-Day. It was captured in late August after the guns had been disabled by their crews. Their type M272 casemates along with the battery's type M262 fire-control bunker are still there.

Villerville, about 3 miles west of Vasouy, was the location of an army coastal battery of six 155 mm guns which, with a range in excess of 13 miles, were capable of firing on the Allied invasion fleet. Their original purpose was the protection of the approaches to the Seine. These guns were in open emplacements which must have made being shelled by *Warspite* from 17 miles at 0530 hrs on D-Day a very unpleasant experience. The Heer battery on Mont Canisy, known to the Allies as the Bénerville battery, was engaged by the 15 in guns of HMS *Ramillies* at the start of the bombardment. About half a mile inland and west of the River Touques, the battery consisted of three 155 mm guns in type 679 casemates in front of its six original open emplacements, only one of which was occupied by another gun of the same calibre at the time of the invasion. The position was protected by a ring of minefields and a number of machine-gun tobruks as well as several 50 mm anti-tank guns in open emplacements. The front of the site was guarded by an emplaced Renault R35 turret. A variety of other bunkers for personnel were dotted about the heart-shaped site, including two fire-control posts.

The battery was silenced by *Ramillies* but it later came back to life and fired on *Warspite* who had to move to avoid the salvoes from Mont Canisy. In fact, this battery was never put out of action. Like the battery at Houlgate 6 miles closer to the invasion beaches, it continued to shell the ships off Sword beach and the beach itself until the end of August following the Normandy breakout and the pursuit of the German army to the Seine. As a result of shelling from the Mont Canisy and Houlgate batteries, the use of Sword to unload supplies was stopped on 25 June. Several times, these batteries were temporarily shelled into silence by battleships and cruisers but they were never destroyed despite more than 1,000 heavy and medium shells being fired at them. They damaged a number of landing ships along with HMS *Locust*, a headquarters ship, and a number of other vessels including a coaster loaded with ammunition which was set ablaze.

The Houlgate battery, manned by troops from the same regiment as those at Mont Canisy and Villerville (HKAA 1255), was basically the same as its Mont Canisy sister but with two casemates rather than three. On the night preceding D-Day, the Houlgate battery was bombed along with many of the other batteries along the invasion coast just before the naval bombardment was to start. About 500 tonnes was dropped on it by RAF heavies and similar quantities were dropped on nine other batteries (Merville, Fontenay, Varreville, la Pernelle, Maisy, Pointe du Hoc, Longues-sur-Mer, Mont Fleury and Ouistreham). While *Warspite* and *Ramillies* were shelling their targets on D-Day, Houlgate was shelled by the monitor HMS *Roberts*, also armed with 15 in guns. It was last shelled towards the end of August by HMS *Erebus* before it was finally captured. Although the Mont Canisy site is easy to get to, the Houlgate battery is much more difficult to reach.

Franceville Plage in front of Merville east of the River Orne was protected by two strongpoints with machine-gun bunkers, tobruks and anti-tank gun bunkers, each strongpoint having a short anti-tank wall facing the sea. The first one had more than a dozen bunkers, including two type 105 machine-gun bunkers and four tobruks, while the second one had about 20 and an emplaced tank turret. These are now in a campsite. These strongpoints were sited to protect the Merville battery about half a mile inland. This battery was believed to have four 150 mm guns with a range of 7.5 miles and capable of inflicting serious damage on Sword beach. Reconnaissance had picked out four casemates and a number of other bunkers within a barbed wire and mined perimeter of about 350 m². For about two months prior to the invasion, the Merville battery and many others were regularly bombed. In all about 1,000 bombs were dropped on Merville but only 50 hit the battery site. A near miss, possibly by a 4,000 lb bomb, cracked the wall of No.1 casemate.

The Allies decided to mount an airborne assault on the battery in the early hours of 6 June with the 750 men and 35 officers of the 9th Parachute Battalion commanded by Lieutenant-Colonel Otway. The operation did not go as planned and Otway had to attack with only 150 officers and men and no heavy equipment because of the wide dispersion of his men in the drop. Prior to the assault, 109 Lancasters dropped 400 tonnes of 4,000 lb Cookies on the village instead of the battery. Nevertheless, Otway took the battery in 30 minutes suffering 70 casualties. The 150 mm guns were not there. All they found were some old 100 mm howitzers which they attempted unsuccessfully to destroy. Fearing that they would be shelled by HMS *Arethusa*, which was due to bombard the battery if the cruiser did not receive a signal to indicate that the battery had been taken, Otway and his men moved off the site before the allotted time. This allowed the remainder of the garrison and the battery commander, Leutnant Steiner, who had been in the battery's fire-control post in one of the Franceville strongpoints when the assault began, to re-occupy the battery. During the assault, Steiner had called in fire from the Houlgate battery on to his own.

A small bunker for a 50 mm anti-tank gun, still in place, at Saint-Aubin-sur-Mer. This was originally an open emplacement that was later converted. (Neil Short)

The battery now attempted to fire on the ships but *Arethusa* returned fire. The battery was bombed on three more occasions and was again shelled by *Arethusa* to support the Commandos trying to retake the battery the next day. The explosions of naval shells and RAF bombs removed the earth that once covered the casemates. No. 1 casemate is now a museum. No. 3 has a defused 4,000-pounder underneath it.

Two more batteries were on the west side of the Orne estuary and at Ouistreham. At Riva-Bella at the front of Ouistreham there were six open emplacements for 155 mm guns at the eastern end of a strongpoint that extended for 1,200 m westwards and was 200 m in depth. Within the eastern half, there were numerous bunkers and tobruks along with a 17 m high command post which is now a museum. Little else remains except for a steel turret on the beach. To the southwest of Ouistreham near a water-tower was a battery with the Allied codename Daimler. This consisted of four 155 mm guns, three of them in type 699 casemates. A third battery, known as Morris, of four 100 mm guns in type 699s, one of which was still under construction, was located nearby at Colleville-sur-Orne (renamed Colleville-Montgomery after the war), while a strongpoint half a mile to the south was known as Hillman. On D-Day, the Riva-Bella battery was shelled by the 7.5 in cruiser HMS *Frobisher*, Daimler by the 6 in cruiser HMS *Danae* and Morris by the Polish 6 in cruiser ORP *Dragon*. These batteries and the strongpoint were taken by ground assault on D-Day, Daimler by the 2nd East Yorkshires with tank support from the 13th/18th Hussars (it held out until 1800 hrs), Morris and Hillman by the Suffolks. Morris surrendered at 1300 hrs without a fight but Hillman was the regimental headquarters of the 736th Grenadier

This photograph was taken four days after D-Day and shows piles of beach obstacles that have been cleared by Canadian engineers ready for demolition. In the foreground are hedgehogs with Belgian gates behind. The flag indicates that some still have live mines attached to them. (Frank L. Dubervill, National Archives of Canada PA131541)

Regiment and was manned by 150 troops. It contained twelve bunkers, some for anti-tank guns while others were for machine-guns. It was about 600 m by 400 m and surrounded by two 3.5 m belts of thick barbed wire. It took the Suffolks more than six hours to secure the position. In 1989, a plaque commemorating the Suffolks' achievement was fixed to the wall of one of the surviving bunkers. Today, there are bunkers at all three sites including one at Morris that has become part of a later house.

A few miles to the west at Douvres-la-Délivrande, there was a Luftwaffe nightfighter radar station that became operational in August 1943. Its radars were located in two linked strongpoints to the west of Douvres-la-Délivrande, the larger one about half a mile to the south of the other. Strongpoint 1 to the south was defended by five 50 mm anti-tank guns, a 75 mm field gun, Flak, mortars and machine-guns in bunkers, tobruks and open emplacements, while the smaller northern strongpoint was only defended by machine-guns in tobruks and by light Flak. The site was fiercely defended and it took several days for the 8th Brigade of the 3rd Canadian Infantry Division to capture it. Most of the bunkers have long since gone but a Würzburg radar dish has been reinstalled as part of a museum in Strongpoint 1.

There were three batteries opposite what was to become Gold beach. Two were located at Ver-sur-Mer, while the third was at la Mare-Fontaine. The battery near Mont Fleury château at Ver-sur-Mer was, like so many batteries along the Normandy coast, still under construction at the time of the invasion. Only two type 679 casemates had been completed and only one of these had its 122 mm gun installed. The casemates had been constructed using prefabricated concrete blocks to make the inner and outer walls between which concrete was then poured. This speeded up the process but produced weaker structures. The technique was used at several sites in Normandy. On D-Day, the battery was shelled by the 6 in cruiser HMS *Orion* which hit it twelve times. The battery did not return fire. The battery near la Mare-Fontaine was further inland and consisted of four type 669 casemates for 100 mm howitzers which were shelled for two hours by the 6 in cruiser HMS *Belfast*. The battery fired eighty-seven rounds before surrendering to the 7th Green Howards who took fifty prisoners.

The 6th Green Howards had the task of capturing the Mont Fleury battery. During their advance on the battery, D Company came under fire from a machine-gun bunker. CSM Stan Hollis took it on by himself, charging 30 yards towards it firing his Sten. On reaching the bunker, he shoved the muzzle through the aperture and fired again. He then lay on the roof and tossed a grenade into the entrance, incapaciting several defenders and killing two. He attempted the same tactic against another bunker but its garrison surrendered before he reached it. This action on D-Day and another act of bravery later in the day led to Hollis being awarded the VC, the only one to be won on D-Day.

Major Anderson of the Special Observer Party landed on D+6 to assess the damage inflicted by Allied naval and air bombardments. His appraisal of the Mont Fleury site showed that although the casemate housing the battery's only operational

A good view of one of the type M272 casemates with its 150 mm Krupp gun still in place at the Longues-sur-Mer battery, which has all four of its original guns. The battery is one of the most frequently visited sites on the Atlantic Wall. (Neil Short)

gun had been hit by a 500 lb bomb the gun was undamaged. On the contrary, he believed that the gun had successfully expended all its ammunition although he conceded that the bombardments had seriously impaired the efficiency of the battery, an optimistic view in the circumstances. Anderson's assessment of resistance nest Wn 34 at Ver-sur-Mer showed that while the air raids had been on target only one machine-gun was damaged. A 50 mm anti-tank gun in an open emplacement was undamaged despite a 1,000-pounder exploding so close that the rim of the crater was a mere 12 m away. Few of the bunkers had been damaged and none significantly. On the other hand, a nearby resistance nest at la Rivière (Wn 33) was more heavily damaged by the naval bombardment although its 88 mm anti-tank gun in a type 677 casemate built into the sea wall survived long enough to shoot up two Crabs and two AVREs before being knocked out by a tank commanded by Captain Bell of the Westminster Dragoons. The casemate still survives.

Between Vers-sur-Mer and Arromanches there were several resistance nests which included numerous bunkers as well as some casemates for field guns. These were surrounded by barbed wire and mines. Some tobruks were built into the sea wall. About 3 miles to the west of Arromanches at Longues-sur-Mer was a Kriegsmarine battery of four 150 mm guns in type M272 casemates which had been built in September 1943, the guns coming from a decommissioned destroyer. They had a range of 12 miles and

The type M262 fire-control post at the Longues-sur-Mer battery from the front. This featured in the film The Longest Day. *The indentations were not caused by battle damage but were built in as camouflage.* (Neil Short)

represented a serious threat to the invasion fleet and the landings. The type M262 fire-control post was on the edge of the cliffs while the four casemates, arranged in an arc, were built about 350 m inland to maximize their fire zone. From late 1943 onwards, the site was bombed several times including two heavy raids in the week preceding D-Day when 1,500 tonnes were dropped on it. At 0530 hrs on D-Day, it was engaged by the cruiser HMS *Ajax* but half an hour later it returned fire on HMS *Bulolo*, a headquarters ship. After a further 20 minutes of bombardment it fell silent but resumed firing soon afterwards on *Bulolo* which was forced to move. *Ajax* was joined by HMS *Argonaut* in shelling the battery which was eventually put out of action at 0845 hrs. Two of the casemates received direct hits, the shells entering the casemates through their embrasures. It had taken 179 6 in and 5.25 in shells from the two cruisers. The two remaining guns opened up again in the late afternoon but were silenced by the French cruiser FFS *Georges Leygues*. The battery's 120 survivors out of 184 surrendered the next day to the British 231st Infantry Brigade. The battery had fired 115 rounds. Today, it is a tourist site and one of the few batteries with casemates that still have their guns.

Before the invasion, the Americans identified 32 strongpoints (actually resistance nests) between the River Vire and Port-en-Bessin but these, like elsewhere along the Normandy coastline, were only a thin crust with no second or third line of defence. Along the Omaha beaches where the Americans were to land, there were 14 resistance nests. Most were sited to protect the beach exits between the dunes. At Colleville, the exits were protected by three resistance nests, while the exits at Saint-Laurent were protected by four. There was another between Colleville and the beach and another two between Saint-Laurent and the beach. A further three protected the exit from the beach at Vierville. Some had no heavy weapons while others had anti-tank guns, Renault R35 tank turrets in tobruks and mortar tobruks. All were defended by machine-guns. One of the nests at Colleville had two 75 mm guns in casemates to enfilade the beach, two 50 mm anti-tank guns in open emplacements, a 50 mm mortar in a tobruk and at least five machine-gun tobruks, plus an anti-tank ditch, while a neighbouring one had an 88 mm gun in a casemate to enfilade the beach, one emplaced 50 mm gun and a tank turret plus one 50 mm mortar in a tobruk in addition to several machine-gun tobruks. Both had several more machine-guns in weapons pits and fire trenches. Various other bunkers were also built on the sites. The 50 mm gun in the nest at the exit between Colleville and Saint-Laurent was in a type 667 bunker. To give the defenders clear fire zones, any houses that obstructed them had been demolished. The beach defences were similar to those along all of the Normandy beaches. Beyond the high water mark there were three lines of obstacles. Furthest out at about 225 m were Belgian gates with Teller anti-tank mines fixed to them. The second line, about 20 m closer to the shore, consisted of mine-tipped logs staked into the sand and pointing out to sea, or log ramps, while the third line 80 m closer still consisted of 1.7 m tall hedgehogs typically made of three sections of steel girder joined together at their centres.

Immediately prior to the naval bombardment on 6 June, 329 Eighth Air Force Liberators bombed these positions with over 1,000 tonnes but due to a number of difficulties the bombs mostly fell too far inland. The defences were then shelled by two battleships, USS *Arkansas* with twelve 12 in guns and USS *Texas* with ten 14 in guns, along with three cruisers, HMS *Glasgow*, FFS *Montcalm* and FFS *George Leygues* which between them had thirty 6 in guns. In addition to these, eight destroyers added their 4 in and 5 in guns to the bombardment, firing 2,000 shells into the resistance nests. Finally, a thousand 5 in rockets from specially equipped landing craft were launched at the resistance nests as the assault waves approached the shore but these failed to hit the targets. The Americans believed that this amount of firepower would overwhelm the defences and that the specialized tanks used by the British 79th Armoured Division would be unnecessary. They were wrong. Even before the American V Corps hit the beaches at 0630 hrs the resistance nests were beginning to wreak havoc, a situation that worsened as more men came ashore and could not move off the beaches. Casualties mounted alarmingly and two hours after getting ashore they were still on the beach. General Bradley considered withdrawing his men but, with aid from destroyers that came to within 800 m of the shore to bombard the resistance nests, men were now starting to get off the beaches. By nightfall, the Wiederstandnester had been overrun and the Americans were up to about a mile inland. It had cost them 2,000 casualties.

Today, little remains of the resistance nests apart from a few isolated bunkers. A casemate at one of the Vierville exits is now a memorial to the National Guard in honour of the 29th Division and still has its 88 mm gun. One of the Colleville exits has its two 75 mm casemates and some bunkers. The American war cemetery is at Colleville.

One of the battle-damaged type 671 casemates on the Pointe du Hoc. (Marcus Massing)

The remains of one of the open gun emplacements on the Pointe du Hoc. The gun was mounted on the circular platform in the centre. (Marcus Massing)

A few miles to the west is Pointe du Hoc (often misspelled as Hoe due to a wartime typing error), a rocky promontory 30 m high on which the Germans had constructed a battery of six 155 mm guns. Open emplacements had originally been built but these were in the process of being replaced by type 671 casemates; two had been built and another two were under construction by D-Day. The fire-control post (type 636) was built at the tip of the promontory and there were various other bunkers on the site which, like most batteries, was protected by light Flak. As it turned out, none of the emplacements or casemates contained guns. These had been withdrawn half a mile inland and camouflaged in an orchard where they had been since an air raid on 15 April. At 0550 hrs on the morning of D-Day, the battery was shelled by the *Texas* from 10 miles off shore before it changed targets to shell the resistance nests along Omaha, firing about 600 14 in shells. The battery was then bombed by eighteen medium bombers of the Ninth Air Force.

The battery was the objective of the 2nd Ranger Battalion who landed on the tiny beach at the foot of the cliff in front of the battery. Unfortunately, they arrived 40 minutes later than scheduled and from a direction parallel with the coast due to having been misdirected to nearby Pointe-de-la-Percée, allowing the battery garrison to spot them and open fire with small arms and 20 mm Flak. Despite the fierce opposition, the Rangers climbed to the top of the cliffs with the fire support of two destroyers, USS *Satterlee* and HMS *Talybont*, which forced the Germans to shelter in

One of the personnel bunkers at the Pointe du Hoc battery. (Marcus Massing)

the bunkers giving the Rangers the few minutes they needed to scale the cliff. The Rangers secured the position but had to withstand a strong counterattack later in the day. They managed to hold on until the 8th when men from V Corps who had landed on Omaha linked up with them but out of 225 men who had set out to take the battery 135 were killed. After the war, the site became a Ranger memorial and has remained much as it was in June 1944, complete with battle damage and bomb craters.

The beaches on the eastern side of the Cotentin peninsula were fortified in much the same way as those along the rest of the Bay of the Seine with numerous Wiederstandnester, sited to protect the beach exits. However, there were fewer defensive positions here than at Omaha. Along Utah beach where the US 4th Division was to land on D-Day there were seven Wiederstandnester and one Stützpunkt to guard three exits between la Grande Dune and les Dunes-de-Varreville. There were three more to the southeast and another three along the coast above the invasion beaches. The exit at la Grande Dune (Exit 2) was protected by two, while the next exit (Exit 3) had one with another at la Madeleine about halfway between the two exits. The exit at les Dunes-de-Varreville (Exit 4) was protected by one. The strongpoint was between Exits 3 and 4.

These were not of equal strength but all were variations on the same theme of combining anti-tank guns in open emplacements with some in casemates to enfilade the beach, tank turrets (the strongpoint had five Renault turrets armed with 37 mm guns), mortar tobruks and numerous machine-gun positions, some in tobruks, some in bunkers. All were protected by barbed wire, mines, anti-tank ditches and, in the case of those against the edge of the beach, with an anti-tank wall. Some, like many elsewhere in France, had automatic flamethrowers.

When the naval bombardment began on D-Day, the cruisers HMS *Hawkins* and HMS *Enterprise*, armed with seven 7.5 in and six 6 in guns respectively, and the Dutch gunboat HNMS *Soemba*, with its three 5.9 in guns, shelled these defences. This was followed half an hour later by 269 Marauders of the Ninth Air Force which dropped 4,400 250 lb bombs on them (small bombs were used to avoid excessive cratering of the beach that would hinder the troops as they came ashore). As at Omaha, specially equipped landing craft then fired salvoes of rockets at the defences as the assault waves moved towards the beaches. Unlike at Omaha, the Wiederstandnester were severely damaged by the shelling and bombing and the landings were much easier despite being further down the beach than intended because of the strong offshore currents. The Americans only had 200 casualties but not all the resistance nests were taken on the first day. The task of taking these beach defences fell to the 3rd Battalion, 22nd Infantry Regiment. The German defenders often waited for the infantry to get very close before opening fire and calling in fire from artillery further inland. This made the taking of these positions costly and slow. When a resistance nest was about to be attacked, naval gunfire was called in. Sometimes, the German garrisons were more than willing to surrender.

The surviving bunkers of the resistance nest astride Exit 2 at la Grand Dune now form a museum. There are two 50 mm guns in open emplacements, a casemate for a 50 mm gun and a number of tobruks including one housing a Renault turret. There are similar relics at the other defended sites.

There were three artillery batteries a little further up the coast at Azeville and Saint-Marcouf, while another was behind the invasion beaches at Saint-Martin-de-Varreville at the opposite end of Exit 4. The Saint-Martin-de-Varreville battery consisted of four 122 mm guns in open emplacements. It was shelled by HMS *Hawkins* on D-Day and taken from an inland assault by paratroopers of the 101st Airborne Division soon afterwards. It was the scene of a little-known event that should have earned the principal player the Congressional Medal of Honour; he had to be content with the Distinguished Service Cross. The battery crew were billeted in about a dozen nearby houses, some of them quite large with many rooms. Staff Sergeant Summers of the 502nd Parachute Infantry, 101st Airborne Division

(Opposite) *Another of the personnel bunkers at the rear of the Pointe du Hoc battery. The casemates are in the background.* (Marcus Massing)

The entrance to one of the ammunition bunkers on the Pointe du Hoc. (Marcus Massing)

attacked these one by one and mostly single-handedly, save for the occasional assistance of one or two other paratroopers, over a period of several hours, killing about 50 of the enemy and capturing another 50 or so. No doubt this act helped the battery to surrender. Little now remains of the site.

The two batteries up the coast proved to be tougher nuts to crack. The Azeville battery, just outside the village to the northeast and astride the road, consisted of four 105 mm guns, two in type 650 casemates and two in type 671 casemates, all of which had been camouflaged as buildings. The 650 casemates were surmounted by 37 mm Flak. There were the usual ammunition bunkers, personnel bunkers and self-defence bunkers and tobruks. The casemates, bunkers and tobruks were linked by underground passages reinforced with concrete. On D-Day, the battery was shelled by the 14 in guns of the battleship USS *Nevada*. This did not silence it.

On 7 June, the battery was approached from the southeast by the 2nd Battalion of the 22nd Infantry Regiment moving up the peninsula parallel with the coast, but they were beaten back by the defenders and a counterattack. Another assault the next day was also counterattacked. On 9 June, the task fell to the 3rd Battalion. First the 44th Field Artillery Battalion shelled it with 1,500 rounds before the infantry

A view from the front of a Renault FT 17 turret in a type R67 bunker on the site of Wn 5 at la Madeleine at Utah beach. (Neil Short)

went in, assisted by a single tank. As Company I approached the first bunker, bazookas were fired at it and the tank fired at it but they only managed to knock chips out of the concrete. A team was sent to blow in the entrance at the back. They emptied a flamethrower at the door and a demolition charge was fired against it, all to little effect. Another two attempts with ever bigger charges achieved nothing. The door remained firmly shut. Another manpack flamethrower was brought up. The operator ran 75 yards towards the bunker under constant fire and jumped into a shell hole only to discover that the ignition system on his flamethrower was inoperable. With remarkable presence of mind he improvised, opening the valve and holding a lighted match in front of the stream of napalm that squirted from the nozzle and directed the flaming jet at the door. This too seemed to have failed but soon the sounds of exploding ammunition inside the bunker could be heard. A white flag was produced and the occupants surrendered. The rest of the battery quickly followed suit.

Another view of the FT 17 turret. The gap between the base and the concrete has occurred because of the way the turret has been re-installed after the war. (Neil Short)

An open emplacement at Utah with anti-tank gun. (Neil Short)

The battery at Saint-Marcouf, also known as Crisbeq battery, had been built in 1941 for the Kriegsmarine. It bore an army coastal battery number, 3/HKAR 1291, because the Kriegsmarine unit that was to operate the battery was absorbed into the Heer unit, HKAR 1291, already at Saint-Marcouf. However, it was under Kriegsmarine command. Originally, the battery had six 150 mm guns in open emplacements but these were upgraded in 1943 to four 210 mm guns, retaining only one of the 150 mm weapons, the rest being reassigned to Fontenay-sur-Mer. The 210 mm guns had a range of 20 miles. By D-Day, two of them had been encased in type 683 casemates with another casemate under construction. A fourth had yet to be started. The sole 150 mm was to be housed in a type M272 but this was still under construction. The large embrasures of the 683 casemates should have been covered by armoured plates but this had not been done. The battery was protected by Flak (six 75 mm and three 20 mm), 15 machine-guns and the customary barbed wire and mines (anti-tank and anti-personnel). There were various other bunkers including the fire-control post for the battery at Azeville, located here because there was a better view of the coast from Saint-Marcouf.

The battery was bombed regularly from April 1944 and 600 tonnes were dropped on it on the night preceding D-Day, which destroyed the Flak and killed some of the battery personnel. Elements of the 502nd Parachute Infantry Regiment of the 101st Airborne attempted to seize the battery that night but failed despite only being faced by middle-aged Kriegsmarine reservists. At H-Hour on D-Day, the 8 in cruiser USS *Quincy* opened up on the battery which returned fire on the *Nevada*, which later turned her guns on the battery. At about 0730 hrs, the battery sank the destroyer USS *Cory* although there is some doubt about this as the ship may have hit a mine. At 0800 hrs one of the battery's guns was damaged and put out of action. An hour later, a shell entered the second casemate's embrasure and destroyed the gun. But before the battery was silenced it had sunk several landing craft and damaged a number of

A 210 mm Skoda in a type 683 casemate at the Saint-Marcouf battery after its capture by the Americans. The casemate was later partially demolished by US engineers. (NARA)

ships. The next day, the damaged gun was back in action and the battery was pounded by three cruisers until it was silent.

That was not the end of the Crisbeq battery, however. The 1st Battalion 22nd Infantry attempted to capture it on 7 June at the same time as the 2nd Battalion was attacking Azeville. It was beaten back by a strong counterattack and fire called in from the Azeville battery by the Saint-Marcouf battery commander Oberleutnant zur See Walter Ohmsen. The following day, the battalion tried again, this time after a 20-minute preliminary bombardment from artillery, mortars and ships. The infantry followed a creeping barrage towards the bunkers. By now the garrison had been reinforced by elements of the 919th Infanterieregiment and the fighting became hand to hand in the trenches. There was another counterattack and again they were shelled by Azeville. They were also hit by Nebelwerfers. After Azeville was captured, the Americans decided to go round Saint-Marcouf and merely contain it for the time being with infantry and tank destroyers while they pressed on up the coast. By 12 June, the 2nd Battalion, 39th Infantry discovered that the battery had been abandoned. The previous night, Ohmsen had been ordered to withdraw. For his stalwart defence of the battery he was awarded the Iron Cross 1st Class on 13 June.

Much of both batteries still exists. At Azeville the two big casemates on one side of the road are in a field but the two smaller ones on the other side are very overgrown. At Saint-Marcouf, American engineers tried to demolish one of the casemates but the other one is more or less intact and has an observation platform on the roof for visitors. The Azeville fire-control post on the Saint-Marcouf site is still there.

There were other batteries up the coast, including one at Quinéville with four 105 mm guns in type 671 and type 650 casemates. The 671 casemates were disguised as houses and had fake gabled roofs with tiles. This battery was shelled by the 8 in cruiser USS *Tuscaloosa* on D-Day. The fortified positions surrendered to the 3rd Battalion, 39th Infantry on the evening of 14 June during the battle for Quinéville. At Crasville there was a battery of four 105 mm guns in type 671 and type 650 casemates. At Morsalines, another 4 miles up the coast, there was another coastal battery. It consisted of six 155 guns in open emplacements and two fire-control posts. The original battery was heavily damaged during an air raid in May 1944 and new positions were still under construction on D-Day when it was shelled by the 5.25 in guns of the cruiser HMS *Black Prince*. The battery was captured during the American advance on Cherbourg.

At la Pernelle there were two batteries, the first one with four 105 mm guns in casemates, the second with three 170 mm guns in open emplacements. The first battery could play little part in attacking the Americans on D-Day because the guns were facing out to sea rather than across the Bay of the Seine. It was bombed several times before D-Day when it was shelled by the monitor HMS *Erebus*. The guns of the second battery, known to the Germans as Essen, were a more serious threat to the landings as they had a greater range than those at the other battery and could fire on the landing beaches. However, Essen lacked the necessary rangefinder and fire-control equipment to fire accurately on moving ships. In a bombing raid on 9 May, one of the guns was damaged and removed to Cherbourg for repair but it was never returned. Following this and other raids, the remaining guns were moved about half a mile inland and hidden. Before the Germans retreated from the area, the guns were spiked without being fired in anger.

The eastern tip of the Cotentin was the site of two more batteries, at Gatteville and Néville-sur-Mer. The Gatteville battery consisted of four 155 mm guns in type 679 casemates which were provided with semi-circular armoured shields that traversed with the gun and kept the embrasure closed. The Kriegsmarine battery at the Pointe de Néville had four 94 mm guns captured from the British, three of them in type M158 casemates with the fourth in a type 671 casemate. There were also four open emplacements for 155 mm guns and a number of tobruks for machine-guns and emplacements for 50 mm anti-tank guns. Many of the structures are now in poor condition.

CHERBOURG

The port of Cherbourg, a designated fortress, was protected by several coastal batteries from Fermanville, about 6 miles to the east, to Gréville-Hague, about 7 miles to the west, including batteries within Cherbourg itself. Some of these batteries mounted very powerful guns. Like other fortresses, Cherbourg was also protected on its landward side, the Germans making use of the ring of old French forts as the basis for a series of strongpoints which the Americans had to take one by one in their final assault on the port.

In the region of Fermanville, there were two batteries, Hamburg battery and Seeadler (sea eagle). Seeadler, a Heer battery, was located above the cliffs at Pointe-du-Brulé. It was originally a French coastal battery, built shortly before the outbreak of war. Equipped with four 94 mm guns in open emplacements, it was simply taken over by the occupiers. The position is now overgrown. Located near les Marettes astride the D612 about half a mile to the east, Hamburg was a Kriegsmarine battery, equipped with four 240 mm guns in steel turrets with a range of nearly 17 miles.

A type 631 casemate, still with its 105 mm gun in place, has been taken over by Americans who have hung their washing across the embrasure. This was part of Kriegsmarine battery 3/MAA 260 in the harbour at Cherbourg. (NARA)

The guns were originally in open emplacements which were still in the process of being converted to casemates when the Americans began their assault on Festung Cherbourg in late June 1944; none of the casemates had roofs. The battery was protected by six 75 mm anti-aircraft guns as well as by light Flak and there were the usual machine-guns for ground defence. Its defences were later strengthened with 75 mm and 50 mm anti-tank guns. The battery's fire-control post was located a couple of miles to the northeast on Cap Lévi.

In air raids preceding the attack on the Cherbourg perimeter, some of the anti-aircraft guns were damaged or destroyed along with some of the personnel bunkers. By 20 June, the Americans were about 5 miles from Cherbourg and Hamburg was on the front line. Unfortunately, the guns pointed in the wrong direction although an attempt had been made to increase the traverse of one of the guns by removing part of the walls of its casemate. The Americans paused to consolidate their forces and resumed their assault on the 22nd. The outlying defences were strafed by rocket-firing Typhoons, then bombed by Mustangs of the Second Tactical Air Force. They were followed by 562 fighter-bombers of the Ninth Air Force. Three days of hard fighting now followed. During the course of this, Hamburg was pounded from the sea. On the 24th, one of its guns was damaged by a shell, resulting in three dead and eleven wounded. The heaviest bombardment of the battery took place the next day when it was engaged by a naval task force that included three battleships and four cruisers as well as a screening force of destroyers. The bombardment was coordinated with the final assault on Cherbourg. Because of effective return fire from several shore batteries, the task force concentrated its efforts on counter-battery work which lasted about 3 hours. Hamburg returned fire and hit the destroyer USS *Barton* but the shell failed to explode. The battery then hit another destroyer, USS *Laffrey*, and again the shell failed to explode. At 1300 hrs, it hit the bridge of the destroyer USS *O'Brien* and this time the shell exploded, killing thirteen and wounding nineteen. The destroyer made smoke and withdrew. Soon afterwards, all the bombarding destroyers were taken out of range of the shore batteries. Hamburg claimed to have sunk more than one cruiser during these duels but there is no evidence to support their hitting even one.

The US 22nd Infantry Division made a concerted drive to take the battery on the 26th. The battery was heavily bombed on the 27th as a prelude to another assault. The defenders had been reinforced by retreating infantry but they had been cut off from the rest of the peninsula. At midnight on the 27th, the defenders surrendered after disabling the guns; 990 Germans went into captivity. The casemates are still there.

The Kriegsmarine used a French fort at les Caplains, just to the east of Tourlaville and about a mile from Cherbourg, as the site of another battery, called Brommy. This consisted of four 150 mm guns in one type M272 casemate, two M175 casemates and a type M195 open emplacement. It had two fire-control posts at the front of the site, one of which was the French battery's own post, and had a number of additional bunkers including a medical bunker at the back of the site. The guns were modern designs developed by Rheinmetal Borsig and the battery could fire up to eight rounds a minute to a range of 13.5 miles. It was captured on 25 June after bombardment by the naval task force and strafing by Ninth Air Force P-47s, the gun crews having been forced to fight as infantry. Much of the battery remains today but it is inside a military area.

Fort Roule was one of the last fortified positions within Fortress Cherbourg to fall. It was on top of a hill with very steep sides, located at the south of the port. It commanded the town, the harbour and its approaches. The bastioned fort dated from the nineteenth century. In the cliffs on the northern face of the hill, 30 m below the French ramparts, the Kriegsmarine built four gun casemates for 105 mm guns with an observation post in the middle, all of which could be reached by interconnecting passages bored through the rock from outside the fort. The back of the fort was protected by a number of machine-gun bunkers (type 634 and type 630) and Flak positions as well as mortars and an anti-tank ditch. Designated by the Americans as Target D, Fort Roule proved to be a tough nut to crack because it could only be approached along a ridge that was well covered by defensive fire. Although it was shelled from the sea and by artillery as well as bombed and strafed by P-47s of the Ninth Air Force, it was the infantrymen of the 314th Infantry Regiment who did most to capture it on 25 June. When Company E was pinned down on the slope at the back of the fort, Corporal John Kelly crawled forward under heavy fire with a 3 m pole charge of 15 lb of TNT and tried to blow up the nearest bunker. The change did little damage. He crawled back for another pole charge. With this Kelly blew off the ends of the enemy guns. He then went back for yet another charge with which he blew in the entrance. Kelly then threw in several grenades and the occupants surrendered. Kelly won the Congressional Medal of Honour for this.

Meanwhile, on the left flank, a similar situation faced First Lieutenant Carlos Ogden when Company K was held up by an 88 and machine-guns. He took an M1 fitted with a grenade launcher and went up the slope under heavy fire towards the bunkers. Although wounded, he reached the 88 and destroyed it with a rifle grenade. He was wounded again but destroyed two machine-guns with hand grenades. He too won the Congressional Medal of Honour. Such acts helped the fort's garrison to surrender. However, this did not include the casemated guns in the cliff which continued to fire on the Americans advancing through the town after the fort had surrendered. Attempts were made to disable the guns by lowering charges down ventilation shafts and on ropes over the side of the cliff, detonating the charges with a trigger. They were all unsuccessful. Anti-tank guns now fired on the embrasures while a demolition team attacked down the tunnels with bazookas and pole charges. It took a day to capture the casemates. They can still be reached through the tunnels. One of the buildings in the fort has been turned into the Musée de Guerre et de la Libération.

There were several batteries to the west of Cherbourg, including one at Fort des Couplets at Equeurdreville, a nearby railway gun battery close to the arsenal between the harbour and Hameau Bourgeois, York battery at Amfreville, a battery at Castel-Vendon and another railway battery at Auderville-Laye. The Fort des Couplets battery consisted of four 155 mm guns with a range of 13 miles in type 679 casemates as well as eight open emplacements and various bunkers and tobruks for self-defence. Two of the guns were re-installed in open emplacements because the casemates had limited elevation and traverse. This battery surrendered to the 47th Infantry on 25 June without putting up much of a fight after being dive-bombed by P-47s and shelled by artillery. The battery near the arsenal had four 240 mm railway guns. This was one of the last positions to surrender. The battery at Auderville-Laye to the west had two 203 mm railway guns with a range of 23 miles. These guns had 11 m diameter concrete platforms which are still there.

York was another Kriegsmarine battery and comprised four 170 mm guns in type M271 casemates. The site was protected by 75 mm anti-tank guns in open emplacements along with several machine-gun and mortar tobruks. York opened fire on the naval task force on 25 June and exchanged fire with the 6 in cruisers HMS *Glasgow* and HMS *Enterprise*. *Glasgow* was hit although it is unclear whether it was a shell from York or another battery. USS *Texas* shelled it but the battery continued to return fire. Like other coastal batteries, it was eventually taken by infantry assault. The Castel-Vendon battery was built on an older French one and consisted of four 150 mm guns in M272 casemates. The Organization Todt had started to construct two emplacements for turrets housing two 380 mm guns but they were never finished.

A 280 mm Kurze Bruno (Little Bruno) railway gun firing in Cherbourg. The battery was based in the port in 1941–2. (MW 1827/71. Bundesarchiv)

SAINT-MALO

The fortress of Saint-Malo included the island of Grand Bé, a small island near the harbour, and the island of Cézembre 2.5 miles northeast of Saint-Malo. Cézembre, only 800 m by 400 m, was itself made into a fortress. The island commanded the approaches to the port. The western end of the island was the site of a battery of three 194 mm guns, while another battery of three was located on the eastern end. All were in open emplacements. To these was added a 150 mm gun about halfway between the two batteries. There were also numerous bunkers and emplacements for Flak ranging in calibre from 20 mm to 75 mm, as well as magazine bunkers, personnel bunkers and a medical bunker. Grand Bé had a battery of four 105 mm guns in type 671 casemates. These island fortresses were the responsibility of the Kriegsmarine.

Within Saint-Malo and its immediate environs there were several strongpoints and batteries, some of them built on existing French fortifications. Grand Bé was one. Others included the Citadel (cité d'Aleth), Fort de la Varde 3 miles northeast of Saint-Malo, and Fort National which was on another small island just beyond the harbour (this was unoccupied at the time of the American assault on Saint-Malo). The Citadel was a Vauban fort, dating from the eighteenth century, on a rocky headland that jutted into the mouth of the River Rance. The Organization Todt went to work on the fort in 1942. Fourteen structures were built inside and outside the fort,

Fort de la Varde with a type 611 casemate (centre). (Marcus Massing)

including bunkers for anti-tank guns and machine-guns and casemates for 105 mm and 75 mm guns. They were all connected by underground passages. The Todt also built anti-tank ditches. In all, about 30,000 m³ of concrete were used. Lengths of upright railway track were planted in the Citadel to prevent glider and paratroop landings. The fortress commander, Oberst Aulock, made this his headquarters. The Fort de la Varde was similarly reinforced with 12 bunkers for anti-tank guns and machine-guns and two casemates for 105 mm guns (a type 611 and a type 669). In addition, there was a mortar tobruk and personnel bunkers (type 622).

At Richardais to the southwest, on the left bank of the Rance, there was a Heer battery of six 122 mm guns in type 669 and type 611 casemates and two 150 mm guns in open emplacements, with another just below Dinard at Ville-es-Mesniers with six 155 mm guns in type 611 casemates. Another was along the beach at Saint-Enogat with four 155 mm guns in type 669 casemates. At la Bodinais to the east of Ville-es-Mesniers, there was another battery of casemated 155 mm guns while at the Pointe de la Vicomté there was a strongpoint overlooking the river. This had seven 50 mm anti-tank guns in type 667 casemates.

A major strongpoint was located at Saint-Joseph hill on the eastern edge of the port. This was a quarry and tunnels had been bored into it and bunkers constructed to make this a formidable obstacle. Before moving his headquarters to the Citadel, Oberst Aulock used this location. At Saint-Ideuc about a mile to the north of Saint-Joseph, there was another strongpoint. This was one of the outer defences for the fort at la Varde and included numerous machine-gun and anti-tank bunkers. About 2½ miles further to the east at Saint-Gilles-Coulomb, there was a Heer battery of four 105 mm guns in type 669 casemates. To the south of the port in the region of Châteauneuf, there was another strongpoint with an anti-tank wall and various bunkers including a type 504 for a 37 mm anti-tank gun.

Following the success of Operation Cobra, the American forces reached Avranches on the 31st. The US VIII Corps commanded by General Middleton approached

A type 667 casemate for a 50 mm anti-tank gun at Fort de la Varde. (Marcus Massing)

The embrasure of a type 653 casemate for a 50 mm anti-tank gun at Fort de la Varde. (Marcus Massing)

Festung Saint-Malo at the beginning of August 1944, believing that the Germans were on the run and would not offer much of a fight. There were more than 12,000 German troops (more than American estimates which put the figure closer to 5,000) in Saint-Malo and Oberst Aulock had no intention of surrendering, promising instead to make it a French Stalingrad (he had fought at Stalingrad). Inspired by Hitler's exhortation for such fortresses to fight to the last man, following the Führer's anger at the speed with which Cherbourg had fallen, Aulock prepared a stubborn defence. The Americans were in for a nasty surprise.

A type 105 machine-gun bunker at Saint-Lunaire, west of Dinard, complete with modern graffiti. (Marcus Massing)

The assault by Task Force A, comprising the 1st Tank Destroyer Brigade, the 6th Tank Destroyer Group and the 159th Engineer Battalion, assisted by the 83rd Infantry Divisioin began on 5 August and almost immediately ran into difficulties although the Châteauneuf strongpoint was overrun. Task Force A was now ordered to break contact, bypass Saint-Malo and head for Brest. The next day, the 83rd Infantry resumed their advance and came within range of the guns on Cézembre. On the 7th, the garrison started to destroy the harbour facilities as had happened at Cherbourg. The same day, the 330th Infantry Regiment attacked the Saint-Joseph Stützpunkt following a short artillery barrage but made no progress. It took two days of constant shelling by artillery and tank destroyers to make the defenders give up; 400 prisoners were taken. The loss of this position led to the strongpoints at Saint-Ideuc and Fort de la Varde being cut off but they refused to surrender. All the time, the Americans were shelled by the guns in the Citadel and on Cézembre.

Saint-Ideuc was shelled for three days during which the 329th Infantry had laboriously to take each bunker with flamethrowers and demolition charges, hand grenades and rifle grenades. The strong point surrendered on the 12th and the Fort de la Varde surrendered the next day. This was a pattern that was repeated throughout the fighting for Saint-Malo. The assaults were constantly given air support from fighter-bombers and mediums of the Ninth Air Force although they were not always

A blasted turret at Saint-Malo. Many turrets along the Atlantic Wall were removed after the war for scrap. (Marcus Massing)

(Opposite) *The steel plate for a machine-gun of a bunker built into an angle of one of the Citadel's bastions. It faced inwards. There is extensive battle damage to the surrounding concrete.* (Marcus Massing)

A smaller turret at Saint-Malo. Note the vision slit (centre) and the lifting lug (bottom left). (Marcus Massing)

effective. On the 16th, the 329th was close enough to Grand Bé to take it by stealth at low water. That left the Citadel and Cézembre. Despite requests for Aulock to surrender, he refused. The Citadel was bombed several times including a heavy raid on the 11th by mediums which dropped incendiaries and semi-armour piercing bombs. Following this raid, a rifle company scaled the walls of the Citadel and dropped demolition charges into vents before being forced to withdraw by heavy machine-gun fire. The Citadel was then pounded by artillery and tank destroyers for two days as well as being bombed twice. Another attempt was made to get into the Citadel by two assault teams with special demolition equipment but they were driven out. The shelling was resumed. On 17 August, Aulock finally surrendered after 8 in artillery shells aimed point-blank at embrasures had destroyed several artillery pieces and machine-guns. An entire division had been held up for nearly two weeks.

But Cézembre fought on. It was bombed repeatedly with high explosive and napalm, strafed with rockets and white phosphorus. The island was shelled

Looking across the east bastion of the Citadel towards Saint-Malo. (Marcus Massing)

constantly by 155 mm and 240 mm artillery. HMS *Warspite* shelled it for 2½ hours on 1 September. It finally surrendered on the 2nd when its water tanks were hit. Everything had been destroyed or damaged including all the island's guns and the garrison had suffered hundreds of casualties.

There are still two personnel bunkers at Saint-Ideuc and various bunkers are in the Fort de la Varde but this is a military area. The steel turrets here and in the Citadel bear numerous gouges from anti-tank rounds, only some of which penetrated. (Those in the Citadel are embossed 1939, suggesting that they were probably taken from bunkers in the West Wall.) There are still bunkers in the Citadel which is now a caravan park. Although the embrasures have been blocked some of the bunkers still have the remains of guns in them. Cézembre is more or less how it was after the battle and the shattered remains of guns are still in some emplacements.

BREST

Brest was one of the most important Kriegsmarine bases in France. It was home to a U-boat flotilla and had been home to *Scharnhorst, Gneisenau* and *Prinz Eugen* from

The Citadel, Saint-Malo. The white plaque commemorates a FFI soldier who died during one of the attempts to take the Citadel, while the darker one to its lower right commemorates the liberation of Saint-Malo in August 1944. (Marcus Massing)

A machine-gun bunker surmounted by a 40 mm Bofors emplacement in the Citadel. The damaged gun remains in place. (Marcus Massing)

March 1941 before their infamous dash up the Channel to Wilhemhelmshaven in February 1942. Consequently, it was very well protected by twenty coastal batteries and as many Flak batteries. These were located from le Conquet in the west to the southern tip of the Crozon peninsula across the Rade de Brest. Because Brest was designated a fortress, it was also protected by a ring of strongpoints and batteries facing inland but these were mostly a response to the Normandy invasion and hastily constructed in the summer of 1944 using existing French forts as their focus, sited to prevent easy access to the port from inland.

The area around le Conquet had several strongpoints because the beaches seemed suitable for an Allied landing. They included one on the headland of Kermorvan and another at Kerlohic. These consisted of the usual bunkers for anti-tank guns and machine-guns as well as personnel bunkers. The Kermorvan strongpoint was based on a Vauban fort. The Kerlohic strongpoint protected two important nearby sites, a radar station and the Kriegsmarine battery, Graf Spee, at Lochrist. Graf Spee had three 280 mm naval guns in turrets mounted in open emplacements and one enclosed in a casemate. These consumed 10,000 m^3 of concrete and 400 tonnes of steel reinforcement. The guns had formerly been on a Friesian island off the northern coast of Germany. Graf Spee's guns could each fire a 283 kg shell 17 miles at the rate of two a minute. The site was protected by various anti-tank guns and fourteen machine-guns in bunkers and emplacements as well as by 75 mm Flak. It had a medical bunker, personnel bunkers and magazines and was manned by 200 troops. The battery's fire-control post was located on a hill about a mile to the west and this was provided with its own protective bunkers and tobruks. There was another Kriegsmarine battery at Pointe Saint-Mathieu with 150 mm guns protected by armoured shields in type M272 casemates. Unusually, its fire-control post was a type 164A, a type rarely used. Although these still exist, the site now belongs to the Marine Nationale.

Much closer to Brest at Toulbroch was an incomplete naval battery of 75 mm guns. This was a very vulnerable position and the Kriegsmarine intended to casemate the guns but the work was never finished and they were not installed by the time of the American assault on Brest. The Pointe du Portzic, the site of an old fort, was the location of three Kriegsmarine batteries (four 105 mm guns, three 152 mm guns and three 88 mm guns), most of them in type 671 casemates. Five more batteries were sited on the crow's foot promontory on the other side of the channel that leads to Brest harbour. They dominated its approaches. These were based on old French forts and included the Pointe des Espagnols which was made into a Stützpunkt with three 105 mm and four 47 mm guns, Pointe de Cornouaille with three 100 mm guns in turrets, Pointe de Capucins with three 240 mm guns and Kerbonn with four 164 mm guns in type M270 casemates and four 75 mm guns in open emplacements. Apart from those at Kerbonn, all but six of the guns dated from 1897; the other three dated from 1908. The fifth battery had four 220 mm guns in open emplacements at Grand Gouin near Carmaret. This was a Heer battery based on a prewar French battery, now provided with additional bunkers and casemates for guns for self-defence.

A type 669 casemate for a 164.7 mm gun near the Pointe de Pen-Hir, Crozon peninsula. The battery of four was part of the protection of Brest. (Neil Short)

If the Americans thought that Saint-Malo was difficult, Brest was worse. On the same day that Paris was liberated, 25 August 1944, VIII Corps of Patton's Third Army began its assault on Brest. Whereas at Saint-Malo the defenders had numbered around 12,000, at Brest there were 35,000 of them and at their core was the 2nd Parachute Division commanded by General Ramcke. Like Aulock, he was prepared to fight to the last man. This was not what Bradley and Patton expected.

The attack was supported by *Warspite* who shelled Graf Spee which quickly returned fire. Eventually, *Warspite* had to make smoke and retire because Graf Spee's shells were getting too close for comfort. The battery had already endured almost daily air raids since July and it was now bombed again, resulting in damage to the muzzle of one of the guns. A 24 cm length had to removed with an oxyacetylene torch. Another of the guns was unable to traverse due to a near miss. Only the casemated gun escaped although its carapace was hit. The battery was later assaulted by tanks and infantry supported by fighter-bombers. It eventually surrendered on 9 September after a hard-fought battle but only after the remaining 280 mm gun was blown up by its crew.

RAF heavies bombed the strongpoints on 25 August and the next day the Eighth Air Force bombed them again. It soon became clear that the infantry would have to use the same tactics as they had used at Saint-Malo to capture the strongpoints – sneaking up on each bunker in turn to squirt flamethrowers, detonate pole charges, toss grenades into apertures and fire rifle grenades into them, combined with point-blank anti-tank and heavy artillery rounds. Typically, a bunker with a machine-gun turret took the patient and persistent efforts of eight men with two flamethrowers and a bazooka along with two Browning automatic rifles to persuade its occupants to give themselves up. A strongpoint at Keranroué to the north of Brest, based on a French fort and defended by about 100, had to be practically obliterated by bombing and shelling before the defenders would surrender. Air support with napalm, white phosphorus and high explosives was used to help reduce the strongpoints. In all, about seventy-five strongpoints had to be reduced like this before Brest was finally captured on 18 September. It had taken VIII Corps six weeks. The Americans suffered 10,000 casualties and took 20,000 prisoners. The effort in capturing the port dissuaded the Americans from repeating the process at Lorient and Saint-Nazaire.

Today, some of the bunkers and casemates along the coast still exist, including those on the Pointe de Kermovan, the Pointe Saint-Mathieu and at the Graf Spee battery. They also survive on the Pointe des Espagnols and at other locations on the Crozon peninsula.

LORIENT

Like Brest, Lorient was an important U-boat base and this was sufficient reason for it to be designated a fortress. And, like Brest, its approaches were well protected by numerous batteries along the coast, some of them with outlying strongpoints. As many as 600 batteries and strongpoints were proposed for the defence of Lorient and its approaches; 400 were completed before the arrival of the Americans. The positions extended from le Pouldu about 8 miles northeast up the coast, down to Plouharnel about 18 miles to the southwest. On the landward side, the defensive positions stretched from Fort Bloqué on the west coast, to north of Ploemeur, to Kerdual north of Lorient, crossed the River Scorff and went east to cross the River Blavet and followed its east bank to the coast. The Flak was formidable, with twenty Kriegsmarine heavy batteries (128 mm and 105 mm guns) arranged in four groups and served by very effective radar posts, as well as another five Luftwaffe batteries.

If all this was not enough, the Ile de Groix about 4 miles off the coast was also turned into a fortress with numerous batteries including the powerful Seydlitz battery at Grognon. This Kriegsmarine battery consisted of two ship turrets each armed with two 203 mm guns with a range of 23 miles. Seydlitz's sister battery was on the mainland at Plouharnel and had four 340 mm guns mounted on circular tracks, similar to those used with railway guns, on which the mountings revolved within the open emplacements.

There were batteries near the village of Kerhop (four 155 mm guns in type 669 and type 611 casemates), near Saint-Fiacre about a mile east of Kerhop (four type 669 casemates for 105 mm guns), Croezhent which was a similar battery to the one at Kerhop, with another at Lann-er-Roch just northwest of Ploemeur which was similar

The tobruk as an independent structure. This one is at Courégan near Lorient. (Jonathan Falconer)

to the one at Saint-Fiacre. There was a battery of four casemated 122 mm guns at Keraude to the northeast of Lann-er-Roch. In the old French fort on the Pointe du Talut, the Kriegsmarine built a battery of four 170 mm guns in type M272 casemates. The French fort of Locqueltas on the western side of the channel that leads to Lorient had four 164 mm guns in M270 casemates. On the Kernevel headland a little further up the channel was Admiral Dönitz's command post in a strongpoint, although after the raid on Saint-Nazaire he decided it was a little too vulnerable and left for Paris. Across the Lorient channel, the sandspit that joined the tiny island of Grâve to the mainland opposite Plouhenic was used to site several batteries.

Although Lorient was bombed regularly because of the submarine pens, the fortress was not reduced by the Americans who merely laid siege after they arrived there on 7 August, permitting themselves occasional sorties against its defences in the manner of a medieval army. Lorient did not surrender until the end of the war nine months later. It is largely for this reason that many of the bunkers and casemates still exist along the coast as well as along the line of inland strongpoints and in the port itself.

SAINT-NAZAIRE

Saint-Nazaire, another naval base, was also a fortress and like Lorient did not surrender until the end of the war, the Americans being content to seal it off. Its defences had been reinforced since the British raid and its Flak defences were as powerful as those at Lorient: seventy-three heavy guns. The defences stretched southeast from la Roche-Bernard on the River Vilaine to Ponchateaux, then south to Donges, northeast of Saint-Nazaire, on the north bank of the River Loire, continuing from Paimboeuf on the opposite side of the river to Saint-Pierre-en-Retz and on to Pornic on Bourgneuf bay. This was a much larger area than Festung Lorient.

The outermost battery was at Pointe du Halguen at the mouth of the Vilaine (two 75 mm guns in type 662 casemates). Croisic bay was protected by three batteries inland of la Turballe and there was a strongpoint on Pen-Bron with three more batteries between Guérande and la Baule-Escoublac. These guns were in both open emplacements and casemates. On the beach near Pen-Bron there are still some tetrahedra. Near Batz-sur-Mer on the peninsula in front of Guérande, several emplacements were built for 240 mm and 305 mm guns but Saint-Nazaire was sealed before the guns arrived. There was, however, a battery of 240 mm railway guns near Kermoisan village for which two concrete platforms were built and there was a

Rommel (left) on a tour of the Atlantic Wall. Here he is at la Baule near Saint-Nazaire on 18 February 1944 in the company of General der Artillerie Fahrmacher (pointing) of the XXV Artillerie Korps. (719/208/13a. Bundesarchiv)

battery of 240 mm guns near Pouligen. There was also a large type S414 fire-control post. Various anti-tank gun casemates and machine-gun bunkers were sited along the beach in front of la Baule.

The Kriegsmarine built a battery of four 170 mm guns in type M270 casemates disguised as houses on the Pointe de Lève, the headland to the southwest of Saint-Nazaire. This was the site of an earlier French battery and the Kriegsmarine made use of the existing fire-control post as well as building one of their own. The four type M270 casemates were disguised as houses with gabled roofs. There were several batteries inland of Saint-Nazaire running northeast to southwest, including one at Ecubues (four 105 mm guns in type 669 casemates) and one in the Roullais quarry which had the same types of casemates and guns, while there were six fire-control posts (types 120 and 613) at le Landreau for various batteries. Near les Arbinais, the Germans built a medical bunker of type 118c. Le Petit-Marsac, north of the port, is the site of a type Fl250 Flak command post, a square tower. In Saint-Nazaire, near the Rue de Vecquerie is a type Fl241 Flak command post. At Minden on the other side of the Loire, there was a 128 mm Flak battery of four guns and further down, near le Pointeau, there was a Kriegsmarine battery of four 105 mm guns in type 671 casemates flanked by two casemates for 150 mm guns.

Saint-Nazaire was sealed by the Americans on 15 August 1944. Like Lorient, Festung Saint-Nazaire was not invested and held out until the end of the war. It was, however, heavily bombed on a regular basis. Some bunkers and casemates still exist although after the war and even as late as the 1960s, a number of attempts were made to demolish them.

LA ROCHELLE

Between Saint-Nazaire and la Rochelle, the main area of defensive works was at les Sables-d'Olonne around which there were several strongpoints and resistance nests. These were far weaker than those around the major ports, however. The islands of Noirmoutier and Yeu were also defended with strongpoints and batteries as these were seen as outposts for the defence of the ports.

La Rochelle was a fortress that included the islands of Ré and Oléron as well as the nearby port of la Pallice which was another U-boat base. The main Kriegsmarine battery for the protection of la Pallice and la Rochelle was on the northwestern end of Ré. Known as Karola battery, this was made up of two turrets taken from the cruiser *Seydlitz*, each mounting two 203 mm guns with a range of 23 miles. Each turret rotated on a double bunker made up of a type S473 and a type S483. Within the same site there was also a 150 mm gun, anti-tank gun and machine-gun bunkers and a lot of Flak emplacements. The fire-control post, a type S497, was surmounted by a cupola for a rangefinder, the whole thing resembling the superstructure of a ship. A battery of four 220 mm guns, known as Kora battery, also shared the site. This island was turned into a fortress and was covered

A tobruk at les Sables-d'Olonne manned by machine-gunners with a French machine-gun. Note the wooden cover on the left. (87/17/291. Bundesarchiv)

Constructing a barbed wire obstacle in front of a machine-gun bunker on the island of Ré off la Rochelle in 1944. The armoured plate and ball joint are visible between the second and third men on the left. (264/1601/29a. Bundesarchiv)

with Flak batteries. Oléron was similarly turned into a fortress with numerous batteries and strongpoints. Its largest guns were only 150 mm and 155 mm but there were four batteries of them in addition to numerous Flak batteries and shore defences. Many of the bunkers and casemates still exist although the turrets are long gone.

La Rochelle and la Pallice were provided with a ring of strongpoints that went as far north as Esnandes nearly 2 miles from la Rochelle, east to the Marans Rochelle canal and south to Angoulins, as well as six artillery batteries such as the one at Angoulins. The Angoulins battery consisted of four 155 mm guns in type 669 casemates, two which were surmounted by Flak emplacements.

La Rochelle was sealed in September 1944 but no major action was taken to invest it until April 1945 when a force that included FFI (French Forces of the Interior, formerly the Maquis) attacked the fortress, including Oléron. The fortress did not surrender, however, until 8 May 1945. Many of the bunkers and casemates have disappeared since the war with little to indicate the sites of many of the strongpoints.

THE GIRONDE

The Gironde was made into two fortresses, one to the north of the estuary, the other to the south. Their purpose was to protect the port of Bordeaux. Once Bordeaux had been taken by the Allies in September 1944, they acquired a new function, that of

One of a group of bunkers and casemates stranded on the beach near Saint-Palais-sur-Mer, this is a type 637 fire-control post in a Wiederstandnest that was part of the North Gironde fortress. Nearly the entire structure is visible. When originally built, it would have been mostly buried. The dark rectangle on its right is a machine-gun embrasure. (Jonathan Falconer)

The rear of the fire-control post showing the entrance (centre) and the access to its tobruk (left). The round apertures are ventilation ports. (Jonathan Falconer)

preventing Allied shipping from reaching Bordeaux. The northern fortress, centred on Royan, included more than thirty strongpoints and resistance nests as well as numerous artillery and Flak batteries, while the southern one included a similar number of defensive works.

The northern fortress consisted of a series of strongpoints along the coast from Ronce-les-Bains to Pointe de Suzac beyond Royan. A miniature fortress was created in the region of la Coubre with at least eight strongpoints within the forest along its southern edge (many of the sites are not now accessible to the public). A line of earthwork defences was also created around Royan in early 1945 because of pressure from local FFI forces. In 1943, a Wiederstandnest was built in the dunes behind the beach of Grande Côte near Saint-Palais-sur-Mer, consisting of two 75 mm guns in type 669 casemates, a type 637 fire-control post and various personnel bunkers, along with a number of tobruks for machine-guns and mortars. The structures are now sinking into the beach at odd angles like beached whales, partly submerged when the tide comes in. A second battery of six captured British 4.5 in guns was located at Saint-Sordolain in type 671 casemates. A third was on the Pointe de Suzac in front of an old French fort. This consisted of four 105 mm guns pointing north, again casemated in type 671, and four more mounted in open emplacements, pointing west.

The rear of one of the type 669 casemates at Grande Côte with the fire-control post behind it and another bunker in the background. (Jonathan Falconer)

A type 669 casemate on the Pointe de Grave. (Jonathan Falconer)

The Kriegsmarine had seven batteries in the north fortress. Two batteries were constructed in the mini-fortress near the Pointe de Coubre. One of these, Coubre 6, was located in the dunes behind the beach at Bonne Anse. This consisted of four 155 mm guns in type M195 open emplacements. Altogether, there were about fifteen bunkers on the site, including two garage-like bunkers (type 672) for 75 mm anti-tank guns and a mortar tobruk. The other battery was constructed in 1942 on a former French naval battery. The Todt built two type M272 and two type M176 casemates for the French 138 mm guns with a fire-control post of type M162a. The most important Kriegsmarine battery, Muschel, consisted of two 240 mm guns in turrets in the middle of Coubre forest (the remains are next to the forester's lodge). Further down the coast, a 105 mm battery was constructed on the Auture promontory, the four type 671 casemates being disguised as houses. The fifth battery was at the Fort du Chay at Royan; this was equipped only with 75 mm guns.

Apart from these, a large number of bunkers and casemates were built in Royan and along the seafront to protect the town, including a strongpoint at Vallières which had Flak bunkers and anti-tank gun casemates. The east side of the town was protected by strongpoints at Vaux, Jaffe and Belmont.

A type M157 Kriegsmarine fire-control post belonging to 4/MAA 618 at the Fort des Arros. It has two observation rooms and a rangefinder room (on the right), one above the other. (263/1581/39. Bundesarchiv)

Across the estuary, the southern fortress was on the Pointe de Grave where the Germans built a large number of strongpoints and batteries for both artillery and Flak down to Montalivet-les-Bains. In the region of the point itself there were nine batteries and strongpoints. The Kriegsmarine Trois Frères battery had four 105 mm guns in type 671 casemates with a type M162 fire-control post and a medical bunker (type 638). Many of these now list drunkenly in the sand. Just outside the Verdon fort on the west side of the Pointe de Grave, the Germans installed two 280 mm railway guns on circular platforms that allowed the guns to be traversed through 360°. They had a range of 17 miles. The battery included ammunition bunkers, a medical bunker and personnel bunkers. In 1942, a radar station with three radar sets was constructed a little further down the Atlantic side on high ground slightly inland. This was protected by light Flak. A fourth radar set, forming a substation, was built closer to the coast. The Fort des Arros was used by the Kriegsmarine for a battery of four 165 mm guns in type M270 casemates with a type M157 fire-control post. The battery was flanked by two 75 mm guns in type 670 casemates to enfilade the beach. In addition, there were anti-tank guns and Flak in a variety of bunkers as well as mortar and machine-gun positions. Altogether, around twenty bunkers and casemates were built.

In early September 1944, both fortresses were encircled by a combined force of American and FFI troops. The batteries and strongpoints were subjected to regular bombing raids and on 5 January 1945 Royan was very heavily damaged. As the end of the war approached, the local French commander wanted to exact revenge on the trapped Germans. The French forces launched an attack on 13 April. The day before, the Coubre defences were bombed and they continued to be bombed with high explosive and napalm for the next few days by American aircraft. The northern fortress surrendered on the 17th while the southern fortress held out for another two days, the resistance being centred around the Arros battery. The position was attacked by 2,400 Somalians as well as by Thunderbolts and Spitfires which dropped napalm and strafed the defenders, resulting in one of the casemates exploding. At the end of the battle for the southern fortress, 600 Germans had been killed and 320 wounded, while about 3,000 became prisoners.

THE SOUTH

Although the likelihood of an Allied invasion somewhere along the beaches of the southern Atlantic coast of France was practically non-existent, nevertheless, the Atlantic Wall continued down the Biscay coast beyond the Gironde all the way to the Spanish border. Moreover, the defences were of similar strength to those on similar stretches of coastline where the danger of landings was more serious and included big-gun batteries as well as resistance nests and strongpoints. They went from Cap Ferret, where the casemates of an artillery battery have now sunk into the sand, to Biarritz, the resort better known for its celebrity guests than its concrete

A type 671 casemate mounting a 105 mm gun belonging to 4b/MAA 286 south of Saint-Jean-de-Luz in 1944. All the battery's casemates were disguised similarly to this one. Windows, shutters, glass, even broken panes, have been painted in. The artist must have had plenty of time on his hands to go to this amount of trouble. Note the table and chairs on the left. Clearly, life here in the south was easy. (264/1622/22. Bundesarchiv)

The painting on this type 671 casemate of the same battery is even more elaborate, with very detailed gabling on the false roof, curtains and corner stones. (264/1622/30. Bundesarchiv)

German prisoners and Canadian wounded in front of one of two 50 mm anti-tank gun bunkers built into the sea wall at Bernières-sur-Mer, photographed on D-Day. Although the barrel is pointing out to sea, the bunker is positioned to enfilade the beach. This position was part of Wn 28 in Canadian landing sector Nan White on Juno. Although Wn 28 was bombed and shelled very little damage was done and the defenders put up a fight when the Queen's Own Rifles landed. The Canadians suffered their highest D-Day casualties on Nan White. The bunker still exists. (Frank L. Dubervill, National Archives of Canada PA 136280)

emplacements and bunkers. At Capbreton, there is another line of sinking concrete, testimony to the transience of coastal defences and the resilience of steel-reinforced concrete.

There were a number of batteries in the region of Arachon, opposite Cap Ferret. In the Bayonne/Biarritz area there were three coastal batteries and in Biarritz a number of bunkers and anti-tank casemates were constructed, including two type 506 casemates for 47 mm anti-tank guns near the Palais hotel. In the Saint-Jean-de-Lutz area, there were six batteries, including one comprising two 240 mm railway guns. The casemates of one of the six batteries, Socoa West, now lie at the foot of the cliffs. On the Pointe de Sainte-Barbe a battery was built into the cliff face with access via tunnels bored through the rock.

The southernmost battery in the Atlantic Wall stood on the Pointe Sainte-Anne, just to the east of Hendaye, next to the Spanish frontier. This consisted of four type 669 casemates for 152 mm guns; six casemated guns had been planned but the other two casemates were never built.

CHAPTER 9

A Successful Failure

Massive concrete monoliths always impress. To have built so much in so short a time along such a distance of coastline was indeed astonishing. It is less astonishing, however, when you consider how it was built; its ability to astonish undergoes a subtle shift when its human cost is considered. It was built by slave labour. Anything can be built if there are enough slaves, the pyramids of Egypt, the Great Wall of China and the Atlantic Wall in France. But unlike the pyramids and the Great Wall, the Atlantic Wall lasted less time than it took to construct it. The truth is that it was ill-conceived. Within a few decades after the end of the Second World War, much of it had already disappeared. Despite the ability of steel-reinforced concrete to weather the passage of time, it will not last like the pyramids and the Great Wall. A thousand years from now it will have long since disappeared and be forgotten.

The Atlantic Wall was in many ways similar to the Great Wall. It was intended to keep out invaders, it was not continuous and it was a solution to the problem of defending a militarily weak border of great length with few troops. The Great Wall, said to be the only man-made structure that is visible from space, did manage to keep China's invaders at bay for a while but it too was a failure. It no more kept out the Mongols than Hadrian's Wall kept out the Picts and Scots. Solid, fixed barriers do not keep out invaders. This lesson was relearned in the last few months of the First World War. The Atlantic Wall was no different. It was breached on 6 June 1944; it took two years to build and two hours to breach. And once breached, the rest of it largely became redundant. It did still prove to be a nuisance at the ports; here it was at its strongest. It gave the defenders time to destroy harbour facilities and deny them to the Allies. But even this was ultimately pointless. The Allies had other means of dealing with their logistics, although they still had problems; lack of fuel, in particular, held up the advance during the late summer and autumn of 1944. But the lack of a port did not halt the advance.

The Atlantic Wall was a manifestation of Hitler's bunker mentality that had grown out of his experience of the First World War. It led him to believe that, as in the First World War, steel-reinforced concrete was the answer to defeating the enemy should he mount a frontal assault. The cost to the enemy would be too great if he attempted it and he would either not try or, if he did, he would sue for peace once he had withdrawn to lick his considerable wounds, having been repulsed by the impregnable fortress. Hitler underestimated the British and the Americans, their ability to find solutions to problems and their determination to crush the Nazi state. Equally, he fell victim to his own propaganda, a failing that grew out of his unwillingness to face the truth. He came to rail against evidence contrary to his views, blaming everyone but himself when plans failed through his own shortcomings. Von Rundstedt recognized that static defences did not work but Rommel also saw that the more reliable method of using mobile reinforcements to counterattack was not feasible in the West because of Allied air superiority. There were not enough troops, nor was there enough time to construct defences in depth. The Atlantic Wall was a compromise, despite Hitler's rhetoric. It represented an unattainable dream to be equally strong everywhere, not only along the Channel and Atlantic coasts but in the West and in the East. The bulk of the German armed forces were in the East fighting the Soviet Union. The bulk of weapons and equipment went East not West. The Atlantic Wall was an attempt to redress the imbalance. It failed.

It is doubtful whether it was as effective as the West Wall, known to Allied soldiers as the Siegfried Line, built in the late 1930s. Although the circumstances were very different, the West Wall proved to be much more difficult for the Allies to overcome when it was confronted a few months later. The Atlantic Wall hamstrung the German defenders all the way up to Hitler, both in a physical sense and psychologically, tying up large reserves of manpower in impotent immobility. Such a heavy reliance on static defences by the German Army in Normandy, was a major factor in its failure to repel the invasion. A similar reliance at the West Wall did not occur when the Allies attempted to penetrate it. The defences were used very differently and, consequently, the West Wall was much more difficult to penetrate.

Following the Normandy breakout and the drive to the German border, the German Army paid dearly for Hitler's insistence that some ports within the Atlantic Wall be classified as fortresses. Some fortified ports such as Saint-Malo and Brest were confronted head-on by the Americans in costly operations. This dissuaded them and the British from mounting similar assaults on other fortresses, choosing merely to contain them instead. Fortress ports such as la Rochelle, Saint-Nazaire, Lorient and Dunkirk, remained isolated pockets until the end of the war. This was not what Hitler had envisaged. His no-surrender orders to these fortresses only succeeded in reducing the fighting strength of the Wehrmacht and made no difference to the outcome of the war. However, it would be a mistake to view Hitler's decisions at this stage of the war as being based on sound military judgement. On the contrary, his objective had become total chaos, to drag the West into the same abyss into which Nazi Germany was inexorably slipping.

There is no doubt that the inability of the Allies to capture an intact port was a hindrance but it was not the insuperable obstacle that Hitler believed it would be. Prior to the invasion neither he nor anyone else at OKW had an inkling of the Mulberry artificial harbours that the Allies brought with them, or the Pipe Line Under The Ocean (PLUTO) for transporting fuel. It can be argued that preventing the Allies from capturing a large port with all its facilities for unloading large ships – which would have shortened the supply lines after the Normandy breakout – was a success of sorts for the Atlantic Wall, but it was a negative one, rather like claiming

Another shot of the anti-tank gun bunker (background, centre left) seen in the previous picture, showing how well it covered the beach. The wall is a sea wall, not an anti-tank wall. (Frank L. Dubervill, National Archives of Canada PA 133754)

good fortune when hit by a bullet in some area of the body that is not immediately lethal.

In terms of raw materials, the Wall was a costly mistake. The steel that was needed for reinforcement, armoured doors, shields and turrets was steel that could have been used for the manufacture of guns, tanks and ammunition. The quantities involved could have made a significant difference to wartime production – although it is doubtful that production could have been increased to such a level that the tide of war would have turned in Germany's favour. It is conceivable that, if more resources had been made available for the Wall and if there had been time to build defences in depth and if the Luftwaffe had been stronger in the West and had not had to devote most of its strength to combat bombing raids, events might have turned out differently. But the 'What if . . .' game is pointless. The fact is, the steel used in the Atlantic Wall was not used to make guns, tanks and ammunition. And the fact is that no one, other than Hitler, really believed that the Atlantic Wall could keep out the

Allies. Although concrete a couple of metres thick was practically impossible to penetrate with conventional weapons, new weapons and new tactics were devised to deal with it – specialized armour, napalm, flamethrowers, teamwork. The Germans themselves knew very well that no concrete defence was secure; they had easily defeated the Belgian fort at Eben Emael. Yet they blindly persisted with the Atlantic Wall as though their defences were superior to those of the Belgians. They were wrong.

The standardization of designs is an illusion created by the use of 'standard design' numbers. Standardization was not rigorously pursued; it was more of a bureaucratic safeguard against interference from party officials than an efficient system for selecting the best designs. Although some so-called standard designs were built in large numbers, many more were not and they were still being introduced in mid-1944. And some standard designs were almost identical to each other. There were also a huge number of non-standard designs. What made the bunkers and casemates effective had less to do with their design than with the thickness of the ferroconcrete. There is no evidence that British, Canadian, French or US troops found any bunker to be more difficult to capture by virtue of its design. On the contrary, all the evidence points to the thickness of the concrete and the determination of the occupants being the decisive factors.

Today, the remains of the Atlantic Wall are a reminder of the folly of believing in the impregnability of permanent defences. This is most graphically demonstrated by the bunkers and casemates that have fallen off cliffs or sunk into the sand. Each bunker is also a memorial to the forced labourers who built the Atlantic Wall.

Atlantic Wall Structures

Key:

A	armour plate
AR	ammunition room
A/T	anti-tank
B	accumulator room
Cat-A	Category A thickness
CR	crew room
E	personnel entrance
GS	gun shelter
HT	howitzer turret
mgT(3)	machine-gun turret (number of embrasures)
moT	M19 mortar turret
O	observation room
OP	observation post
oT	observation turret
P	periscope
PM	pedestal mount
R	rangefinder room
RC	rangefinder in cupola
RR	radio room
S	armoured shutter
sd/mg	self-defence machine-gun
SS	searchlight shelter
tb	tobruk
TE	telephone exchange
th	operating theatre
Tl	telegraphy room
TR	treatment room
Tw	tower
W	medical ward

Design (date)	Function	Features	Concrete/steel used (m³/t)	Length (m)	Width (m)	Height (m)	Number built (approx)
105 (1939)	Mg bunker, enfilade	2A, CR, E, oT, sd/mg	564	11.8	12.3	4.9	85
110 (1939)	Mg bunker	CR, E, sd/mg(A), mgT(3)	610	13.35	12.4	5.1	12
112 (1939)	Mg bunker	CR, E, mgT(6), sd/mg	660	14.5	9.65	6.3	5
114a new (1942)	Mg bunker	Cat-A, CR, E, mgT(6), sd/mg	1,700	17.4	16.5		41
117 (1939)	Battalion/regiment command post	6CR, 2E, sd/mg, oT	1,092	21.7	12.0	4.9	31
118 (1939)	Medical bunker	2CR, 2E, th, 2W	856	22.2	12.8		26
119 (1939)	Battery command post	2CR, 2E, P, sd/mg	999	19.5	12.5		32
120a (1939)	Artillery observation post	2CR, E, sd/mg, oT	650/45.5	11.5	14.2	5.8	8
121 (1939)	Artillery observation post	2CR, E, sd/mg(A), oT	1,692	14.6	14.1	7.2	5
127 (1939)	Personnel bunker	CR, E	406	9.9	8.6		3
128 (1939)	Personnel bunker	2CR, 2E	655	17.6	8.6		
132 (1939)	Mg bunker	Cat-A, CR, E, mgT(3), sd/mg					323
134 (1942)	Magazine (type I)	2AR, 2E	490	11.1	10.8		3
135 (1939)	M19 mortar bunker	2CR, 2 floors, E, moT, oT	990	11.75	12.2	9.15	5
139 (1940)	47 mm A/T gun & mg casemate, enfilade	2A, AR, CR, E, P, sd/mg	1,070	18.8	11.9	5.3	15
142 (1942)	Accumulator bunker	2B, CR, E	786	17.0	12.1		422
143 (1942)	Observation post	CR, E, oT	510	13.6	8.9		395
501 (1939)	Personnel bunker	CR, E	356	9.9	9.0		55
502 (1939)	Personnel bunker	2CR, 2E, P	629	14.8	9.5		33
504 (1939)	A/T bunker	2CR, E, GS, P	537	14.3	8.8		24
505 (1939)	A/T gun casemate, enfilade	A, AR, CR, E, E, P, sd/mg	550/38	11.9	13.0	4.8	100
506 (1939)	47 mm A/T gun casemate	AR, CR, E, P	778	11.8	13.0	8.3	82
515 (1939)	Mg bunker, enfilade	A, AR, CR, E, P	383	10.7	8.0		26
600 (1942)	50 mm A/T gun emplacement	AR, CR, E	555	9.9	10.0	6.0	11
601 (1942)	A/T gun bunker	AR, CR, E, GS, tb	600	11.2	11.0	5.7	3
602 (1942)	Tank bunker	CR, E, GS, tb	810	13.8	12.0		49
603 (1942)	Tank bunker	2GS, tb	1,150	14.0	12.0		7
604 (1942)	Gun bunker	AR, CR, E, GS, P, tb	800	14.8	11.5		14
605 (1942)	Gun bunker	CR, E, 2GS, P, 2S, tb	910	16.0	13.2		190
606 (1942)	60 cm searchlight bunker	CR, E, SS, tb	680	11.5	10.0		
607 (1942)	Magazine (type II)	2AR, 2E	740	15.0	11.0		

Design (date)	Function	Features	Concrete/steel used (m³/t)	Length (m)	Width (m)	Height (m)	Number built (approx)
608 (1942)	Battalion/regiment command post	3CR, 2E, P, sd/mg, tb	990	14.0	15.1		86
609 (1942)	Battalion/regiment command post	3CR, 2 floors, 2E, P, sd/mg, tb	1,470	17.0	13.7		12
610 (1942)	Company/battery command post	3CR, 2E, P, sd/mg, tb	860	13.1	13.1		47
611 (1942)	Field-gun casemate	2AR, E, CR, P, sd/mg, tb	1,330	17.5	16.5	7.9	98
612 (1943)	Field-gun casemate, enfilade	2AR	385	9.0	9.0		397
613 (1942)	Artillery observation post	3CR, E, sd/mg, oT	750	14.6	12.0	5.1	15
614 (1942)	Artillery observation post	2 floors, 3CR, E, sd/mg, oT	950/47.5	13.3	10.0	8.2	3
615 (1942)	Artillery observation post	A, 2CR, E, P, sd/mg	590	13.8	11.8	5.0	
616 (1942)	Switchboard	CR, E, sd/mg	590	11.0	10.0		8
617 (1942)	Signals post	CR, 2E, P, sd/mg, tb	850	17.0	12.8		18
618 (1942)	Staff signals post	2E, RR, sd/mg, tb	1,110	20.5	13.7		14
619 (1942)	Machinery bunker	E, sd/mg	1,040	17.2	12.0		5
620 (1943)	Mg bunker, enfilade	A, AR, CR, E, tb	590	12.8	8.2		8
621 (1943)	Personnel bunker	CR, 2E, tb	480	9.8	9.6		385
622 (1942)	Personnel bunker	2CR, 2E, tb	660	12.6	11.5		449
623 (1942)	Mg bunker, enfilade	A, Ar, Cr, E, sd/mg, tb	600	11.0	10.4		15
624 (1942)	Mg bunker, enfilade	A, 2AR, CR, E, sd/mg, tb	590	11.2	10.4	5.1	15
625 (1943)	75 mm A/T gun casemate, enfilade	AR, CR, E, sd/mg, tb	770	18.7	9.7		32
625B (1943)	75 mm A/T gun casemate	AR, CR, E, sd/mg	800	18.4	12.1		1
626 (1942)	75 mm A/T gun casemate, enfilade	A, AR, CR, E, sd/mg, tb	665	9.6	15.75	5.9	29
627 (1942)	Artillery OP	CR, E, sd/mg	630	13.8	11.8	5.0	28
628 (1942)	Personnel bunker	CR, 2E, P, tb	600	9.8	10.3		10
629 (1942)	A/T gun bunker	CR, E, GS, tb	675	11.2	11.0		20
630 (1942)	Mg bunker, enfilade	A, AR, CR, E, sd/mg, tb	610	10.7	10.4		215
630B (1943)	Mg bunker, enfilade	A, AR, CR, E, P, sd/mg	730	12.5	9.0		17
631 (1942)	47 mm A/T casemate, enfilade	AR, CR, E, P, sd/mg, tb	730	11.5	11.1	5.3	51
631b (1943)	47 mm A/T gun casemate, enfilade	AR, CR, E, sd/mg	815	14.0	10.0		11
632 (1942)	Mg bunker	CR, E, mgT(3), sd/mg, tb	590	14.4	8.9	6.4	15
633 (1942)	M119 mortar bunker	AR, CR, E, moT, sd/mg	765/40	16.3	13.25	5.1	37
634 (1942)	Mg bunker	CR, E, mgT(6), sd/mg	620/31	11.4	10.7	5.1	71
635 (1942)	Personnel bunker	2CR, 2E, tb	855	16.8	9.4		10

Design (date)	Function	Features	Concrete/steel used (m³/t)	Length (m)	Width (m)	Height (m)	Number built (approx)
636 (1942)	Fire-control post	CR, E, O, R, sd/mg	960	18.4	15.5	6.8	43
636a	Fire-control post	2CR, E, O, R, sd/mg	1,250	17.3	16.0	7.4	2
637 (1942)	Measuring post	CR, E, R, sd/mg, tb	445	11.5	8.3	5.1	35
638 (1942)	Medical bunker	2E, tb, th, 2W	900/61	15.5	14.0	5.1	27
639 (1942)	Medical bunker	2E, tb, th, 2W	1,300/71	21.0	14.0	5.8	8
640 (1943)	37/42 mm A/T gun casemate, enfilade	A, AR, CR, E, sd/mg, tb	680	8.0	14.0	5.10	4
641 (1943)	Magazine (type III)	2AR, 2E, tb	940	17.6	13.0		3
642 (1943)	47 mm A/T gun & mg casemate, enfilade	2A, AR, CR, E, P, sd/mg, tb	1,020/58	15.3	12.4	5.6	5
643 (1943)	Mg bunker	CR, E, mgT(3), sd/mg, tb	1,460	16.25	12.8		9
644 (1943)	Mg bunker	CR, E, mgT(6), sd/mg, tb	1,730/89	14.7	19.2	7.9	19
645 (1943)	Kitchen bunker	CR, E, tb	605	11.5	11.5	5.1	12
647 (1943)	Mg bunker	CR, 2E, 2mgT(1), P, sd/mg, tb	905	15.0	11.0		
646 (1943)	Water bunker	E	330	8.4	8.4		31
648 (1943)	Mg bunker	CR, E, mgT(1), sd/mg	605	12.7	9.2	5.5	
649 (1943)	Casemate	90° trav, 2AR, CR, 2E, PM, sd/mg, tb	1,090/54	18.2	15.0	5.1	4
650 (1943)	Casemate	120° trav, 2AR, CR, E, PM, sd/mg, tb	1,080	17.7	15.0	5.4	16
651 (1943)	Casemate	90° trav, 2AR, E, PM, sd/mg, tb	880	16.2	13.0		2
652 (1943)	Casemate	120° trav, 2AR, E, PM, sd/mg, tb	880	16.2	13.0	8.0	8
653 (1943)	50 mm A/T gun casemate	AR, CR, E, P, sd/mg, tb	830	8.3	14.8		9
653B	50 mm A/T gun casemate, emfilade	AR, CR, E, sd/mg		12.2	13.9		
654 (1943)	50 mm A/T gun, enfilade	AR, E, P, sd/mg, tb	610	10.0	10.0	4.7	3
655 (1943)	Personnel bunker	AR, CR, E, tb	500	10.0	10.0		9
656 (1943)	Personnel bunker	CR, 2E, P, 2tb	570	11.7	10.0		27
657 (1943)	Kitchen bunker	CR, E, tb	700	14.0	12.0		3
658 (1943)	Water bunker	E	460	11.6	9.5		26
659 (1943)	Water bunker	Cat-A, E	1,175	14.6	12.5		3
660 (1943)	Accumulator bunker	B, CR, 2E, P, sd/mg, tb	720	14.6	13.2		2
661 (1943)	Medical bunker	2E, tb, 2TR	660	12.6	12.0		17
663a	100 mm gun casemate	A, AR, CR, 2E, oT, sd/mg, tb	3,375/155	27.5	21.4	10.4	1
663b	100 mm gun & mg casemate	A, AR, CR, 2E, oT, sd/mg, tb	3,180	26.5	20.4	10.4	1
664 (1943)	105 mm howitzer bunker	CR, E, HT, sd/mg, tb	2,500/110	17.0	20.0	7.5	7

Design (date)	Function	Features	Concrete/steel used (m³/t)	Length (m)	Width (m)	Height (m)	Number built (approx)
665 (1943)	Infantry OP	CR, E, oT, sd/mg, tb	700	13.4	11.0	6.3	5
666 (1943)	Infantry OP	E, oT, tb	370/17	11.6	7.4	6.6	6
667 (1943)	50 mm A/T gun casemate, enfilade	E	165	6.8	6.4	4.6	430
668 (1943)	Personnel bunker	CR, E	210	7.7	7.0		296
669 (1943)	Field-gun casemate	60° trav, 2AR	495	12.0	11.0	5.3	544
670 (1943)	Casemate	90° trav, 2AR, E, PM	310	9.6	10.0	5.1	28
671 (1943)	Casemate	120° trav, 2AR, E, PM	300	9.6	10.0		219
672 (1943)	Gun bunker	GS	340	11.5	6.5		5
673 (1943)	Gun bunker	GS, S	430	13.2	7.0		1
674 (1943)	Magazine	AR, E	230	7.65	7.65		41
675 (1943)	Water bunker	E	230	7.65	7.65		17
676 (1943)	47 mm A/T gun casemate, enfilade	E	355/18.2	9.4	8.1	4.6	37
677 (1943)	88 mm A/T gun casemate, enfilade	2AR	380	9.5	9.8	5.1	116
679 (1943)	Casemate	120° trav, 2AR, E, PM, S	560/31.2	10.1	13.0	6.6	41
680 (1943)	75 mm A/T gun casemate, enfilade	2AR	440	8.8	9.0		122
681 (1943)	Mg bunker, enfilade	A, E	280	7.8	8.0		3
682 (1943)	Bunker for small generator	E	230	7.65	7.65		2
683 (1944)	Casemate for 210 mm gun	120° trav, 2AR, Cat-A, E, PM	2,000	21.6	16.0		
686 (1944)	Casemate for 194 mm gun	2AR, E, PM	685	14.1	12.5		
688 (1944)	Casemate for 170 mm gun	120° trav, 2AR, Cat-A, E, PM	1,750	19.2	17.4	8.9	22
689 (1944)	Casemate for 170 mm gun	120° trav, 2AR, Cat-A, E, PM	1,400	15.5	13.5		7
691 (1944)	Signals post	2CR, E, 2RR, sd/mg	1,350	25.1	13.0		
693 (1944)	Flash-spotting post	E, O	140	6.3	5.5	4.4	3
697 (1944)	Measuring post	CR, E, O	140	10.8	7.0	4.4	
700 (1944)	75 mm A/T gun casemate		230	7.6	9.6		4
701 (1944)	A/T gun bunker	GS	380	12.6	6.7		1
702 (1944)	Personnel bunker	CR, 2E	385	9.0	9.0		
703 (1944)	88 mm A/T gun casemate, enfilade	2AR	370	9.3	7.5		23
704 (1944)	Casemate	2AR, PM	305	7.7	7.5		
Fl241 (1942)	Flak command post	E, sd/mg	1,500	24.45	16.3	7.4	8
Fl242 (1942)	Medium/heavy flak emplacement	Ar, CR, E	640	10.45	11.0	6.4	28

Design (date)	Function	Features	Concrete/steel used (m³/t)	Length (m)	Width (m)	Height (m)	Number built (approx)
Fl243 (1942)	Heavy flak emplacement	CR, E	647/30.7	19.6	12.6	5.3	
Fl243a (1942)	Heavy flak emplacement	E	200	11.6	11.6		38
Fl244 (1942)	Heavy flak fire-control post	6CR, E, O, R	1,400	25.4	17.9	5.6	6
Fl245 (1942)	Machinery bunker	E	850	14.0	13.4		
Fl246 (1942)	Magazine	4AR, 2E	1,540	23.5	15.2		25
Fl247 (1942)	Light flak emplacement	AR, 2CR, E	600	18.2	9.5	5.3	
Fl248 (1942)	Flak emplacement	Cr, 2E	750/7.3	13.1	11.1	6.7	1
Fl249 (1942)	Heavy flak fire-control post	CR, E	645	18.8	19.6	6.1	
Fl250 (1942)	Flak command post	E, sd/mg, Tw	2,500	25.0	23.8	20.0 (Tw)	2
Fl255 (1942)	Heavy flak fire-control post	2E, R, sd/mg	1,600	21.4	17.75	7.2	
Fl256 (1942)	Machinery bunker	E	570	11.2	10.8		
Fl277 (1943)	150 cm searchlight bunker	CR, E, sd/mg, SS	920	13.0	12.8		
Fl300a (1944)	Flak command post	2E, 2sd/mg	4,000	28.1	23.1	9.4	
Fl304 (1943)	Heavy flak fire-control post	E, 2O, R	500	13.8	11.2	5.7	15
Fl311 (1943)	Flak fire-control post	3CR, E, 2O, R, sd/mg		27.0	14.4	6.2	
Fl314 (1944)	Heavy flak fire-control post	CR, 2E, R, sd/mg	1,300	17.8	14.5		
Fl317 (1944)	Magazine for 128 mm flak	4AR, 2E	1,500	22.4	17.0		
Fl331 (1944)	Flak command post	2sd/mg	5,600				
Fl351 (1944)	Heavy flak fire-control post	E, 2O, R	1,100	10.9	11.2	6.5	
Fl354a (1944)	Flak command post	2E, Tw		19.0	16.0	15.0 (Tw)	
L401 (1942)	88/105 mm flak emplacement	AR, CR, 2E	660	14.8	11.1	6.2	46
L401A (1942)	88/105 mm flak emplacement	AR, CR, 2E, sd/mg	840	14.8	13.6	6.75	28
L402 (1942)	20 mm flak emplacement	AR, CR, E	450	9.6	10.1	6.3	26
L403 (1942)	Heavy flak fire-control post	5CR, 2E, R	1,400	19.4			13
L403A (1943)	Heavy flak (BII) fire-control post	3CR, 2E, R, sd/mg	1,150	19.35	15.1	6.6	
L404 (1942)	Heavy flak (BI) fire-control post		1,400	18.5		6.4	6
L404A (1943)	Flak (BI) fire-control post	3CR, 2E, R, sd/mg	1,140	19.35	15.1		
L405 (1942)	Radar bunker	CR, E	700	12.5	10.1	5.1	6
L405A (1943)	Flak radar bunker	CR, 2E, tb	740	15.4	10.1		3
L406 (1943)	Machinery bunker for 105 mm flak battery	CR, E	630	12.6	10.1		8
L406A (1942)	150/200 cm searchlight bunker	CR, 2E, SS, tb	785	15.3	11.5		1

Design (date)	Function	Features	Concrete/steel used (m³/t)	Length (m)	Width (m)	Height (m)	Number built (approx)
L407 (1942)	Magazine for 88 mm or 105 mm flak	2AR, 2E	700	13.0	12.7		12
L407A (1943)	Magazine	3AR, 2E, tb	800	13.9	12.6		7
L408 (1942)	Command post	2E, sd/mg	1,340	18.5	17.6		6
L408A (1943)	Command post	3E, sd/mg	1,685	19.1	17.8		4
L409 (1942)	37 mm flak emplacement	AR, CR, E	525	11.7	10.1	6.3	78
L409a (1942)	37 mm flak emplacement	AR, CR, E	1,010	13.7	12.1	6.8	3
L409A (1942)	20/37 mm flak emplacement	AR, CR, 2E	635	11.0	11.0	6.8	61
L410 (1942)	37 mm flak emplacement	AR, 2CR, E	700	15.9	10.1		31
L410A (1942)	37 mm flak emplacement	AR, 2CR, 2E, sd/mg	886/51.4	15.7	13.5	6.6	36
L411 (1942)	60 cm searchlight bunker	CR, SS	600	11.8	11.4	6.3	31
L411A	60 cm searchlight bunker	CR, E, SS, tb	680	13.0	10.6		16
L412 (1943)	Light flak fire-control post	CR, E	1,050	15.5	12.0		3
L412A (1943)	Flak fire-control post	3CR, 3E, sd/mg	1,080	17.2	12.7		2
L413 (1942)	Magazine for 37 mm flak	AR, E	370	10.2	8.0		44
L413A (1943)	Magazine for light flak	3AR, 2E, tb	625	12.1	10.9		7
L414	Water bunker	E		6.5	6.5		
L415	Water bunker	E		8.0	6.0		
L416	Command post	2E, sd/mg		31.2	18.0		1
L416A	88 mm flak casemate	4AR, tb	500	7.6	11.2		
L417	Command post	2E		18.5	17.6		
L418	105 mm flak emplacement	AR, CR, 2E		11.0	14.1		6
L419	37 mm flak emplacement	2CR, 2E		9.2	8.8		2
L419A (1943)	20/37 mm flak emplacement	AR, CR, 2E	470	10.9	8.0	6.8	7
L420	60 cm searchlight bunker	CR, SS		9.3	9.0		1
L420A (1943)	60 cm searchlight bunker	SS, T	490	10.6	9.0		1
L421A (1943)	Flak fire-control post	CR, 3E, sd/mg	655	12.5	12.6		2
L422	Heavy flak emplacement	CR, 2E		11.4	9.0		4
L422A (1943)	88/105 mm flak emplacement	AR, CR, 2E	650	11.2	11.1	6.6	
L424	Flak (BI) fire-control post	2E	640	11.8	11.6		
L424A (1944)	Flak (BI) fire-control post	CR, 2E, R	650	10.0	11.8	6.7	
L425	Flak (BII) fire-control post	CR, 2E		11.8	11.9		
L425A (1944)	Flak (BII) fire-control post	CR, 2E, R	650	10.0	11.8	6.7	

Design (date)	Function	Features	Concrete/steel used (m³/t)	Length (m)	Width (m)	Height (m)	Number built (approx)
L426	Radar bunker	CR		11.9	9.0		
L427	Machinery bunker	2E		9.4	8.4		
L428 (1942)	Bunker for command post personnel	3CR, 2E, sd/mg	950	17.6	12.0		
L429	Bunker for command post personnel	3CR, 2E		17.6	12.0		
L430A	150/200 cm searchlight bunker	CR, 2E, 2SS	890	19.7	16.1	5.2	6
L435A (1942)	Bunker light AA personnel	2CR, 2E, P, tb	795	18.8	11.2		4
L436 (1943)	88 mm flak emplacement	AR, CR, 2E, sd/mg	760	145.4	12.6	6.75	
L470	37 mm flak emplacement + command post	AR, 2CR	700	15.9	10.1		2
L480 (1942)	Wassermann radar bunker	E, sd/mg	1,890	27.4	12.2	6.8	6
L485 (1943)	Mammut radar bunker	E, sd/mg	2,520	25.2	23.9	6.5	12
L486 (1943)	Radar bunker	CR, 2E, sd/mg, tb	1,300	26.0	13.5	5.3	14
L489 (1943)	Signals post	CR, 2E, sd/mg, tb	1,280	24.2	12.8		
L490 (1943)	Signals post	E, sd/mg, tb	545	10.5	9.0		
M120 (1942)	Fire-control post for 170 mm battery	CR, 2 floors, E, R, 2T	1,400	23.5	16.6	6.2	6
M123 (1943)	Machinery bunker	2E	580	13.2	9.0		1
M132 (1943)	Fire-control post for 170 mm battery	CR, 3 floors, E, R, 2T		25.2	17.4	8.2	5
M145 (1942)	Magazine	4AR, 2E	1,450	18.5	17.7		17
M151 (1942)	Personnel bunker	2CR, 2E	970	16.3	14.0		24
M157 (1942)	Fire-control post for medium & heavy batteries	E, 2O, R, sd/mg	1,325	23.8	14.9	8.9	7
M158 (1942)	Light gun emplacement	AR, E	600	19.2	12.4	4.8	13
M159 (1942)	Medical bunker	2E, th	1,000	16.0	12.8		4
M160 (1942)	Personnel bunker	CR, E	500	13.3	9.8		23
M162a (1942)	Fire-control post for light batteries	E, O, R, sd/mg, tb	1,000	20.0	13.6	7.6	17
M163 (1942)	Machinery bunker for medium battery	2E, tb	920	14.65	14.3		
M170 (1943)	Casemate	90° trav, 2AR, E, sd/mg	1,335	20.1	12.8		34
M176 (1943)	Casemate	120° trav, 2AR, E, sd/mg		21.3	12.8		8
M178 (1943)	Fire-control post	E, O, R, sd/mg	2,300	22.8	14.8	9.8	2
M180 (1944)	Emplacement	4AR, CR, E	700	18.0	18.4	5.6	
M182 (1943)	Searchlight emplacement	SS		11.5	7.5	5.8	1
M183 (1944)	Machinery bunker	E, sd/mg	800	13.8	13.45		6
M195 (1943)	Emplacement	2AR, E, tb	830	21.0	11.6	5.0	6
M262 (1943)	Fire-control post for light battery	E, O, R, sd/mg	720	17.0	11.4	7.8	7

Design (date)	Function	Features	Concrete/steel used (m³/t)	Length (m)	Width (m)	Height (m)	Number built (approx)
M270 (1944)	Casemate	120° trav, 2AR, E, sd/mg	1,950	18.8	12.8	6.8	46
M271 (1943)	Casemate	2AR, E	930	13.5	12.5	7.1	7
M272 (1943)	Casemate	2AR, E	760				38
M283 (1944)	Machinery bunker	E	210	8.45	7.0		3
M383 (1944)	Machinery bunker	E	310	8.1	8.0		3
S100 (1942)	Fire-control post for heavy battery	4CR, 2 floors, E, RC, oT		28.6	20.6	8.4	1
S169 (1941)	Turretted-gun emplacement	8AR, 2E		49.5	33.2	6.8	
S302 (1943)	Magazine	2AR, 2E		16.8	12.6		
S384 (1944)	Turretted-gun emplacement	8AR, 2E, 2sd/mg		47.0	36.8	10.2	4
S412 (1942)	Bunker for heavy-gun turret	5AR, CR, E	1,800	26.1	28.8	6.2	3
S414 (1942)	Fire-control post for medium & heavy batteries	3 floors, E, 2O, R	1,300	25.6	15.1	12	2
S446 (1943)	Fire-control post	2E, O, RC, sd/mg		21.8	16.0	5.4	
S448 (1942)	Fire-control post	E, RC, 2sd/mg, Tw	4,800	29.0	23.5	27.1 (Tw)	
S448a (1942)	Magazine for 280 mm or 305 mm	4AR, 2E	4,192	27.0	23.4		1
S449 (1942)	Measuring post	CR, E, O, sd/mg	550	16.25	9.4	5.4	
S468 (1943)	Magazine	3AR, 2E	5,130	27.8	17.5		
S497 (1944)	Fire-control post	2E, 2sd/mg, Tw	5,400	20.5	20.6	14.2 (Tw)	1
V134 (1943)	Light flak emplacement	AR, 2CR, 2E	800	18.75	9.6	6.2	1
V142 (1942)	Signals post	2E, RR, sd/mg, tb, TE, Tl	1,750	21.0	19.8		7
V143 (1942)	Mammut radar bunker	2e, 2sd/mg, 2tb	1,800	20.5	18.2	5.3	4
V148 (1942)	Medical staff bunker	E	400	11.25	7.9		1
V151 (1942)	Signals post	3CR, 2E, sd/mg, Tw	1,000	18.5	13.5	10.0 (Tw)	
V152 (1942)	Command post	E, sd/mg	1,100	18.0	12.6	5.85	10
V157 (1944)	Aircraft reporting centre	2E, sd/mg	1,300	22.0	14.2	7.6	
V174 (1944)	Radar bunker	CR, E, sd/mg, Tw	850	14.7	10.2	13.8 (Tw)	
V192 (1944)	Machinery bunker	E, sd/mg		18.34	14.0		2
V193 (1944)	Radar coordination centre	2E, sd/mg	2,144	30.2	17.3		
V194 (1943)	Radar coordination centre	E, sd/mg	920	16.4	13.5		
V196 (1944)	Command post	2E, sd/mg, tb	2,372	24.5	23.6		
V206 (1944)	Radar bunker			16.5	13.0		
V214 (1944)	Signals post	CR, E, O, sd/mg, Tw	1,515	14.25	13.0	11.8 (Tw)	2

APPENDIX B

Coastal Batteries

Key:

AA	*Artillerie Abteilung*
AR	*Artillerie Regiment*
EB	*Eisenbahn Batterie*
HAA	*Heeres Artillerie Abteilung*
HAB	*Heeres Artillerie Batterie*
HKAA	*Heeres Künsten Artillerie Abteilung*
HKAR	*Heeres Künsten Artillerie Regiment*
LAR	*Luftwaffe Feld Division Artillerie Regiment*
MAA	*Marine Artillerie Abteilung*
OA	*Ost Abteilung*

Dunkirk to Normandy (Fifteenth Army)

Unit	Armament	Location (battery name)
LAR 18	4 × 155 mm	Uxem
1/LAR 18	4 × 76.2 mm	Ferme Bayard
2/LAR 18	4 × 76.2 mm	les Mottes
3/LAR 18	4 × 76.2 mm	Ferme Mathieux
4/LAR 18	4 × 155 mm	Coudekerque
5/LAR 18	4 × 155 mm	Canal de Mardyck
6/LAR 18	4 × 155 mm	Loon Plage
7/LAR 18	4 × 155 mm	Basse Plaine
8/LAR 18	4 × 155 mm	Lefrinckouke
9/LAR 18	4 × 155 mm	Ferme Deldrève
1/HKAA 1244	6 × 155 mm	le Clipon
2/HKAA 1244	6 × 155 mm	Oye
3/HKAA 1244	6 × 155 mm	Mardyck
4/HKAA 1244	4 × 88 mm	Ferme Lebecque
5/HKAA 1244	4 × 88 mm	Canal aux Chats
6/HKAA 1244	4 × 88 mm	Ferme Noël
MAA 204	4 × 105 mm	Zuydcoote
MAA 204	4 × 164.7 mm	Saint-Pol
MAA 204	4 × 150 mm	les Huttes d'Oye
MAA 204	4 × 210 mm	Ferme Masson
EB 688	2 × 280 mm	Coquelles
EB 696	2 × 280 mm	Saint-Pol
EB 710	2 × 280 mm	Nieulay
EB 765	2 × 280 mm	Frethun
AR 147	4 × 155 mm	Wissant
AR 147	4 × 155 mm	Wimereux
1/AR 147	4 × 76.2 mm	Coquelles
2/AR 147	4 × 76.2 mm	le Beau Marais
3/AR 147	4 × 76.2 mm	Camp de l'Alma

Unit	Armament	Location (battery name)
4/AR 147	4 × 100 mm	Mont Lambert
5/AR 147	4 × 100 mm	Saint-Etienne
6/AR 147	4 × 94 mm	Outreau
7/AR 147	4 × 100 mm	Herquelingue
8/AR 147	3 × 150 mm	Noirbenne
9/AR 147	4 × 155 mm	Maninghen
10/AR 147	4 × 155 mm	Coquelles
1/AA 179	4 × 105 mm	Bonningues
2/AA 179	4 × 105 mm	Peuplingues
1/MAA 242	4 × 155 mm	Wissant (M3)
2/MAA 242	4 × 280 mm	Framzelle (Grosser Kurfürst)
3/MAA 242	3 × 170 mm	Cap Gris Nez (M4)
4/MAA 242	4 × 380 mm	Haringzelles (Todt)
5/MAA 242	3 × 150 mm	Waringzelle
1/MAA 244	2 × 240 mm	Waldam (M1)
2/MAA 244	3 × 194 mm	Moulin Rouge (Oldenburg)
3/MAA 244	4 × 164.7 mm	Bastion II
4/MAA 244	2 × 280 mm	Fort Lapin
5/MAA 244	3 × 406 mm	Sangatte (M2)
6/MAA 244	4 × 150 mm	Sangatte (Lindemann)
	4 × 170 mm	Sangatte (Prinz Heinrich)
1/HAA 1143	4 × 105 mm	le Colombier
2/HAA 1143	4 × 105 mm	Peuplingues
3/HAA 1143	4 × 105 mm	Beuvrequen
4/HAA 1143	4 × 105 mm	Inglevert
1/AA 70	2 × 150 mm	Loulinghon-Bernes
2/AA 70	4 × 155 mm	Bernes
1/AA 105	4 × 100 mm	Audembert
2/AA 105	4 × 105 mm	Ferques
EB 701	1 × 210 mm	Hydrequent
EB 712	2 × 280 mm	Pointe aux Oies
EB 713	3 × 280 mm	Hydrequent
1/MAA 240	2 × 75 mm	Boulogne, north mole
1/MAA 240	2 × 75 mm	Boulogne, mole caisson
2/MAA 240	3 × 305 mm	la Trésorerie (Friedrich August)
3/MAA 240	4 × 194 mm	la Crèche I
4/MAA 240	4 × 105 mm	la Crèche II
5/MAA 240	3 × 138 mm	Mont de Couppe
6/MAA 240	1 × 150 mm	le Portel
7/MAA 240	4 × 94 mm	la Tour d'Ordre
10/MAA 240	4 × 105 mm	Stella Plage
1/AR 149	4 × 105 mm	Beauregard, south
2/AR 149	4 × 105 mm	Beauregard, north
3/AR 149	4 × 105 mm	Etaples
4/AR 149	4 × 100 mm	Hardelot
5/AR 149	4 × 100 mm	Mont Saint-Frieux
6/AR 149	4 × 100 mm	Mont de Neufchatel
7/AR 149	4 × 155 mm	Nesles
8/AR 149	4 × 155 mm	le Cucq
9/AR 149	4 × 155 mm	Merlimont
10/AR 149	4 × 122 mm	Airon

Unit	Armament	Location (battery name)
1/HKAR 1245	6 × 155 mm	Saint-Gabriel
2/HKAR 1245	6 × 155 mm	Hardelot Plage
3/HKAR 1245	6 × 155 mm	le Touquet
4/HKAR 1245	4 × 170 mm	Mont Saint-Frieux
5/HKAR 1245	3 × 170 mm	Quend
6/HKAR 1245	3 × 170 mm	Berck
7/HKAR 1245	3 × 170 mm	Saint-Firmin
8/HKAR 1245	3 × 170 mm	Etaples
9/HKAR 1245	4 × 105 mm	Fort Mahon
10/HKAR 1245	4 × 105 mm	Berck
11/HKAR 1245	4 × 105 mm	Saint-Quentin
12/HKAR 1245	3 × 170 mm	Berck
EB 655	4 × 150 mm	Montreuil
AR 344	4 × 155 mm	Fort Mahon
1/HAA 1146	4 × 122 mm	Waben
2/HAA 1146	4 × 122 mm	la Plaine
3/HAA 1146	4 × 122 mm	Flandre
1/HKAR 1252	3 × 170 mm	Ault
2/HKAR 1252	3 × 170 mm	Neuville
3/HKAR 1252	4 × 105 mm	Mers-les-Bains
4/HKAR 1252	4 × 220 mm	Thibermont
5/HKAR 1252	4 × 88 mm	Mont de la Chapelle
6/HKAR 1252	4 × 88 mm	Friaucourt
7/HKAR 1252	4 × 88 mm	Neuville
1/AR 348	4 × 76.2 mm	Brutelles
2/AR 348	4 × 76.2 mm	Woignarue
3/AR 348	4 × 76.2 mm	Lanchères
1/HAA 1147	4 × 150 mm	Calmont
2/HAA 1147	4 × 150 mm	Neuville
3/HAA 1147	4 × 150 mm	Roumesnil
1/HAA 1148	4 × 100 mm	Saint-Quentin
2/HAA 1148	4 × 100 mm	Appeville
3/HAA 1148	4 × 100 mm	Saint-Quentin
4/HAA 1148	4 × 100 mm	Blingues
1/AR 245	4 × 76.2 mm	le Beau Fournier
2/AR 245	4 × 76,2 mm	Bourg Dun
3/AR 245	4 × 76.2 mm	Chapelle Dun
4/AR 245	4 × 76.2 mm	Ingouville
5/AR 245	4 × 76.2 mm	Cailleville
6/AR 245	4 × 76.2 mm	Saint-Riquier
7/AR 245	4 × 122 mm	Brunville
8/AR 245	4 × 122 mm	Berneval
9/AR 245	4 × 122 mm	Glicourt
10/AR 245	4 × 122 mm	Greny
1/HAA 1151	4 × 80 mm, replaced by 4 × 122 mm	Colombe
2/HAA 1151	4 × 80 mm, replaced by 4 × 122 mm	Mesnil Durdent
1/OA 621	4 × 76.2 mm	Theuville
2/OA 621	4 × 76.2 mm	Angerville
3/OA 621	4 × 122 mm	Colleville
1/LAR 17	4 × 105 mm	Epreville
2/LAR 17	4 × 105 mm	Froberville

Unit	Armament	Location (battery name)
3/LAR 17	4 × 105 mm	Ganzeville
4/LAR 17	4 × 150 mm	Beaurepaire
5/LAR 17	4 × 150 mm	Pifolet
6/LAR 17	4 × 150 mm	Tilleul
3/HKAA 799	6 × 155 mm	Criqueboeuf
1/HKAA 1253	6 × 155 mm	Ectot
2/HKAA 1253	6 × 155 mm	Fécamp
3/HKAA 1253	6 × 155 mm	Yport
4/HKAA 1253	4 × 105 mm	Heuqueville
1/MAA 266	3 × 380 mm	Bléville
2/MAA 266	4 × 155 mm	Ferme Valentin
3/MAA 266	4 × 150 mm	Nice Havrais
4/MAA 266	2 × 105 mm	le Havre, north mole
5/MAA 266	3 × 94 mm	le Havre, south mole
6/MAA 266	3 × 138 mm	le Havre, petrol mole
7/MAA 266	2 × 75 mm	le Havre, central mole
8/MAA 266	2 × 105 mm	le Havre, quay
9/MAA 266	3 × 150 mm	Vasouy
1/HKAR 1254	4 × 105 mm	Ecqueville
2/HKAR 1254	4 × 105 mm	Fort Sainte-Adresse
3/HKAR 1254	3 × 170 mm	Bléville (Goldbrunner)
4/HKAR 1254	4 × 105 mm	Cap de la Hève
1/HAA 1149	4 × 155 mm	les Monts Trottins
2/HAA 1149	4 × 150 mm	Févretot
3/HAA 1149	4 × 150 mm	Petit Bléville
4/HAA 1149	4 × 75 mm	Octeville
1/HAA 1150	4 × 155 mm	Rouelles
2/HAA 1150	4 × 155 mm	Craville
3/HAA 1150	4 × 155 mm	Château Montgeon
1/HKAA 1255	6 × 155 mm	Villerville
2/HKAA 1255	6 × 155 mm	Mont Canisy
3/HKAA 1255	6 × 155 mm	Houlgate
4/HKAA 1255	4 × 105 mm	Manoir Normand
1/AR 1711	4 × 76.2 mm	Barneville
2/AR 1711	4 × 76.2 mm	Croix Sonnet
3/AR 1711	4 × 76.2 mm	Champs Rabats
4/AR 1711	4 × 76.2 mm	Marie Antoinette
5/AR 1711	4 × 155 mm	Carrefour David
6/AR 1711	4 × 155 mm	Gonneville
7/AR 1711	4 × 155 mm	Mont des Grangues
8/AR 1711	4 × 155 mm	Croix Sonnet

Normandy to Saint-Nazaire (Seventh Army)

Unit	Armament	Location (battery name)
1/HKAA 1260	6 × 155 mm	Riva-Bella
2/HKAA 1260	6 × 155 mm	Pointe du Hoc
3/HKAA 1260	4 × 122 mm	Mont Fleury
4/HKAA 1260	4 × 150 mm	Longues-sur-Mer
1/AR 1716	4 × 100 mm	Merville
2/AR 1716	4 × 100 mm	Colleville
3/AR 1716	4 × 100 mm	Bréville

Unit	Armament	Location (battery name)
4/AR 1716	4 × 155 mm	Ouistreham
5/AR 1716	4 × 100 mm	Crépon
6/AR 1716	4 × 100 mm	Mare Fontaine
7/AR 1716	4 × 100 mm	Beny-sur-Mer
8/AR 1716	4 × 100 mm	Maisy
9/AR 1716	4 × 155 mm	Maisy
10/AR 1716	3 × 150 mm	Surrain
1/HKAR 1261	4 × 122 mm	Saint-Martin-de-Varreville
2/HKAR 1261	4 × 105 mm	Azeville
3/HKAR 1261	3 × 210 mm	Saint-Marcouf
4/HKAR 1261	4 × 105 mm	Quinéville
5/HKAR 1261	4 × 105 mm	Crasville
6/HKAR 1261	4 × 155 mm	Morsalines
7/HKAR 1261	4 × 155 mm	Gatteville
8/HKAR 1261	4 × 155 mm	les Couplets
9/HKAR 1261	4 × 105 mm	la Pernelle
10/HKAR 1261	3 × 170 cm	la Pernelle
5/AR 1709	4 × 105 mm	Fermanville
6/AR 1709	4 × 155 mm	Digosville
7/AR 1709	4 × 155 mm	le Mesnil-Val
9/AR 1709	4 × 76.2 mm	Varouville
10/AR 1709	4 × 76.2 mm	Val Bourgin
11/AR 1709	4 × 76.2 mm	Cosqueville
1/MAA 260	4 × 94 mm	Fort Central
2/MAA 260	4 × 94 mm	Néville (Blankensee)
3/MAA 260	2 × 105 mm	Cherbourg, harbour station
4/MAA 260	4 × 105 mm	Bastion II
5/MAA 260	4 × 105 mm	Fort du Roule
6/MAA 260	4 × 150 mm	Castel Vendon
7/MAA 260	4 × 150 mm	les Caplains (Brommy West)
8/MAA 260	4 × 17 mm	Amfreville (York)
9/MAA 260	4 × 240 mm	Fermanville (Hamburg)
2/AR 1709	4 × 100 mm	Ozouville
4/AR 1709	4 × 105 mm	Sainte-Croix-Hague
1/HKAR 1262	4 × 155 mm	Auderville-la-roche
2/HKAR 1262	4 × 105 mm	Biville
3/HKAR 1262	2 × 203 mm	Auderville-Laye
4/HKAR 1262	3 × 170 mm	Flamanville
5/HKAR 1262	4 × 122 mm	Carteret
6/HKAR 1262	4 × 105 mm	Siouville
7/HKAR 1262	4 × 105 mm	Houel
8/HKAR 1262	4 × 105 mm	Pointe de Rozel
1/MAA 608	6 × 194.7 mm	Cézembre
2/MAA 608	4 × 105 mm	Grand Bé
3/MAA 608	4 × 120 mm	Pointe du Roc
1/HKAR 1266	4 × 105 mm	Saint-Gilles-Coulomb
2/HKAR 1266	4 × 105 mm	Paramé
3/HKAR 1266	6 × 122 mm	la Richardais
1/AR 346	6 × 155 mm	Villas Mesniers
2/AR 346	4 × 155 mm	la Broussette
3/AR 346	4 × 100 mm	Pointe Bellefard

Unit	Armament	Location (battery name)
4/AR 346	4 × 155 mm	Pleneuf
5/AR 346	4 × 155 mm	Pleneuf
6/AR 346	4 × 100 mm	Erquy
EB 532	2 × 203 mm	Paimpol
1/AR 266	4 × 76.2 mm	Saint-Pol
2/AR 266	4 × 76.2 mm	Saint-Pol
3/AR 266	4 × 155 mm	Saint-Pol
4/AR 266	4 × 155 mm	Saint-Michel-en-Grève
5/AR 266	4 × 122 mm	Pleumeur
7/AR 266	4 × 76.2 mm	Paimpol
9/AR 266	4 × 122 mm	Pordic
10/AR 266	4 × 155 mm	Lezardrieux
4/AR 353	4 × 105 mm	Pleumeur Bodou
5/AR 353	4 × 105 mm	Servel
6/AR 353	4 × 105 mm	Kerblat
7/AR 353	4 × 105 mm	Lanmeur
8/AR 353	4 × 105 mm	Guimaëc
9/AR 353	4 × 105 mm	Plouézoch
1/AR 343	4 × 155 mm	Pen ar Menez
2/AR 343	4 × 155 mm	Kerveneur
3/AR 343	4 × 155 mm	Tremadic
4/AR 343	4 × 155 mm	Kergounan
5/AR 343	4 × 155 mm	Kerizaouen
6/AR 343	4 × 100 mm	Villeneuve
7/AR 343	4 × 76.2 mm	Plounevez
8/AR 343	4 × 76.2 mm	Kerlouan
9/AR 343	4 × 76.2 mm	Treflez
1/HAA 1161	4 × 150 mm	Landeda
2/HAA 1161	4 × 150 mm	Ranorgat
1/HKAA 1273	4 × 105 mm	Plouider
2/HKAA 1273	4 × 105 mm	Flescou Lannilis
1/MAA 262	4 × 150 mm	Rospects (Holtzendorff)
2/MAA 262	4 × 105 mm	Portzic
3/MAA 262	4 × 75 mm	Toulbroch
4/MAA 262	4 × 164.7 mm, 4 × 75 mm	Kerbonn
5/MAA 262	4 × 164.7 mm, replaced by 4 × 150 mm	Cap de la Chèvre
6/MAA 262	3 × 88 mm, 3 × 152 mm	Portzic
7/MAA 262	4 × 280 mm	Lochrist (Graf Spee)
1/HAA 1162	4 × 105 mm	Arsenal
2/HAA 1162	4 × 105 mm	Saint-Pierre-de-Quibignon
1/HKAA 1274	4 × 220 mm	Pointe du Gouin
2/HKAA 1274	4 × 105 mm	Pointe du Minou
1/AR 265	4 × 76.2 mm	Ploneour
2/AR 265	4 × 76.2 mm	Ploneour
3/AR 265	4 × 76.2 mm	Treluant
4/AR 265	4 × 76.2 mm	le Resto
5/AR 265	4 × 76.2 mm	Plouhinec
6/AR 265	4 × 76.2 mm	Kergouric
7/AR 265	4 × 122 mm	Kerbernes
8/AR 265	4 × 122 mm	Ploemeur
10/AR 265	4 × 122 mm	Keraude

Unit	Armament	Location (battery name)
1/HAA 1163	4 × 155 mm	Kerhope
2/HAA 1163	4 × 105 mm	Saint-Fiacre
3/HAA 1163	4 × 155 mm	Kerhar
4/HAA 1163	4 × 122 mm	Lann er Roc'h
1/MAA 264	4 × 170 mm	le Talud (Jade West)
2/MAA 264	4 × 164.7 mm, 2 × 150 mm	Locqueltas
3/MAA 264	4 × 105 mm	Gavres
4/MAA 264/EB 673	3 × 340 mm	Plouharnel
5/MAA 264	4 × 203 mm	Grognon, Ile de Groix (Seydlitz)
4a/MAA 683	2 × 75 mm	Pointe de Taillefer, Belle Ile (Leurbtges)
4b/MAA 683	3 × 75 mm	Pointe de Taillefer, Belle Ile (Gunter)
4c/MAA 683	4 × 105 mm	Pointe de Taillefer, Belle Ile (Siegfried)
4a/MAA 688	4 × 138 mm	Pointe de Taillefer, Belle Ile (Thomas)
4b/MAA 688	2 × 75 mm	Pointe de Taillefer, Belle Ile (Roland)
4c/MAA 688	3 × 75 mm	Pointe de Taillefer, Belle Ile (Lothar)
4a/MAA 681	4 × 105 mm	Fort Surville, Ile de Groix
4b/MAA 681	4 × 75 mm	Kerlivio, Ile de Groix
4c/MAA 681	4 × 75 mm	Kerlivio, Ile de Groix
12/AR 275	4 × 150 mm	Carnac
11/AR 275	4 × 150 mm	Carnac
10/AR 275	4 × 150 mm	Kergonan
1/AR 275	4 × 105 mm	Betz
2/AR 275	4 × 105 mm	Ecobues
3/AR 275	4 × 105 mm	Rouallais
4/AR 275	4 × 105 mm	Guérande (Dora)
5/AR 275	4 × 105 mm	Canevé (Emil)
6/AR 275	4 × 105 mm	Escoublac Fritz
7/AR 275	4 × 105 mm	Coipéans (Adolf)
8/AR 275	4 × 105 mm	Brézéan (Berta)
9/AR 275	4 × 105 mm	Signolais (*Cäsar*)
4/HAA 1162	4 × 105 mm	Landreau
HAB 1164	4 × 150 mm	Sainte-Marguerite
1/MAA 280	4 × 75 mm	Saint-Gildas
2/MAA 280	4 × 105 mm	le Pointeau
3/MAA 280	4 × 170 mm	L'Eve (Behncke)
4/MAA 280	2 × 240 mm	Batz-sur-Mer
5/MAA 280	2 × 240 mm	Préfailles

Vendée to Spain (First Army)

Unit	Armament	Location (battery name)
5a/MAA 684	4 × 75 mm	la Guérinière, Ile de Noirmoutier
5a/MAA 684	2 × 105 mm	la Lande, Ile de Noirmoutier
5b/MAA 684	2 × 75 mm	Pré Pelé, Ile de Noirmoutier
5b/MAA 684	2 × 75 mm	Guérande, Ile de Noirmoutier
5c/MAA 684	4 × 155 mm	Moulin de l'Echelle, Ile de Noirmoutier
5c/MAA 684	2 × 155 mm	Grand Viel, Ile de Noirmoutier
Battery 826	4 × 76.2 mm	Saint-Gilles
1/HKAR 1280	4 × 105 mm	la Chaume
1/HAA 1181	4 × 155 mm	la Pironnibre
4/AA 213	4 × 105 mm	Olonne-sur-Mer

Unit	Armament	Location (battery name)
5/AA 213	4 × 105 mm	Chateau-d'Olonne
2/HAA 1181	4 × 155 mm	la Tranche-sur-mer
1/AA 763	3 × 170 mm	Vairé
2/AA 763	3 × 170 mm	Saint-Mathurin
3/AA 763	3 × 170 mm	Gros Breuil
5d/MAA 684	10 × 75 mm	les Chiens Perrins, Ile d'Yeu
5d/MAA 684	3 × 75 mm	Pointe Gauthier, Ile d'Yeu
5d/MAA 684	3 × 75 mm	Pointe Corbeaux, Ile d'Yeu
2/MAA 685	3 × 75 mm	Marais Sales, Ile d'Yeu
3/AA 764	3 × 170 mm	la Sauzaie
1/AA 764	3 × 170 mm	Dompierre
2/AA 764	3 × 170 mm	Hautes Branches
1/AA 18	4 × 105 mm	Minimes
2/AA 18	4 × 105 mm	Lagord
3/AA 18	4 × 105 mm	Puilboreau, la Rochelle
3/HAA 1181	4 × 155 mm	Bonnedeau
4/HAA 1181	4 × 155 mm	Angoulins
5/MAA 282	4 × 88 mm	la Pallice
2/HAA 1180	4 × 100 mm	Soumard
1/MAA 282	3 × 150 mm	la Couarde, Ile de Ré (Herta)
2/MAA 282	4 × 75 mm	Sainte-Marie, Ile de Ré (Ella)
3/MAA 282	4 × 75 mm	Lizay, Ile de Ré (Lola)
4/MAA 282	4 × 203 mm	Ars, Ile de Ré (Karola)
2/HKAR 1280	4 × 220 mm	Ars, Ile de Ré (Kora)
2/MAA 686	3 × 75 mm	Sainte-Marie, Ile de Ré
4/MAA 686	4 × 75 mm	Saint-Martin, Ile de Ré (Anna Agatha)
5a/MAA 686	4 × 75 mm	le Bois Plage, Ile de Ré (Fanny)
5a/MAA 686	2 × 75 mm	Saint-Clément, Ile de Ré (Karla)
5b/MAA 686	6 × 75 mm	Conche des Baleines, Ile de Ré (Klara Kuni)
5c/MAA 686	4 × 155 mm	la Couarde, Ile de Ré (Hilde)
1/HAA 1180	4 × 100 mm	le Douhet, Ile d'Oléron (Adler)
3/HAA 1180	4 × 150 mm	Saint-Denis, Ile d'Oléron (Taube)
4/HAA 1180	4 × 150 mm	Pointe de, Ile d'Oléron Chaucre (Puma)
2/MAA 687	2 × 75 mm	Vert Bois, Ile d'Oléron (Kondor)
4/MAA 687	4 × 75 mm	la Cotinibre, Ile d'Oléron (Mammut)
5a/MAA 687	2 × 155 mm	Saint-Trojan Plage, Ile d'Oléron (Iltis)
5a/MAA 687	4 × 75 mm	Chassiron, Ile d'Oléron (Schwalbe)
5b/MAA 687	4 × 75 mm	Chassiron, Ile d'Oléron (Qualle)
5c/MAA 687	4 × 155 mm	la Perroche, Ile d'Oléron (Luchs)
5d/MAA 687	4 × 75 mm	Grande Plage, Ile d'Oléron (Krokodile)
1/HKAA 1282	4 × 105 mm	Grande Côte
2/HKAA 1282	6 × 114 mm	Saint-Sordolin
3/HKAA 1282	4 × 105 mm	Suzac
4/HKAA 1282	4 × 105 mm	Pointe de Grave
5/HKAA 1282	6 × 152 mm	la Claire
EB 721	2 × 280 mm	le Verdon
1/MAA 284	3 × 75 mm	Fort du Chay, Royan
2/MAA 284	4 × 138 mm	la Coubre, east
3/MAA 284	4 × 150 mm	la Coubre, west

Unit	Armament	Location (battery name)
4/MAA 284	4 × 164.7 mm	les Arros
5/MAA 284	2 × 240 mm	la Coubre (Muschel)
6/MAA 284	4 × 105 mm	Puy de l'Auture
7/MAA 284	4 × 75 mm, 4 × 105 mm	les Trois Fréres, Pointe de Grave
1/MAA 618	4 × 150 mm	Hounin
2/MAA 618	4 × 88 mm	Contis
3/MAA 618	4 × 88 mm	le Porge
4/MAA 618	4 × 88 mm	Careens 11
5/MAA 618	4 × 150 mm	Carcans I
6/MAA 618	4 × 88 mm	Hossegor
Battery 950	4 × 75 mm	Lacanau
1/AA 993	4 × 122 mm	Lège
2/AA 993	4 × 122 mm	le Porge
3/AA 993	4 × 122 mm	Lacanau
1/HKAR 1287	4 × 105 mm	Cap Ferret
2/HKAR 1287	6 × 152 mm	Gaillouneys
3/HKAR 1287	4 × 105 mm	Cap Breton
4/HKAR 1287	6 × 152 mm	Chiberta
5/HKAR 1287	4 × 105 mm	Sainte-Barbe
6/HKAR 1287	6 × 152 mm	Pointe Sainte-Anne
1/HAA 1182	4 × 155 mm	Castillon
2/HAA 1182	4 × 155 mm	Labenne
3/HAA 1182	4 × 155 mm	Biscarosse
4/HAA 1182	4 × 155 mm	Vieux Boucau
5/HAA 1182	4 × 170 mm	Biscarosse
6/HAA 1182	4 × 210 mm	Cazaux
7/HAA 1182	4 × 210 mm	Lacanau
1/AA 9	4 × 105 mm	Mimizan
2/AA 9	4 × 105 mm	Lège
3/AA 9	4 × 155 mm	Biscarosse
4/AA 9	4 × 155 mm	le Moulleau
1/MAA 286	4 × 150 cm, 4 × 164.7 mm	Adour, north
2/MAA 286	4 × 155 mm	Socoa, west
3/MAA 286	6 × 75 mm	Adour, south
4a/MAA 286	4 × 75 mm	Socoa, east
4b/MAA 286	4 × 105 mm	Bordagain
EB 664	2 × 240 mm, 4 × 100 mm	Guethary
EB 674	3 × 240 mm, 4 × 100 mm	Mondeguy

Atlantic Wall Museums

Todt Battery
Framzelle

Le Mémorial, Musée pour la Paix
Esplanade D.D. Eisenhower
14066 Caen

Musée de la Batterie de Merville
Avenue de la Batterie de Merville
Merville 14810

Musée No. 4 Commando
Place Alfred Thomas
14150 Ouistreham

Musée du Mur de l'Atlantique
Boulevard du 6 Juin
14150 Ouistreham
Riva-Bella

Musée Radar
14440 Douvres la Delivrande

Musée America-Gold Beach
2 Place Amiral Byrd
Ver-sur-Mer

Musée du Débarquement
Place du 6 Juin
14117 Arromanches

Musée Mémorial de la Bataille de Normandie
Boulevard Fabian Ware
14400 Bayeux

Batterie de Longues
14400 Longues-sur-Mer

Musée des Epaves Sous-marines du
    Débarquement
Route de Bayeux
Commes
14520 Port-en-Bessin

Musée des Rangers
14450 Grandcamp-Maisy

Musée du Débarquement (Utah Beach)
50480 Sainte-Marie du Mont

Musée de la Libération
Fort du Roule
50100 Cherbourg

Musée de la Liberté
50310 Quinéville

Mémorial 1939–45
Cité d'Alet
Saint-Malo

Bibliography

BOOKS

Anon. *Omaha Beachhead*, Historical Division, Department of the Army, 1946
Bando, Mark A. *The 101st Airborne at Normandy*, Motorbooks International, 1994
Chazette, Alain. *Atlantikwall, Le Mur de l'Atlantique en France 1940–1944*, Editions Heimdal, 1995
Chicken, Stephen. *Overlord Coastline*, Spellmount, 1993
Ellis, Major LF. *Victory in the West*, Vol 1, *The Battle of Normandy*, HMSO, 1962
——. *Victory in the West*, Vol 2, *The Defeat of Germany*, Imperial War Museum, 1994
Kaufmann, J.E. and R.M. Jurga, *Fortress Europe*, Combined Publishing, 1999
Kershaw, Robert J. *D-Day, Piercing the Atlantic Wall*, Ian Allan, 1993
Majdalany, Fred. *Fall of Fortress Europe*, Hodder & Stoughton, 1969
Montgomery, Viscount. *El Alamein to the River Sangro; Normandy to the Baltic*, Barrie & Jenkins, 1973
Partridge, Colin. *Hitler's Atlantic Wall*, DI Publications, 1976
Ramsey, Winston G. *D-Day, Then and Now*, 2 Vols, Battle of Britain Prints International, 1995
Rolf, Rudi. *Atlantic Wall Typology*, Fortress Books, 1998
Rolf, Rudi & Peter Saal. *Fortress Europe*, Airlife, 1988
Ruppenthal, Major Roland G. *Utah Beach to Cherbourg*, Historical Division, Department of the Army, 1947
Speer, Albert. *Inside the Third Reich*, Phoenix, 1995
Speidel, Lt-Gen Hans. *We Defended Normandy*, Herbert Jenkins, 1951
Zimmermann, R Heinz. *Der Atlantikwall von Dünkirchen bis Cherbourg*, Schild-Verlag, 1996
——. *Der Atlantikwall von Brest bis Biarritz*, Schild-Verlag, 1997
——. *Der Atlantikwall von Cherbourg bis Brest mit dem Kanalsinseln*, Schild-Verlag, 2000

PART WORKS

Thompson, R.W. 'Fortress Europe', *History of the Second World War*, Vol 4, Purnell/BPC, 1972

REPORTS

Report on Engineer survey of heavy German coastal batteries, Calais – Boulogne area, DFWS, 1945

JOURNALS

Galbraith, Ian. 'Operation "Wellhit": the Capture of Boulogne', *After the Battle*, No. 86, 1994
Ramsey, Winston G, Ed. 'Dieppe 1942', *After the Battle*, No. 5, 1974
——. 'St.Malo 1944', *After the Battle*, No. 33, 1981
Reed, John. 'The Cross-Channel Guns', *After the Battle*, No. 29, 1980
Smith, Lt-Col Sherwood B. 'Defences of the Normandy Peninsula', *The Royal Engineers Journal*, June 1946

INTERNET SITES

www.geocities.com/Athens/Olympus/65550 – Atlantikwall Website
www.siteo.net–Site O
www.wovij.vuurwerk.nl – Dutch Atlantic Wall site

Index